RICHARD WISEMAN

59 Seconds

Richard Wiseman is based at the University of Hertfordshire in the United Kingdom and has gained an international reputation for research into quirky areas of psychology, including deception, humor, and luck. He is the author of *The Luck Factor, Quirkology,* and numerous other books. Wiseman is well-known for his media appearances, high-profile talks, live demonstrations, and mass-participation studies. Wiseman also regularly acts as a creative consultant for print, broadcast, and new media.

www.richardwiseman.com

ALSO BY RICHARD WISEMAN

Quirkology

Did You Spot the Gorilla?

The Luck Factor

Laughlab

59 seconds

59 seconds

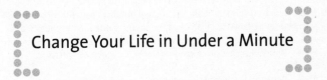

Change Your Life in Under a Minute

RICHARD WISEMAN

ANCHOR BOOKS

A DIVISION OF RANDOM HOUSE, INC.

NEW YORK

To Jeff

CONTENTS

59 seconds

introduction

Self-help exposed,

Sophie's question, and the

potential for rapid change

DO YOU WANT TO IMPROVE an important aspect of your life? Perhaps lose weight, find your perfect partner, obtain your dream job, or simply be happier? Try this simple exercise. . . .

Close your eyes and imagine the new you. Think how great you would look in those close-fitting designer jeans, dating Brad Pitt or Angelina Jolie, sitting in a luxurious leather chair at the top of the corporate ladder, or sipping a piña colada as the warm waves of the Caribbean gently lap at your feet.

The good news is that this type of exercise has been recommended by some in the self-help industry for years. The bad news is that a large body of research now suggests that such exercises are, at best, ineffective and, at worst, harmful. Although imagining your perfect self may make you feel better, engaging in such mental escapism can also have the unfortunate side effect of leaving you unprepared for the difficulties that crop up on the rocky road to success, thus increasing the chances of your faltering at the first hurdle rather than persisting in the face of failure. Fantasizing about heaven on earth may put a smile on your face, but it is unlikely to help transform your dreams into reality.

Other research suggests that the same goes for many popular techniques that claim to improve your life. Attempting to "think yourself happy" by suppressing negative thoughts can make you obsess on the very thing that makes you unhappy. Group brainstorming can produce fewer and less original ideas than individuals working alone. Punching a pillow and screaming out loud can increase, rather than decrease, your anger and stress levels.

Then there is the infamous "Yale Goal Study." According to some writers, in 1953 a team of researchers interviewed Yale's graduating seniors, asking them whether they had written down the specific goals that they wanted to achieve in life. Twenty years later the researchers tracked down the same cohort and found that the 3 percent of people who had specific goals all those years before had accumulated more personal wealth than the other 97 percent of their classmates combined. It is a great story, frequently cited in self-help books and seminars to illustrate the power of goal setting. There is just one small problem—as far as anyone can tell, the experiment never actually took place. In 2007 writer Lawrence Tabak, from the magazine *Fast Company,* attempted to track down the study, contacting several writers who had cited it, the secretary of the Yale Class of 1953, and other researchers who had tried to discover whether the study had actually happened.[1] No one could produce any evidence that it had ever been conducted, causing Tabak to conclude that it was almost certainly nothing more than an urban myth. For years, self-help gurus had been happy to describe a study without checking their facts.

Both the public and the business world have bought into modern-day mind myths for years and, in so doing, may have significantly decreased the likelihood of achieving their aims and ambitions. Worse still, such failure often encourages people to believe that they cannot control their lives. This is especially unfortunate, as even the smallest loss of perceived control can have a dramatic effect on people's confidence, happiness, and life span. In one classic study conducted by Ellen

Langer at Harvard University, half of the residents in a nursing home were given a houseplant and asked to look after it, while the other residents were given an identical plant but told that the staff would take responsibility for it.[2] Six months later, the residents who had been robbed of even this small amount of control over their lives were significantly less happy, healthy, and active than the others. Even more distressing, 30 percent of the residents who had not looked after their plant had died, compared to 15 percent of those who had been allowed to exercise such control. Similar results have been found in many areas, including education, career, health, relationships, and dieting. The message is clear—those who do not feel in control of their lives are less successful, and less psychologically and physically healthy, than those who do feel in control.

A few years ago I was having lunch with a friend named Sophie. Sophie is a bright, successful thirtysomething who holds a senior position in a firm of management consultants. Over lunch Sophie explained that she had recently bought a well-known book on increasing happiness, and she asked me what I thought of the industry. I explained that I had serious reservations about the scientific backing for some of the techniques being promoted, and described how any failure to change could do considerable psychological harm. Sophie looked concerned and then asked whether academic psychology had produced more scientifically supported ways of improving people's lives. I started to describe some of the quite complex academic work in happiness, and after about fifteen minutes or so Sophie stopped me. She politely explained that interesting though it was, she was a busy person, and she asked whether I could come up with some effective advice that didn't take quite so much time to implement. I asked how long I had. Sophie glanced at her watch, smiled, and replied, "About a minute?"

Sophie's comment made me stop and think. Many people are attracted to self-development and self-improvement because of the lure of quick and easy solutions to various issues in their lives. Unfortunately, most academic psychology either fails to address these issues or presents far more time-consuming and complex answers (thus the scene in Woody Allen's film *Sleeper,* in which Allen's character discovers that he has awakened two hundred years in the future, sighs, and explains that had he been in therapy all this time he would almost be cured). I wondered whether there were tips and techniques hidden away in academic journals that were empirically supported but quick to carry out.

Over the course of a few months I carefully searched through endless journals containing research papers from many different areas of psychology. As I examined the work, a promising pattern emerged, with researchers in quite different fields developing techniques that help people achieve their aims and ambitions in minutes, not months. I collected hundreds of these studies, drawn from many different areas of the behavioral sciences. From mood to memory, persuasion to procrastination, resilience to relationships, together they represent a new science of rapid change.

There is a very old story, often told to fill time during training courses, involving a man trying to fix his broken boiler. Despite his best efforts over many months, he simply can't mend it. Eventually, he gives up and decides to call in an expert. The engineer arrives, gives one gentle tap on the side of the boiler, and stands back as it springs to life. The engineer presents the man with a bill, and the man argues that he should pay only a small fee as the job took the engineer only a few moments. The engineer quietly explains that the man is not paying for the time he took to tap the boiler but rather the years of experience involved in knowing exactly where to tap. Just like the expert engineer tapping the boiler, the techniques described in this book demonstrate that effective change does not have to be time-consuming. In fact, it can take less than a minute and is often simply a question of knowing exactly where to tap.

happiness

Why positive thinking often fails and

how the real route to happiness involves a pencil,

keeping the perfect diary,

small acts of kindness, and

developing the gratitude attitude

WHY IS IT IMPORTANT TO BE HAPPY? Well, for one thing, by definition, you will feel better. But there is more to it than that. Happiness does not just make you enjoy life more; it actually affects how successful you are in both your personal life and your professional life.

A few years ago Sonja Lyubomirsky at the University of California and her colleagues set about the mammoth task of reviewing hundreds of studies in which experimenters cheered up selected people and then monitored the effects of their subjects' newfound joy.[1] All sorts of procedures were employed to make participants feel happy, including having them smell fresh-cut flowers, read out positive affirmations ("I really am a good person"), eat chocolate cake, dance, or watch a funny film. Sometimes the experimenters resorted to trickery, telling participants that they had performed especially well on an IQ test or ensuring that they "accidentally" found some money in the street. Regardless of the method used, the overall result was clear—happiness doesn't just flow from success; it actually causes it.

After trawling the data from hundreds of studies involving more than a quarter of a million participants, Lyubomirsky discovered impressive benefits to being happy. Happiness makes people more sociable and altruistic, it increases how much they like themselves and others, it improves their ability to resolve conflict, and it strengthens their immune systems. The cumulative effect means that people have more satisfying and successful relationships, find more fulfilling careers, and live longer, healthier lives.

Given the emotional and tangible benefits of happiness, it is not surprising that everyone wants a slice of the pie. But what is the most effective way of putting a permanent smile on your face? Ask most people the question, and you are likely to receive a two-word answer: more money. In survey after survey, the need for a fatter wallet consistently tops the "must have" list for happiness.[2] But is it really possible to buy happiness, or do financial aspirations set you on the road to despair?

Part of the answer comes from a remarkable study conducted in the 1970s by Philip Brickman from Northwestern University and his colleagues.[3] Brickman wanted to discover what happens to people's happiness when their financial dreams come true. Does a huge windfall really create a long-term smile, or does the initial thrill quickly fade away as newfound fortune becomes commonplace? Brickman contacted a group of people who had won a major prize in the Illinois State Lottery, including several who had hit the million-dollar jackpot. For a control group, he randomly selected people from the Illinois telephone directory. Everyone was asked to rate how happy they were at that moment and how happy they expected to be in the future. In addition, they were asked to say how much pleasure they derived from everyday activities in life, such as chatting with friends, hearing a funny joke, or receiving a compliment. The results provide a striking insight into the relationship between happiness and money.

Contrary to popular belief, those who had won the lottery were no more or less happy than those in the control group. There was also no significant difference between the groups when it came to how happy they expected to be in the future. In fact, there was only one difference—compared to those who had won the lottery, the people in the control group derived significantly more pleasure from the simple things in life.

Clearly, winning the lottery is a rather unusual way of obtaining financial security, but psychologists have also examined the relationship between income and happiness among those who have worked for their wealth.

Some of this work has involved carrying out large-scale international surveys by having people rate how happy they are (usually using standard ten-point scales that run from "very unhappy" to "very happy") and then plotting countries' average happiness ratings against their gross national product (GNP).[4] The results suggest that although people in very poor nations are not as happy as those in wealthier countries, this disparity vanishes once a country has achieved a relatively modest GNP. Research examining the possible link between salary and happiness found the same type of pattern. One study, conducted by Ed Diener from the University of Illinois and his colleagues, revealed that even those on the Forbes 100 list of the wealthiest people are only slightly happier than the average American.[5] All of this adds up to one simple message: when people can afford the necessities in life, an increase in income does not result in a significantly happier life.

So why should this be the case? Part of the reason is that we all get used to what we have very quickly. Buying a new car or a bigger house provides a short-term feel-good boost, but we quickly become accustomed to it and sink back to our pre-purchase level of joy. As psychologist David Myers once phrased it, "Thanks to our capacity to adapt to ever greater fame and fortune, yesterday's luxuries can soon become today's necessities and tomorrow's relics."[6] If money can't buy happiness, what is the best way of putting a long-term smile on your face?

The bad news is that research shows that about 50 percent

of your overall sense of happiness is genetically determined, and so cannot be altered.[7] The better news is that another 10 percent is attributable to general circumstances (educational level, income, whether you are married or single, etc.) that are difficult to change. However, the best news is that the remaining 40 percent is derived from your day-to-day behavior and the way you think about yourself and others. With a little knowledge, you can become substantially happier in just a few seconds.

The problem is that the advice offered in some self-help books and courses is at odds with the results of scientific research. Take, for example, the power of positive thinking. Does the road to happiness really depend on people's being able to simply push negative thoughts out of their mind? Actually, research suggests that such thought suppression may be far more likely to increase, rather than decrease, misery. In the mid-1980s Harvard psychologist Daniel Wegner chanced upon an obscure but intriguing quote from Dostoyevsky's *Winter Notes on Summer Impressions*: "Try to pose for yourself this task: not to think of a polar bear, and you will see that the cursed thing will come to mind every minute." Wegner decided to carry out a simple experiment to discover if this was true. Each person from a group of willing volunteers was made to sit alone in a room and told to think about anything, but NOT to imagine Dostoyevsky's white bear. Everyone was then asked to ring a bell each time the banned bear sprang to mind. Within moments a cacophony of bells indicated that Dostoyevsky was right—attempting to suppress certain thoughts makes people obsess on the very topic that they are trying to avoid.

Other work has shown how this effect operates in real life, with one study, conducted by Jennifer Borton and Elizabeth Casey at Hamilton College in New York State, providing a dramatic demonstration of how it influences people's moods and self-esteem.[8] Borton and Casey asked a group of people to describe their most upsetting thought about themselves. The researchers then had half of the group spend the next eleven days trying to push this thought out of their minds, while the remaining participants were asked to carry on with life as usual. At the end of each day, everyone indicated the degree to which they had dwelled upon their upsetting thought, and rated their mood, anxiety level, and self-esteem. The results were conceptually similar to those obtained by Wegner's "white bear" experiment. The group attempting to actively suppress their negative thoughts actually thought more about them. Compared to those going about their business as usual, the suppression group also rated themselves as more anxious, more depressed, and having lower self-esteem. More than twenty years of research have demonstrated that this paradoxical phenomenon occurs in many different aspects of everyday life, showing, for example, that asking dieters not to think about chocolate causes them to consume more of it and asking the public not to elect fools to positions in government encourages them to vote for George Bush.[9]

So, if thought suppression is not the answer, what can you do? One possibility is to distract yourself. Perhaps spend time with your family, go to a party, get more involved in your work, or take up a new hobby. Although this technique can often provide an effective short-term boost, it will probably not lead to a long-term sense of contentment. For that, research suggests, you need to know how to use a pencil, how to keep the perfect diary, how to carry out small acts of kindness, and how to develop the gratitude attitude.

CREATING THE PERFECT DIARY

All of us will experience unpleasant events during our lives. Perhaps the breakup of a long-term relationship, the death of a loved one, getting laid off, or, on a really bad day, all three. Both common sense and many types of psychotherapy suggest that the best way forward is to share your pain with others. Those adopting this "a problem shared is a problem halved" approach believe that venting your feelings is cathartic and helps you release negative emotions and move forward. It is a nice idea and one that holds tremendous intuitive appeal. Indeed, surveys show that 90 percent of the public believes that talking to someone else about a traumatic experience will help ease their pain.[10] But is that really the case?

To investigate, Emmanuelle Zech and Bernard Rimé at the University of Louvain in Belgium carried out an important study.[11] A group of participants was asked to select a negative experience from their past. To make the study as realistic as possible, they were asked to avoid the trivial stuff, such as missing a train or not being able to find a parking space, and instead think about "the most negative upsetting emotional event in their life, one they still thought about and still needed to talk about." From death to divorce, and illness to abuse, the issues were serious. One group of participants was then asked to have a long chat with a supportive experimenter about the event, while a second group was invited to chat about a far more mundane topic—a typical day. After one week, and then again after two months, all the participants went back to the lab and completed various questionnaires that measured their emotional well-being.

Those who had spent time talking about their traumatic event thought that the chat had been helpful. However, the questionnaire results told a very different story. In reality, the chat had had no significant impact at all. Participants thought that it was beneficial to share their negative emotional experiences, but in terms of the difference it made in how well they were coping, they might just as well have been chatting about a typical day.

So, if talking about negative experiences to a sympathetic but untrained individual is a waste of time, what can be done to help ease the pain of the past? As we saw at the start of this section, trying to suppress negative thoughts can be just as unhelpful.[12] Instead, one option involves "expressive writing."

In several studies, participants who have experienced a traumatic event have been encouraged to spend just a few minutes each day writing a diary-type account of their deepest thoughts and feelings about it.[13] For example, in one study participants who had just been laid off were asked to reflect on their deepest thoughts and feelings about their job loss, including how it had affected both their personal and their professional lives.[14] Although these types of exercises were both speedy and simple, the results revealed that participants experienced a remarkable boost in their psychological and physical well-being, including a reduction in health problems and an increase in self-esteem and happiness. The results left psychologists with something of a mystery. Why would talking about a traumatic experience have almost no effect but writing about it yield such significant benefits?

From a psychological perspective, thinking and writing are very different. Thinking can often be somewhat unstructured, disorganized, and even chaotic. In contrast, writing encourages the creation of a story line and structure that help people make sense of what has happened and work toward a solution. In short, talking can add to a sense of confusion, but writing provides a more systematic, solution-based approach.

This is clearly helpful for those who have been unfortunate enough to experience real trauma in their lives, but can the same idea also be used to promote everyday happiness? Three different, but related, bodies of research suggest that that this is indeed the case.

The Gratitude Attitude

One of the most important writing techniques for boosting happiness revolves around the psychology of gratitude. Present an individual with a constant sound, image, or smell, and something very peculiar happens. The person slowly gets more and more used to it, and eventually it vanishes from their awareness. For example, if you walk into a room that smells of freshly baked bread, you quickly detect the rather pleasant aroma. However, stay in the room for a few minutes, and the smell will seem to disappear. In fact, the only way to reawaken it is to walk out of the room and come back in again. Exactly the same concept applies to many areas of our lives, including happiness. Everyone has something to be happy about. Perhaps they have a loving partner, good health, great kids, a satisfying job, close friends, interesting hobbies, caring parents, a roof over their heads, clean water to drink, a signed Billy Joel album, or enough food to eat. As time passes, however, they get used to what they have and, just like the smell of fresh bread, these wonderful assets vanish from their consciousness. As the old cliché goes, you don't know what you've got till it's gone.

Psychologists Robert Emmons and Michael McCullough wondered what would happen to people's happiness levels if they were asked to carry out the conceptual equivalent of leaving the bread-smelling room and coming back in again. The researchers wanted to discover the effect of reminding people of the good things that were constantly present in their lives.[15] Three groups of people were asked to spend a few moments each week writing. The first group listed five things for which they were grateful, the second noted five things that annoyed them, and the third jotted down five events that had taken place during the previous week. Everyone scribbled away, with the "gratitude" group remarking on seeing the sunset on a summer day and the generosity of their friends, the "annoyed" group listing taxes and their children arguing, and the "events" group detailing making breakfast and driving to work. The results were startling. Compared to those in either the "annoyed" or the "events" group, those expressing gratitude ended up happier, much more optimistic about the future, and physically healthier—and they even exercised more.

Your Inner Perfect Self

When trying to write your way to a happier life, expressing gratitude is just the tip of the iceberg. There is also the notion of getting in touch with your inner perfect self. In the introduction I noted that a large body of research shows that visualizing a wonderful future is unlikely to increase the chances of achieving your goals. However, other work suggests that when it comes to putting a smile on your face, such exercises are more likely to prove beneficial. In a classic study conducted by Laura King at Southern Methodist University,[16] participants were asked to spend a few minutes during four consecutive days describing their ideal future. They were asked to be realistic but to imagine that all had gone as well as it possibly could and that they had achieved their goals. Another group was asked to imagine a traumatic event that had happened to them, and a third group simply wrote about their plans for the day. The results revealed that those who had described their best possible future ended up significantly happier than those in the other groups. In a follow-up study, King and her colleagues repeated the experiment, this time having people describe on paper the most wonderful experience in their lives.[17] Three months later, assessments revealed that compared to a control group, those reliving an intensely happy moment were significantly happier.

Affectionate Writing

Finally, another body of research has examined the idea of "affectionate writing." It may come as no great surprise to learn that being in a loving relationship is good for your physical and psychological health. However, are these benefits the result of receiving love, expressing love, or both? To find out, Kory Floyd, from Arizona State University, and his colleagues[18] asked some volunteers to think about someone they loved and spend twenty minutes writing about why this person meant so much to them. As a control, another group was asked to write about something that had happened to them during the past week. Each group repeated the writing exercise three times over the course of five weeks. Once again, this simple procedure had a dramatic effect, with those who spent just a few minutes engaged in affectionate writing showing a marked increase in happiness, a reduction in stress, and even a significant decrease in their cholesterol levels.

In short, when it comes to an instant fix for everyday happiness, certain types of writing have a surprisingly quick and large impact. Expressing gratitude, thinking about a perfect future, and affectionate writing have been scientifically proven to work—and all they require is a pen, a piece of paper, and a few moments of your time.

IN 59 SECONDS

To help you incorporate effective writing techniques into your life, I have put together a rather unusual diary. Instead of keeping a record of the past, this diary encourages you to write about topics that will help create a happier future. The diary should be completed on five days of the week, with each entry taking just a few moments. Maintain the diary for one week. According to scientific studies, you should quickly notice the difference in mood and happiness, changes that may persist for months.[19] If you feel the effects wearing off, simply repeat the exercise.

Monday: Thanksgiving
There are many things in your life for which to be grateful. These might include having close friends, being in a wonderful relationship, benefiting from sacrifices that others have made for you, being part of a supportive family, and enjoying good health, a nice home, or enough food on the table. Alternatively, you might have a job that you love, have happy memories of the past, or recently have had a nice experience, such as savoring an especially lovely cup of coffee, enjoying the smile of a stranger, having your dog welcome you home, eating a great meal, or stopping to smell the flowers. Think back over the past week and list three of these things.

1

2

3

Tuesday: Terrific Times

Think about one of the most wonderful experiences in your life. Perhaps a moment when you felt suddenly contented, were in love, listened to an amazing piece of music, saw an incredible performance, or had a great time with friends. Choose just one experience and imagine yourself back in that moment in time. Remember how you felt and what was going on around you. Now spend a few moments writing a description of that experience and how you felt. Do not worry about your spelling, punctuation, or grammar. Instead, simply commit your thoughts to paper.

Wednesday: Future Fantastic

Spend a few moments writing about your life in the future. Imagine that everything has gone really well. Be realistic, but imagine that you have worked hard and achieved all of your aims and ambitions. Imagine that you have become the person that you really want to be, and that your personal and professional life feels like a dream come true. All of this may not help you achieve your goals, but it will help you feel good and put a smile on your face.

Thursday: Dear . . .

Think about someone in your life who is very important to you. It might be your partner, a close friend, or a family member. Imagine that you have only one opportunity to tell this person how important they are to you. Write a short letter to this person, describing how much you care for them and the impact that they have had on your life.

Friday: Reviewing the Situation

Think back over the past seven days and make a note of three things that went really well for you. The events might be fairly trivial, such as finding a parking space, or more important, such as being offered a new job or opportunity. Jot down a sentence about why you think each event turned out so well.

1

2

3

THE POWER OF PURCHASES

Out of the blue, two words suddenly pop into your mind: "retail" and "therapy." Seconds later, you find yourself heading to the nearest shoe shop or gadget emporium, convinced that your forthcoming purchases will lead to a more blissful existence. But is that really the case? Will you actually feel better after you have bought that new pair of shoes or the latest high-tech music player? And, if so, just how long will your newfound joy last? The results from recent research have yielded clear and consistent answers to these questions. Perhaps more important, they have also revealed the wisest way to spend your money in order to put a smile on your face.

Psychologists Leaf Van Boven and Thomas Gilovich[20] examined whether, when attempting to buy happiness, you are better off spending your money on goods (that latest dress or an impressive new smartphone) or an experience (going out for a meal, buying a ticket for a concert, or booking a vacation). In one study the duo conducted a national survey in which people were asked first to think of an object or experience that they had bought with the aim of increasing their happiness, and then to rate the degree to which the purchase had cheered them up. In another experiment, the researchers randomly divided people into two groups, asked one group to think about an object they had recently bought and the other to describe an experiential purchase, and then asked both groups to rate their current mood on two scales, one ranging from −4 (bad) to +4 (good) and another ranging from −4 (sad) to +4 (happy). The results from both studies clearly indicated that in terms of short- and long-term happiness, buying experiences made people feel better than buying products.

Why? Our memory of experiences easily becomes distorted over time (you edit out the terrible trip on the airplane and just remember those blissful moments relaxing on the beach). Our goods, however, tend to lose their appeal by becoming old, worn-out, and outdated. Also, experiences promote one of the most effective happiness-inducing behaviors—spending time with others. Sociability might be part of the experience itself, or it might happen when you tell people about the occasion afterward. In contrast, buying the latest or most expensive new product can sometimes isolate you from friends and family who may be jealous of the things that you have.

But choosing experiences over goods is only part of the story when trying to buy happiness. Time for a quick questionnaire.[21] Take a few moments to read the following ten statements and assign each of them a rating indicating the degree to which it describes you. Don't spend too long thinking about each statement. Just answer honestly—and no peeking at the answers.

Assign each item a rating between 1 ("strongly disagree") and 5 ("strongly agree").

1 I am impressed by people who own expensive   1 2 3 4 5
   cars and houses.

2 I tend to judge how well I am doing in life by the   1 2 3 4 5
   possessions that I buy.

3 I like to buy things that I don't really need.   1 2 3 4 5

4 I like to be surrounded by expensive items.   1 2 3 4 5

5 I think that my life would be better if I owned   1 2 3 4 5
   more luxury items.

6 I am sometimes bothered by the fact that   1 2 3 4 5
       I can't afford to buy certain luxury goods.

7 Buying expensive items makes me feel good   1 2 3 4 5
       about myself.

8 I seem to put more emphasis on material   1 2 3 4 5
       things than most of my friends and family do.

9 I am prepared to pay significantly more   1 2 3 4 5
       money for branded items.

10 I enjoy owning items that others find impressive.   1 2 3 4 5

Now add up your ratings. Low scores are between 10 and 20, medium scores between 21 and 39, and high scores between 40 and 50.

It may come as no great surprise that this questionnaire is designed to measure your level of materialism. People who obtain high scores clearly tend to place a great deal of importance on the acquisition of possessions, frequently view such items as central to their happiness, and judge their own success, and the success of others, on the basis of what they have. In contrast, those with low scores value experiences and relationships more than possessions. As is so often the case, those with middling scores are of little interest to anyone.

Researchers have spent a great deal of time looking at the link between people's scores on these types of questionnaires and happiness.[22] The findings are as consistent as they are worrisome—high scores tend to be associated with feeling unhappy and unsatisfied with life. Of course, this is not the case with every single materialist, so if you did get a high score, you might be one of the happy-go-lucky people who buck the trend. (However, before adopting that viewpoint, bear in mind that studies carried out by psychologists also suggest that whenever we are confronted with negative results from tests, we prove to be extremely good at convincing ourselves that we are an exception to the rule.)

So what explains this general trend? You might think that the answer lies in the financial consequences of continually having to have the latest thing. But in fact the problem is not about the spending of money per se. It's about who benefits from the cash.

Materialists tend to be somewhat self-centered. Studies show that when presented with a hypothetical $40,000, materialists spend, on average, three times as much on things for themselves as they do on things for others. Also, when they are asked to rate statements about the degree to which they care for others ("I enjoy having guests stay in my house," "I often lend things to my friends"), they end up giving far more self-centered responses. As research by Elizabeth Dunn, from the University of British Columbia, shows, seen from the perspective of happiness, this self-centeredness can have a detrimental effect on people's happiness.

Dunn and her colleagues have conducted several studies on the relationship between income, spending, and happiness.[23] In one national survey, participants were asked to rate their happiness, state their income, and provide a detailed breakdown of the amount spent on gifts for themselves, gifts for others, and donations to charity. In another study Dunn measured the happiness and spending patterns of employees before and after they each received a profit-sharing bonus of between $3,000 and $8,000. Time and again, the same pattern emerged. Those who spent a higher percentage of their income on others were far happier than those who spent it on themselves.

Of course, a skeptical materialist might argue that researchers have the direction of causality wrong, that it is not spending money on others that makes you happy but rather it is that happy people spend more on others. It is an interesting point, and one tackled in a clever experiment conducted by Dunn and her team. In a simple but innovative study, participants were given an envelope containing either $5 or $20 and asked to spend the money by five o'clock that evening. They were randomly assigned to one of two groups. One group was instructed to spend the money on themselves (perhaps treating themselves to a self-indulgent present), while the second group was asked to spend their unexpected windfall on someone else (perhaps purchasing a present for a friend or family member). The predictions made by the "happy people spend more on themselves" brigade proved unfounded. In fact, participants who spent the money on their friends and family ended up feeling significantly happier than those who treated themselves to luxury gifts.

Why should this be the case? The answer, it seems, lies deep within your brain. Macroeconomist William Harbaugh from the University of Oregon and colleagues[24] gave participants $100 in a virtual bank account and asked them to lie in a brain scanner. Participants first saw some of their money being given to help those in need via a mandatory taxation; they were then asked to decide whether to donate some of their remaining balance to charity or keep it for themselves. The scanning results revealed that two evolutionarily ancient regions deep in the brain—the caudate nucleus and the nucleus accumbens—became active when participants witnessed some of their money going to those in need, and were especially busy when they donated money voluntarily. These two brain regions also spring into action when our most basic needs are met, such as when we eat tasty food or feel valued by others, suggesting a direct brain-based link between helping others and happiness.

So, scientifically speaking, if you want some real retail therapy, help yourself by helping others. It has a direct effect on your brain that in turn makes you feel happier.

Of course, you might argue that you really don't have enough money to donate to others. Once again, however, help is at hand. A few years ago happiness researcher Sonja Lyubomirsky and her colleagues arranged for a group of participants to perform five nonfinancial acts of kindness each week for six weeks.[25] These were simple things, such as writing a thank-you note, giving blood, or helping a friend. Some of the participants performed one of the acts each day, while others carried out all five on the same day. Those who performed their kind acts each day showed a small increase in happiness. However, those who carried out all their acts of kindness on just one day each week increased their happiness by an incredible 40 percent.

IN 59 SECONDS

Buy Experiences, Not Goods.

Want to buy happiness? Then spend your hard-earned cash on experiences. Go out for a meal. Go to a concert, movie, or the theater. Go on vacation. Go and learn how to pole dance. Go play paintball. Go bungee jumping. In fact, get involved in anything that provides an opportunity to do things with others, and then tell even more people about it afterward. When it comes to happiness, remember, it is experiences that represent really good value for the money.

'Tis Better to Give Than to Receive.

Long-term happiness is not just about gyrating around a pole to raunchy music or plummeting toward the ground while screaming like a baby. Ask people whether they will be happier after spending money on themselves or others, and the vast majority will check the "me" box. The science shows that exactly the opposite is true—people become much happier after providing for others rather than themselves. The good news is that you really do not have to divert a huge proportion of your income to charity, friends, family, and colleagues. In fact, the smallest gifts can quickly result in surprisingly large and long-lasting changes in happiness. A few dollars spent on others may be one of the best investments that you ever make. And if you really can't afford to donate your hard-earned cash, remember that carrying out five nonfinancial acts of kindness on a single day also provides a significant boost to happiness.

THE ROOTS OF MATERIALISM

What makes people materialistic? Is a love of possessions the result of personality, childhood experiences, or events later in life? According to research by psychologists Lan Nguyen Chaplin and Deborah Roedder John, materialism takes root in early childhood, and is driven mainly by low self-esteem.[26]

In a two-part study, the researchers first arranged for a group of children between the ages of eight and eighteen to complete a standard self-esteem questionnaire (rating statements such as "I am happy with the way I look"). Next, they presented the children with display boards containing lots of images relating to five general topics: hobbies (such as "camping," "skateboarding"), sports ("soccer," "tennis"), material things ("new shoes," "my own computer"), people ("friends," "teacher"), and achievements ("getting good grades," "learning to play an instrument"). The children were asked to look at the boards and use any of the images to create a collage around the theme "What makes me happy." This fun task allowed the researchers to calculate each child's level of materialism by counting the percentage of images that each child took from the "material things" display board. The results revealed a strong link between self-esteem and materialism, with children who were low in self-esteem being far more materialistic than their friends.

But could the cause and effect be the other way around? Could materialism cause low self-esteem? To test this possibility, the researchers had a group of children write nice things about one another on paper plates, and then they presented each child his or her very own plateful of praise and positivity. This simple "nice things about me" plate significantly increased the children's self-esteem and, more important, subsequently caused them to halve the number of materialistic images that they used when creating their "What makes me happy" collage. All of these results add up to compelling evidence that low self-esteem causes materialistic tendencies and that such tendencies take root at a very young age. The good news is that the work also demonstrates that just like spending a small amount of money on others or carrying out a few acts of kindness, it takes only a few seconds and a paper plate to change the way people think and behave.

HAPPINESS IS A PENCIL

People behave in highly predictable ways when they experience certain emotions and thoughts. When they are sad, they cry. When they are happy, they smile. When they agree, they nod their heads. So far, no surprises, but according to an area of research known as "proprioceptive psychology," the process also works in reverse. Get people to behave in a certain way and you cause them to feel certain emotions and have certain thoughts. The idea was initially controversial, but fortunately it was supported by a series of compelling experiments.[27]

In a now classic study, people in one group were asked to furrow their brows (or, as the researchers put it, "contract their corrugator muscle"), while those in another group were asked to adopt a slight grin ("extend their zygomaticus muscle"). This simple act of facial contortion had a surprisingly large effect on participants' moods, with the grinning group feeling far happier than those who were frowning.

Participants in a different study were asked to fixate on various products moving across a large computer screen and then indicate whether the items appealed to them.[28] Some of the items moved vertically (causing the participants to nod their heads while watching), and others moved horizontally (resulting in a side-to-side head movement). Participants preferred vertically moving products without being aware that their "yes" and "no" head movements had played a key role in their decisions.

Exactly the same idea applies to happiness. People smile when they are happy, but they also feel happier because they are smiling. The effect even works when people are not aware that they are smiling. In the 1980s, Fritz Strack and his colleagues asked two groups of people to judge how funny they found Gary Larson's *The Far Side* cartoons and then rate how happy they felt, in one of two rather bizarre circumstances.[29] One group was asked to hold a pencil between their teeth, but to ensure that it did not touch their lips. The other group supported the end of the pencil with just their lips, but not their teeth. Without realizing it, those in the "teeth only" condition had forced the lower part of their faces into a smile, while those in the "lips only" condition had made themselves frown. The results revealed that the participants tended to experience the emotion associated with their expressions. Those who had their faces forced into a smile felt happier and found the *Far Side* cartoons much funnier than those who were forced to frown. Other work has demonstrated that this increase in happiness does not immediately drain away when people cease smiling.[30] It lingers, affecting many aspects of their behavior, including interacting with others in a more positive way and being more likely to remember happy life events.

The message from this type of work is simple: if you want to cheer yourself up, behave like a happy person.

IN 59 SECONDS

Smile.

There are a number of happiness-inducing behaviors that can be quickly incorporated into your everyday life. Most important of all, smile more. This shouldn't be a brief, unfelt smile that ends in the blink of an eye. Instead, research suggests that you should try to maintain the expression for between fifteen and thirty seconds. To make the grin as convincing as possible, try to imagine a situation that would elicit a genuine smile. Perhaps you have just met a good friend, heard a hilarious joke, or found out that your mother-in-law isn't coming to visit after all. Also, consider creating a signal to remind you to smile regularly. Set your watch, computer, or PDA to beep on the hour, or use a more random cue, such as your telephone ringing.

Sit Up.

Your posture is equally important. In a study conducted by Tomi-Ann Roberts at Colorado College, participants were randomly split into two groups and asked to spend three minutes either sitting up straight or slumping in their chairs.[31] Everyone was then given a math test and asked to assess their mood. Those who had sat upright were much happier than those who had slouched, and they even made higher scores on the math test. Interestingly, the result didn't hold for many of the female participants, causing Roberts to speculate that the act of sitting upright and pushing their chests forward may have made them feel self-conscious.

Act Happy.

Research by Peter Borkenau from Bielefeld University and others has revealed that happy people move in a very different way than unhappy people do.[32] You can use this information to increase your sense of happiness by acting like a happy person. Try walking in a more relaxed way, swinging your arms slightly more and putting more of a spring in your step. Also, try making more expressive hand gestures during conversations, nod your head more when others are speaking, wear more colorful clothing, use positively charged emotional words more (especially "love," "like," and "fond"), use fewer self-references ("me," "myself," and "I"), have a larger variation in the pitch of your voice, speak slightly faster, and have a significantly firmer handshake. Incorporating these behaviors into your everyday actions will enhance your happiness.

PUTTING IN THE EFFORT

According to researchers Kenneth Sheldon and Sonja Lyubo-mirsky, happiness does not come easily.[33]

In several experiments, the duo recruited participants who had recently experienced one of two types of change in their life. The first type, labeled "circumstantial change," involved relatively important alterations to their overall circumstances, including, for example, moving, getting a raise, or buying a new car. The second type, labeled "intentional change," involved changes that required effort to pursue a goal or initiate an activity, including, for example, joining a new club, starting a new hobby, or embarking on a different career. Both sets of participants were asked to rate their happiness levels for several weeks. The results consistently showed that although people in both groups experienced an immediate increase in happiness, those who had experienced a circumstantial change quickly reverted back to their initial levels, while those who had made an intentional change remained happier for a much longer period of time. Why?

According to Sheldon and Lyubomirsky, it is the result of a phenomenon known as "hedonistic habituation." Unsurprisingly, humans derive a great deal of enjoyment from any new form of positive experience. However, give them the same wonderful experience time and again and they quickly become familiar with their new source of joy and so cease to derive anywhere near as much pleasure from it. Unfortunately, circumstantial changes frequently produce hedonistic habituation. Although the initial thrill of a new house, a raise, or a new car is wonderful, the positive feelings caused by the change tend to be the same day after day, and so the initial enjoyment quickly fades away. In contrast, intentional changes tend to avoid hedonistic habituation by creating a constantly changing psychological landscape. Whether it is starting a new hobby, joining an organization, initiating a project, meeting new people, or learning a novel skill, the brain is fed with ever-changing positive experiences that prevent habituation and so prolong happiness.

So, to maximize happiness, choose intentional change over circumstantial change. Make the effort to start a new hobby, begin a major project, or try a sport that you have never tried before. Choose activities that fit your personality, values, and abilities. It might help to think about what you already enjoy doing, identify the core elements that make this activity so pleasurable, and try other activities involving the same elements. If, for example, you enjoy drawing, try taking up watercolors. If you like playing tennis, consider taking up badminton or squash. If you are good at Sudoku, try turning your hand to crossword puzzles. Whatever you decide to pursue, make a real effort to change what you do and when you do it. It may sound like hard work, but research suggests that when it comes to happiness, it is well worth the effort.

persuasion

Why rewards fail,

how to give the flawless interview,

improve your social life by making mistakes,

never lose your wallet again, and

convince anyone of anything by using your pet frog

HOW DO YOU PERSUADE a child to complete a homework assignment, an employee to perform better in the workplace, or people to care more about the environment? Many believe that the most effective way is to dangle the biggest possible carrot in front of their noses. But does research suggest this is really an incentive, or is it just a myth?

In one famous study, Stanford psychologist Mark Lepper and colleagues asked two groups of schoolchildren to have fun creating some drawings.[1] Before being allowed to play with the crayons and paper, one group was told that they would receive an elaborate "good player" medal for drawing, while the other group was not promised any reward. A few weeks later the researchers returned, handed out drawing paper and crayons, and measured how much the children played with them. Surprisingly, the children who had received the medals on the first occasion spent significantly less time drawing than their classmates did.

Why did this happen? According to Lepper, the children who were offered the medals thought something along these lines: "Well, let me see here, adults usually offer me rewards when they want me to do something that I don't like doing. An adult is offering me a gold medal for drawing, therefore I must not like drawing." The effect has been replicated many times, and the conclusion is clear: if you set children to an activity that they enjoy and reward them for doing it, the reward reduces the enjoyment and demotivates them. Within a few seconds you transform play into work.

It could be argued that this outcome applies only to activities that people enjoy and that rewards actually encourage people with respect to tasks that they dislike. To test this theory, a few years ago I ran a study in which two groups of people were asked to take part in an experiment spending an afternoon picking up litter in a park.[2] Participants were told that they were taking part in an experiment examining how best to persuade people to look after their local parks. One group was paid handsomely for their time, while the other was given only a small amount of cash. After an hour or so of backbreaking and tedious work, everyone rated the degree to which they had enjoyed the afternoon. You might think that those clutching a large amount of well-earned cash would be more positive than those who had given their time for very little money.

In fact, exactly the opposite happened. The average enjoyment rating of the handsomely paid group was a measly 2 out of 10, while the modestly paid group's average rating proved to be a whopping 8.5. It seemed that those who had been paid well had thought, "Well, let me see, people usually pay me to do things that I don't enjoy. I was paid a large amount, so I must dislike cleaning the park." In contrast, those who received less money thought, "I don't need to be paid much to do something I enjoy. I did the cleaning for very little, so therefore I must have enjoyed cleaning the park." According to the results of this study, it seems that excessive rewards can even have a detrimental effect on tasks that people don't enjoy.

These findings have been replicated time and again. Almost regardless of the nature of the rewards or tasks, those who are offered a carrot tend not to perform as well as those who don't expect to receive anything.[3] Some of the studies have shown short-term boosts in performance, but over the long haul rewards tend to destroy the very behavior they are designed to encourage.

As we've seen, what does *not* work is to motivate people with the promise of a reward. So what form of incentive does work? To encourage people to do more of something they enjoy, try presenting them with the occasional small surprise reward after they have completed the activity or praising the fruits of their labor. When it is something that they don't enjoy, a realistic, but not excessive, reward is effective at the start, followed by feel-good comments that encourage them to pursue the activity ("If only everyone was a good park-cleaning citizen like you").

However, there are methods of persuasion other than praise, modest rewards, and cheesy comments. For quick and effective techniques, whether in negotiations or help in an emergency or getting the odd favor or two, think about putting your foot in the door, understanding groupthink, and realizing why it really is better to give than to receive.

GIVING THE PERFECT INTERVIEW

Just how do you go about trying to persuade someone to offer you a job? There is an old joke about a man being interviewed for a new job and being told, "You know, in this job we really need someone who is responsible." The man thinks for a moment, then replies, "I am perfect for you. In my last job lots of things went badly wrong, and they always said that I was responsible."

Unfortunately, disastrous replies are common in actual interviews—but help is at hand. Over the past thirty years, psychologists have investigated the key factors that impress interviewers, and the work has resulted in several quick and effective techniques that can significantly increase your chances of being offered your dream job.

Ask any employer to explain why they choose one applicant in preference to another, and they will tell you that it is a matter of which candidate has the best qualifications and personal skills for the job. To make the process as rational and fair as possible, many draw up a list of key skills that the successful candidate must possess, study each applicant's résumé for evidence of those skills, and then use a face-to-face interview to discover a little more information. But research conducted by Chad Higgins from the University of Washington and Timothy Judge from the University of Florida suggests that interviewers are often deluding themselves about how they make up their minds. In reality they are unconsciously swayed by a mysterious and powerful force.[4]

Higgins and Judge followed the fortunes of more than a hundred former students as they tried to obtain their first job after college. At the start of the study, the researchers examined the résumé of each student, measuring the two factors that interviewers consistently claim play a key role in separating successful and unsuccessful candidates—qualifications and work experience. After each job interview, students completed a standard questionnaire about how they had behaved, including whether, for example, they made the most of their positive points, took an interest in the company, or asked the interviewers about the type of person they were looking for. The research team also contacted the interviewers and asked them to provide feedback on several factors, including the candidate's performance, how well they would fit in with the organization, whether they possessed the necessary skills for the job, and, perhaps most important of all, whether they would be offered the job.

After analyzing the mass of data, the research team exploded some of the myths about why interviewers choose candidates for a job, discovering a surprising reality. Did the likelihood depend on qualifications? Or was it work experience? In fact, it was neither. It was just one important factor—did the candidate appear to be a pleasant person? Those who had managed to ingratiate themselves were very likely to be offered a position, and they charmed their way to success in several different ways.

A few had spent time chatting about topics that were not related to the job but that interested the candidate and the interviewer. Some had made a special effort to smile and maintain eye contact. Others had praised the organization. This barrage of positivity had paid dividends, convincing the interviewers that such pleasant and socially skilled applicants would fit well in the workplace and so should be offered a job.

Higgins and Judge's study clearly demonstrates that in order to get your dream job, going out of your way to be pleasant is more important than qualifications and past work experience. However, try explaining away twelve counts of murder and two convictions for major corporate fraud, and you will quickly discover that such ingratiation has its limitations. With respect to your weaknesses, then, what is the best way of dealing with the less-impressive side of your résumé? Should you mention weaknesses toward the start of the interview, or hope to make a good first impression and introduce possible problems only at the end?

This issue was investigated in an important study conducted in the early 1970s by psychologists Edward Jones and Eric Gordon from Duke University.[5] Participants were presented with a tape recording of a man (actually an accomplice of the experimenters) talking about his life. They were then asked to rate the degree to which he sounded likeable. During the interview the man told how he had not completed a school semester because he had been caught cheating and had been expelled. The researchers edited the tape so that half of the participants heard this bombshell toward the beginning, while the others heard it toward the end. This manipulation had a large impact on how much the participants liked the man. When the cheating was mentioned toward the start of the tape, the man appeared far more likeable than when it was mentioned toward the end. Additional work has confirmed exactly the same effect in other contexts, with, for example, lawyers being judged to have a stronger case when presenting a weakness in their argument at the beginning of a trial.[6]

It seems that presenting weaknesses early is seen as a sign of openness. This is a lesson that many politicians, such as Bill Clinton, have yet to learn. Interviewers believe that they are dealing with someone who has the strength of character and integrity to bring up potential difficulties at the outset, and they therefore conclude that the applicant is not attempting to mislead them.

Can the same be said of the more positive aspects of your résumé? Actually, no. In another part of the same study, participants heard a positive reason for the skipped semester ("I was awarded a prestigious scholarship to travel around Europe"), with the information presented either early or late on the tape. Now the effect was reversed, with the man appearing far more likeable when he mentioned the award later. It seems that modesty, rather than honesty, is critical for positive aspects of your past. By delaying mention of such details, you appear to prefer letting your strengths emerge naturally, while playing your cards early is seen as boastful.

So, you have polished up your ingratiating skills, are willing to declare your weaknesses early, and intend to leave the best till last. Does that mean that you are guaranteed to be a success? Unfortunately, no. Despite the best of intentions and the most extensive preparations, we all make mistakes. Perhaps you will knock a glass of water into your lap, inadvertently insult your interviewer, or give an answer that is as bumbling as it is unconvincing. The fact is, you need to be able to cope with the odd unexpected disaster or two. To help, Thomas Gilovich of Cornell University and his colleagues undertook a series of studies in which they forced people to wear Barry Manilow T-shirts.[7]

In a typical study, Gilovich arranged for five participants to arrive at the same time at his laboratory. Everyone was led into a room, asked to sit along one side of a table, and to complete a questionnaire. The group began to check off various boxes, unaware that the researchers had arranged for another participant to arrive five minutes late. This latecomer was met before entering the room and told to wear a T-shirt bearing a large picture of Barry Manilow. Why Manilow? Well, the study was about the psychology of embarrassment, and carefully controlled pretesting had revealed that the majority of Cornell students wouldn't be caught dead in a Barry Manilow T-shirt. Moments after putting on the T-shirt, the latecomer was bundled into the room, only to be confronted by a row of staring fellow students. After a few moments, the experimenter explained that it might be better to wait outside for a while, and promptly escorted the latecomer out of the room.

Two things happened next. Everyone in the room was asked if they had noticed the image on the latecomer's T-shirt, while the latecomer was asked to estimate the percentage of students who would have noticed the embarrassing image. The results from a series of experiments revealed that on average about 20 percent of the people in the room noticed Barry. However, the latecomers were convinced that the image had been far more eye-catching, and they estimated that on average about 50 percent of the group would have noticed the T-shirt. In short, the latecomers significantly overestimated the impact of their embarrassing encounter.

This bias, known as the "spotlight" effect, has been found in many different settings. From assessing the effects of a bad-hair day to performing poorly in a group discussion, those who feel embarrassed are convinced that their mistakes are far more noticeable than they actually are. Why? It seems that we focus on our own looks and behavior more than on those of others, and so we are likely to overestimate the impact of our situation. So, if you make a mortifying mistake in an interview, think about the man in the Barry Manilow T-shirt and remember that it probably feels far worse than it is.

IN 59 SECONDS

Increase your chances of giving a great interview in three easy steps.

First
Remember that likeability is more important than academic achievements and work experience, so . . .
- find something that you truly like about the organization, and let your opinion be known
- feel free to give a genuine compliment to the interviewer
- chat about a non-job-related topic that you and the interviewer find interesting
- show interest in the interviewer. Ask what type of person is being sought and how the position fits into the overall organization
- be enthusiastic about the position and the organization
- smile and maintain eye contact with the interviewer

Second

When you do have weaknesses, don't wait until late in the interview to reveal them. Instead, give your credibility a boost by getting them into the conversation toward the start of the interview. And remember, for positive aspects, modesty is vital, so retain something strong until the very last minute.

Third

If you make what seems like a major mistake, don't overreact. The chances are that it is far more noticeable to you than to others, and your excessive response or apologizing could just draw more attention to it. Instead, acknowledge the mistake, if appropriate, and then continue as if nothing has happened.

THREE QUICK TIPS FOR PERSUASION

Choose the Middle Way. If you want to increase your chances of making a good impression in a meeting, sit toward the middle of the table. Psychologists Priya Raghubir and Ana Valenzuela analyzed episodes of the television game show *The Weakest Link*.[8] In the show, contestants stand in a semicircle, and during each round one contestant is voted off by the other players. Contestants standing at the central positions in the semicircle reached the final round, on average, 42 percent of the time and won the game 45 percent of the time. Those standing at the more extreme positions reached the final round just 17 percent of the time and won just 10 percent of the time. In another experiment, participants were shown a group photograph of five candidates for a business internship and asked to choose which candidate should be awarded the position. Candidates in the center of the group were chosen more frequently than those at the edges. The researchers, labeling the phenomenon the "center stage" effect, concluded that when looking at a group, people use a basic rule of thumb— "Important people sit in the middle."

K.I.S.S. When thinking about the name of a new project, campaign, or product, keep it simple. Adam Alter and Daniel Oppenheimer, of Princeton University, tracked the fortunes of companies on the stock market and found that those with simple and memorable names, such as Flinks, Inc., tended to outperform companies with awkward names such as Sagxter, Inc.[9] Further research showed that the effect resulted not from larger companies' tending to have simpler names but from a natural tendency of people to be drawn to words that are easy to remember and straightforward to pronounce.

Mind Your Language. Who hasn't been tempted to slip the odd overcomplicated word into a report or letter to make themselves sound especially intelligent and erudite? According to other research conducted by Daniel Oppenheimer, an unnecessary love of the thesaurus may have exactly the opposite effect.[10] In a series of five studies, Oppenheimer systematically examined the complexity of the vocabulary used in passages from various kinds of texts (including job applications, academic essays, and translations of Descartes). He then asked people to read the samples and rate the intelligence of the person who allegedly wrote them. The simpler language resulted in significantly higher ratings of intelligence, showing that the unnecessary use of complex language sent out a bad impression. Oppenheimer described the results of the research in a paper titled "Consequences of Erudite Vernacular Utilized Irrespective of Necessity: Problems with Using Long Words

Needlessly." Among his findings was that passages presented in a font that was difficult to read lowered people's evaluations of the author's intelligence. These results suggest that you can increase how bright people think you are by merely writing legibly and simplifying your language.

FAVORS, PRATFALLS, AND GOSSIP

Likeability matters. The Gallup organization has examined the public perception of American presidential candidates since 1960, focusing on the impact of issues, party affiliation, and likeability.[11] From these factors, only likeability has consistently predicted the winning candidate. Similarly, research on relationships, by Phillip Noll at the University of Toronto, shows that likeable people are about 50 percent less likely to get divorced. Indeed, likeability might even save your life, as other studies indicate that doctors urge likeable patients to stay in touch and to return for more frequent checkups.

But what is the best way to ensure that you top the likeability league? Self-help guru Dale Carnegie has rightly pointed out that one way of increasing your popularity is to express a genuine interest in others. In fact, Carnegie argues, people will win more friends in two months by developing a genuine interest in those around them than in two years of trying to make others interested in them. Other writers have suggested alternative quick and easy routes, which include giving sincere compliments, matching people's body language and style of speech, appearing to be modest, and being generous with your time, resources, and skills. No doubt these kinds of commonsense techniques work. According to research, however, there are other, more subtle ideas that can also help you win friends and influence people. All it takes is a little advice from Benjamin Franklin, the ability to trip up once in a while, and an understanding of the power of gossip.

Eighteenth-century American polymath and politician Benjamin Franklin was once eager to gain the cooperation of a difficult and apathetic member of the Pennsylvania state legislature. Rather than spend his time bowing and scraping to the man, Franklin decided on a completely different course of action. He knew that the man had a copy of a rare book in his private library, and so Franklin asked whether he might be able to borrow it for a couple of days. The man agreed and, according to Franklin, "when we next met in the House, he spoke to me (which he had never done before), and with great civility; and he ever after manifested a readiness to serve me on all occasions." Franklin attributed the success of his book-borrowing technique to a simple principle: "He that has once done you a kindness will be more ready to do you another than he whom you yourself have obliged." In other words, to increase the likelihood that someone will like you, get that person to do you a favor. A century later, Russian novelist Leo Tolstoy appeared to agree, writing, "We do not love people so much for the good they have done us, as for the good we do them."

In the 1960s psychologists Jon Jecker and David Landy set out to discover if this two-hundred-year-old technique still worked in the twentieth century.[12] They arranged for participants in an experiment to win some money. Then, soon after the participants had left the laboratory, a researcher caught up with some of them and asked a favor. He explained that he had used his own funds for the study, was running short of cash, and wondered if the participants would mind returning the money. A second researcher, the departmental secretary, accosted another group of participants and made the same request, but this time explained that it was the psychology department that had financed the experiment, not personal money, and that the department was now a bit low on cash. Afterward, all of the participants were asked to rate how much they liked each researcher. Just as predicted by Franklin and Tolstoy all those years before, the participants liked the researcher who asked for help on a personal basis far more than they liked the researcher who made the request on behalf of the department.

Although it may sound strange, this curious phenomenon, referred to as the "Franklin" effect, is theoretically sound (at least when it comes to small favors—large requests can have the opposite effect, making people either respond begrudgingly or simply refuse). Most of the time people's behavior follows from their thoughts and feelings. They feel happy and so they smile, or they find someone attractive and so look longingly into the person's eyes. However, the reverse can also be true. Get people to smile and they feel happier, or ask them to look into someone's eyes and they find that person more attractive. Exactly the same principle applies for favors. To encourage others to like you, ask for their help.

The Franklin effect is not the only counterintuitive route to likeability. There is also the technique that helped John F. Kennedy become one of the most popular presidents in American history.

In 1961 Kennedy ordered troops to invade Cuba at the Bay of Pigs. The operation was a fiasco, and historians still view the decision as a huge military blunder. However, a national survey taken after the failed invasion showed that the public actually liked Kennedy more than earlier despite his disastrous decision. Two factors could account for this seemingly strange finding. Kennedy didn't try to make excuses or pass the buck for the botched operation; instead he immediately took full responsibility. Also, until that point in time, Kennedy had been seen as a superhero—a charming, handsome, powerful man who could do no wrong. The Bay of Pigs disaster made him appear far more human and likeable.

Elliot Aronson and his colleagues at the University of California decided to take an experimental approach to the issue in an effort to discover whether making a mistake or two is actually good for your popularity.[13] In one part of their study, participants listened to one of two audiotapes. Both tapes detailed a student's participation in a general-knowledge quiz, followed by him talking about his background. The student performed very well on the quiz, correctly answering more than 90 percent of the questions, and then he modestly admitted to a lifetime of success. However, in one of the two editions, toward the end of the recording, the participants heard the student knock over a cup of coffee and thereby ruin a new suit. All of the participants were asked to rate how likeable they found the student. Despite the only difference between the tapes being the fictitious knocking over of coffee, the student who had committed the blunder was considered far more likeable, just like Kennedy after the Bay of Pigs invasion. Interestingly, the effect emerges only when someone runs the risk of being seen as too perfect. In another part of the Aronson experiment, the researchers made two audiotapes of a more normal-sounding student who averaged just 30 percent correct answers on the quiz, and then outlined a series of more mediocre achievements. Under these conditions, spilling the coffee in his lap sent him plummeting to the bottom of the likeability scale, because he was perceived as a total loser.

This strange phenomenon, often referred to as the "pratfall" effect, may work well for presidents, and when heard on audiotapes, but does it also operate in other situations? To find out, I recently helped restage a version of Aronson's experiment, but this time the setting was a shopping center.[14]

We gathered a crowd and explained that they were going to see two trainees demonstrating how to make a fruit drink using a new type of blender. First was Sara, who played the role of our "perfect" person. Sara had spent the night before coming to grips with the device and learning a convincing script. In went the fruit, on went the lid, zoom went the liquidizer, and out came a perfect drink. The crowd rewarded Sara with a well-deserved round of applause and then eagerly awaited our second demonstrator, Emma, who was playing the part of our "less than perfect" person. This time, in went the fruit, on went the lid, zoom went the blender, off came the lid, and Emma ended up covered in fruit drink. Shaking the remains of the drink from the bottom of the blender into a glass, she received a sympathetic round of applause from the crowd.

After the first part of the experiment, it was time to explore the issue of likeability. We interviewed audience members about the two demonstrations. Which impressed them more? Were they more likely to buy a blender after seeing the first or the second demonstration? Most important of all, did they most like Sara or Emma? Although the public tended to find Sara's demonstration more professional and convincing, it was Emma who topped the likeability scale. When asked to explain their decision, people said that they found it difficult to identify with Sara's flawless performance but warmed to Emma's more human display. Although not the perfect experiment (for example, Emma and Sara were not identical twins, so maybe their looks influenced the crowd's judgment), it provides further support that the occasional trip-up can be good for your social life.

The third, and final, route to likeability involves a very human trait—the desire to gossip. Most people like to pass on a juicy bit of information about friends and colleagues, but is such behavior good for them? John Skowronski, from Ohio State University at Newark, and his colleagues investigated the downside of spreading malicious gossip.[15] Participants watched videotapes of actors talking about a third party (a friend or acquaintance of the actor). Some of the actor's comments about his friend were very negative, such as "He hates animals. Today he was walking to the store and he saw this puppy. So he kicked it out of his way." Afterward, the participants were asked to rate the personality of the speaker. Remarkably, even though it was obvious that the person on the videotape was criticizing someone else, the participants consistently attributed the negative traits to the speaker. This effect, known as "spontaneous trait transference," reveals the pluses and minuses of gossiping. When you gossip about another person, listeners unconsciously associate you with the characteristics you are describing, ultimately leading to those characteristics' being "transferred" to you. So, say positive and pleasant things about friends and colleagues, and you are seen as a nice person. In contrast, constantly complain about their failings, and people will unconsciously apply the negative traits and incompetence to you.

IN 59 SECONDS

Self-help gurus have argued that it is possible to increase your likeability by becoming more empathetic, modest, and generous. They are probably right. But there are also three other surprising factors that can promote popularity.

The Franklin Effect
People like you more when they do a favor for you. The effect has its limits, however, and is more likely to work with small favors rather than more significant requests that make people either respond begrudgingly or, even worse, refuse.

The Pratfall Effect
The occasional slipup can enhance your likeability. However, remember that the effect really works only when you are in danger of being seen as too perfect.

Gossip
Know that whatever traits you assign to others are likely to come home to roost, being viewed as part of your own personality.

QUICK PERSUASION TIPS

Make It Personal. In 1987 the public contributed $700,000 to assist a baby who had fallen into a well in Texas, and in 2002 they gave $48,000 to help a dog stranded on a ship in the Pacific Ocean. In contrast, organizations constantly struggle to raise funds to help prevent the 15 million or so deaths from starvation that occur each year, or the ten thousand annual child deaths in America resulting from car accidents. Why? In a recent study, researchers paid people for their involvement in an experiment and then presented them with an opportunity to contribute some of the money to the Save the Children charity. Before making any contribution, half of the participants were shown statistics about the millions facing starvation in Zambia, while the other half saw a story about the plight of just one 7–year-old African girl.[16] Those who saw the story of the girl contributed more than twice the

---

amount given by those who saw only statistics. Irrational as it is, people are swayed far more by the individual than by the masses.

"Yes, yes, yes." Research conducted in the 1980s, by psychologist Daniel Howard from Southern Methodist University, supported the persuasive impact of positive utterances. Howard arranged for researchers to telephone randomly selected people and ask whether a representative of the "Hunger Relief Committee" could visit their home and try to sell them some cookies for charity.[17] Half of the researchers started their conversations with a simple question designed to get a positive answer, asking "How are you feeling this evening?" As expected, the vast majority of people responded favorably ("Great," "Fine, thanks"). More important, this act had a dramatic influence on whether they would allow a salesperson into their house. Of those who were in the "How are you feeling?" group, 32 percent accepted the offer, compared to just 18 percent in the control "no question" group. The message is that people are more likely to agree with you when they have already said something positive.

"Let me get this." In a series of studies during the 1930s, psychologist Gregory Razran discovered that people developed a special fondness for other people, objects, and statements if they were introduced to them while eating a meal.[18] The effect may be attributable to the fact that good food puts people in a happy mood and can cause them to make faster, and more impulsive, decisions.[19] More recently, researchers discovered that people who have just consumed caffeinated drinks were more likely to be swayed by arguments about various controversial topics.[20] In short, it's good evidence that there really is no such thing as a free lunch, or an innocent cup of coffee.

Save Your Time, Persuade by Rhyme. In his influential book *The Gay Science*, German philosopher Friedrich Nietzsche argued that rhyming poetry originally appealed to the primitive mind because it appeared to have magical connotations and represented a way of speaking directly with the gods. Although this view has not been universally accepted, recent research does suggest that rhymes can be surprisingly effective. Psychologists Matthew McGlone and Jessica Tofighbakhsh (try finding a rhyme for that) showed people well-known rhyming sayings ("Caution and measure will win you treasure" and "Life is mostly strife") and some non-rhyming counterparts ("Caution and measure will win you riches" and "Life is mostly a struggle") and instructed the readers to rate how accurately they described human behavior.[21] The rhymes were viewed as significantly more accurate than the non-rhyming statements. The authors suggested that this was the outcome because they were more memorable, likeable, and repeatable. The effect is frequently used in advertising ("The best part of waking up is Folgers in your cup") and has even made its way into the courtroom, as when attorney Johnnie Cochran defended O. J. Simpson by using the phrase "If the gloves don't fit, you must acquit."

Peas in a Pod. For persuasion, the research points to a simple fact: similarity works. For example, Randy Garner, of Sam Houston State University, mailed surveys, varying the information on the cover sheet to ensure that the first name of the addressee either matched or didn't match the experimenter's first name.[22] So in the "matching name" group, a participant named Fred Smith might receive a survey from researcher Fred Jones, while in the "non-matching name" group, participant Julie Green might get a survey from Amanda White. This remarkably simple manipulation affected the response rate, with 30 percent in the non-matching name condition returning the survey, compared to 56 percent returned from those who saw their own first name on the cover. Other work suggests that people are far more likely to support, and agree with, those who appear to be like them. In one study, more than six thousand American voters rated their own personalities and how they perceived the personalities of John Kerry and George W. Bush.[23] Both sets of voters agreed that Kerry was far more open to new ideas and concepts than Bush, but they thought that Bush was more loyal and sincere than Kerry. However, exactly the same pattern of traits emerged in the voters' assessments of themselves, with those who voted for Kerry rating themselves as more open-minded than the Bush voters and Bush supporters seeing themselves as more trustworthy than those who voted for Kerry. Regardless of whether the similarity is in dress, speech, background, age, religion, politics, drinking and smoking habits, food preferences, opinions, personality, or body language, we like people who are like us, and we find them far more persuasive than others.

Remember to Mention Your Pet Frog. When it comes to persuading others, try lightening up. In a study conducted by Karen O'Quinn and Joel Aronoff, participants were asked to negotiate with a seller over the purchase price of a piece of art.[24] Toward the end of the negotiation, the seller made a final offer in one of two ways. Half of the time they said that they would accept $6,000, while the other half of the time they gave the same final price but also added a little humor ("Well, my final offer is $6,000, and I'll throw in my pet frog"). Those few moments of attempted humor had a large effect, as participants made a much greater compromise in their purchase price when they heard about the frog. The effect worked just as well with men and women, regardless of the degree to which the seller's final price was above the amount originally offered by the participant. It seemed that the brief humorous aside momentarily put the participant in a good mood and encouraged them to be more giving. So, next time you're trying to get what you want, remember to mention your pet frog.

WHY TOO MANY COOKS LEADS TO NO COOKING AT ALL, AND WHAT CAN BE DONE ABOUT IT

On March 13, 1964, a young woman named Kitty Genovese was returning to her apartment in New York City's borough of Queens when she was the victim of a random and vicious attack. Although she parked her car less than a hundred feet from her door, she was overpowered by a total stranger during the short walk to her apartment and repeatedly stabbed. Despite the ordeal, Genovese managed to scream for help and stagger toward her apartment. Unfortunately, her attacker caught up with her and inflicted a second set of injuries that proved fatal.

On March 27, the *New York Times* ran a front-page article about the attack, describing how a large number of respectable, law-abiding citizens" had either witnessed or heard the attack but had not telephoned the police during the assault. The detective in charge of the case reportedly could not understand why so many witnesses did so little. The story was quickly picked up by other media, and most journalists concluded that Genovese's neighbors simply didn't care enough to get involved and characterized the incident as damning evidence of how modern-day American society had lost its way. The tragic story caught the public imagination, and it has since inspired several books, films, and songs, and even a sensitively titled musical drama *The Screams of Kitty Genovese.*[25]

The witnesses' lack of involvement also puzzled two social psychologists working in New York at the time. Bibb Latané and John Darley were unconvinced that the apparent widespread apathy reflected a lack of empathy, and they set about investigating some of the other factors that could have caused the witnesses to turn their backs rather than pick up the telephone. The two researchers reasoned that the large number of witnesses may have played a pivotal role, and they carried out a series of ingenious experiments that have since been described in almost every social psychology textbook published in the last thirty years.[26]

In their first study, Latané and Darley had a student fake an epileptic seizure on the streets of New York and observed whether passersby took the time to help. As they were interested in the effect that the number of witnesses might have on the likelihood of any one of them helping, the researchers staged the fake seizure again and again in front of different numbers of people. The results were as clear as they were counterintuitive. As the number of witnesses increased, the chances that any one of them would help decreased. The effect was far from trivial: the student received assistance 85 percent of the time when there was one other person present but only about 30 percent of the time when five others were present.

In another study, the researchers moved off the streets and turned their attention to groups of people sitting in a waiting room.[27] Rather than faking an epileptic seizure, they created another apparent emergency: smoke seeping under the waiting room door, suggesting that a fire had broken out in the building. Once again, the larger the group, the smaller the chance of anyone raising the alarm. Of people sitting on their own, 75 percent reported the smoke, versus just 38 percent when there were three people in the room. Other work revealed exactly the same effect, regardless of whether the need for assistance was large or small. For example, the team arranged for 145 stooges to take 1,497 elevator rides, in each of which they dropped some coins or pencils. A total of 4,813 people shared the elevators with them.[28] When accompanied by just one other person, the researchers' coins and pencils were picked up 40 percent of the time, whereas when they were sharing the elevator with six others, the rate of assistance went down to just 20 percent.

From helping a stranded motorist to donating blood to reporting a shoplifter or making an emergency telephone call, exactly the same pattern has emerged time and again. It seems that the witnesses to the Kitty Genovese attack were not especially uncaring or selfish—there were just too many of them.

Why should the urge to help others decrease as the number of people in the room increases? When faced with a relatively uncommon event, such as a man falling down in the street, we have to decide what's going on. Often there are several options. Maybe it really is a genuine emergency and the man is having a real epileptic fit, or maybe he has just tripped, or perhaps he is faking it as part of a social psychology experiment, or maybe he is part of a hidden-camera stunt show, or perhaps he is a mime just about to start his street show. Despite the various possibilities, we have to make a quick decision. But how do we do that? One way is to look at the behavior of those around us. Are they rushing to help, or are they continuing to go about their daily business? Are they telephoning for an ambulance or still chatting with their friends? Unfortunately, because most people are reluctant to stand out from the crowd, everyone looks to everyone else for pointers, and the group can end up deciding to do nothing. Even if a clear and present need for help exists, there is still the issue of responsibility. In most everyday situations, there is no clear chain of command. Is it your job to help, or should you leave it to the guy over there (not him, the guy behind him)? Everyone in the group thinks in the same way, which can result in no one helping at all.

The situation is very different when you are on your own. Suddenly you are carrying all the weight on your shoulders. What if the guy who has just fallen over really is in need of help? What if the building really is on fire? What if that woman in the elevator really does need that pencil to put between her teeth before a particularly gloomy meeting? Are you prepared to be the person who turned their back and walked away? Under these circumstances, most people are far more likely to find out if there is a problem and, if necessary, provide a helping hand.

Latané and Darley's groundbreaking studies of what has become known as the "bystander" effect were initiated by the behavior of thirty-eight witnesses who saw or heard the tragic murder of Kitty Genovese but didn't lend a helping hand. Interestingly, recent work suggests that the original media reports of the murder may have exaggerated the alleged apathy, with one of the attorneys involved saying that they could find only about half a dozen good witnesses, that none of them actually reported seeing Genovese being stabbed and at least one claimed that the incident *was* reported to the police while it was happening.[29] Regardless of the reactions that took place on that particular night, however, the experiments that followed from the media reports of the murder provide compelling insight into why being surrounded by strangers in a moment of need provides no guarantee of receiving help.

IN 59 SECONDS

The message from the bystander effect is clear—the more people who are around when a person is apparently in need of assistance, the lower the likelihood that any one person will actually help.

So, if you are unfortunate enough to require assistance in the street, what can you do to increase your chances of obtaining help? According to persuasion expert Robert Cialdini, the answer is to pick out a friendly face in the crowd and clearly tell them what is happening and what they need to do. It might be a question of saying that you think you are having a heart attack and that they need to call an ambulance, or that you are diabetic and need sugar as soon as possible. Do anything that short-circuits the diffusion of responsibility underlying the problem and helps transform a bystander from a faceless member of the crowd into a fully functioning human being.

An understanding of the diffusion of responsibility may also help you to persuade people in other situations. For example, when trying to get people to help you via e-mail, do not send your message to an entire group. When people see that an e-mail has been sent to lots of others, the same diffusion effect can arise, with everyone thinking that it is everyone else's responsibility to respond.[30] To increase the chances of getting people to help, send the message to each person individually.

EVERY PENNY HELPS

Is it possible to increase the amount donated to good causes by creating the perfect "donation box"? To find out, I teamed up with Borders bookstores and conducted a weeklong secret study. Participating stores were sent four donation boxes. The boxes were identical in shape and size, and all advertised the same charity—the National Literacy Trust. Each carried one of four messages that psychologists believed would be effective: "Please give generously," "Every penny helps," "Every dollar helps," and "You can make a difference." Managers were asked to place each box at one of four randomly selected registers and monitor the amount collected at each location.

Did our different messages make an impact on the cash donated to charity? Yes. At the end of the experiment, the four types of boxes contained very different amounts of money. "Every penny helps" worked best, accounting for an impressive 62 percent of all contributions, while "Every dollar helps" trailed, with just 7 percent of the total take. Why should such a small change have such a big effect? According to work by psychologist Robert Cialdini at Arizona State University,[31] many people are concerned that putting a very small amount of money into a box will make them look cheap, and so they end up giving nothing at all. "Every penny helps" legitimates, and therefore encourages, the smallest of contributions. In contrast, "Every dollar helps" has the reverse effect—people who would have contributed less are suddenly concerned that their donation will appear paltry, and so they end up giving nothing at all.

In another part of the experiment we varied the color of the boxes and discovered that red was by far the most effective, perhaps because it elicits a sense of urgency. Interestingly, large variations in donations emerged between regions.

All told, the results show that donation boxes can become up to 200 percent more effective by being painted red and labeled "Every penny counts."

ON THE IMPORTANCE OF SCRATCHING BACKS

According to the Bible, it is better to give than to receive. This notion is also supported by research into the psychology of persuasion, albeit in ways that might not have been intended by the Good Book.

In December 1970 psychologists Phillip Kunz and Michael Woolcott conducted perhaps the simplest social psychology experiment ever.[32] Over the course of a couple of weeks, they popped some Christmas cards in the mail. However, Kunz and Woolcott did not send the cards to their friends, family, or colleagues; instead they randomly selected the recipients' names and addresses from a local telephone directory. The two intrepid researchers, interested in the psychology of reciprocity, wondered whether the act of receiving a greeting card from a total stranger would be enough to persuade people to send a card back. The answer was a resounding yes. Kunz and Woolcott quickly received cards from the majority of those on their random list of complete strangers.

The principle of reciprocity has been explored by those interested in the science of persuasion. Perhaps not surprisingly, the work hasn't tended to focus on persuading strangers to send Christmas cards. Instead, it has examined whether the same technique also influences more important aspects of people's behavior.

In the 1970s psychologist Dennis Regan invited people to help out with an experiment exploring aesthetics and art. Willing volunteers were asked to come to an exhibition one at a time and were told that on arrival they would be met by another participant. Together, they would then have to rate each of the paintings being shown.[33] Now, if you take part in a social psychology experiment and are asked to meet another participant, you can bet your bottom dollar that your newfound friend is actually working for the experimenter. True to form, this was the case in Regan's study. The stooge had been given very careful instructions. When accompanying the genuine participants around the gallery, he was suddenly to become thirsty and head toward the free-drinks table. He would return refreshed, but half of the time he would be empty-handed; the other half of the time he would carry a bottle of cola that he had picked up for the genuine participant.

Now, if you take part in a psychology experiment, and your fellow "participant" helps you in any way at all, you can bet that you are just moments away from being asked a favor. Again, Regan didn't break with tradition. After all the paintings had been rated, the stooge turned to the genuine participant, explained that he was selling raffle tickets and had only a handful left. They were 25 cents each, and if he sold the last few tickets he would win a $50 prize. He asked them to contribute: "Any would help, the more the better."

Even though the cola had not actually cost the stooge anything, it had a large impact on participants' behavior, with those in the "I picked this bottle up for you" group buying twice as many raffle tickets as those who did not receive the cola.

Several other studies have also illustrated how apparently spontaneous favors can elicit a powerful need to reciprocate. In one especially elegant and effective experiment, psychologist David Strohmetz and his colleagues arranged for waiters to hand customers their checks with or without candy, and examined the impact on tipping.[34] In the control group, diners were unlucky enough to receive their checks without any sweets at all. A second group was given a single piece of candy with their bills. This simple gesture of kindness resulted in a measly 3 percent increase in tips compared to the control group. A third group received two sweets each and, again compared to the control group, gave 14 percent larger tips. Not bad. However, here comes the really clever part. In the fourth and final group, the waiters were asked to present the check to customers along with one piece of candy each, then, just as they were turning away from the table, reach into their pocket and quickly hand everyone a second piece. In terms of candy per customer, everyone ended up with exactly the same number of candies as those in the third group. But psychologically speaking, this was very, very different. The waiter had just done the customers an unnecessary and nice favor, and because of that, tips increased by an impressive 23 percent.

Why do these kinds of small favors produce such big results?

According to sociologists, there are only a handful of rules that are absolutely central to the well-being of any society. These rules have been found in almost every culture and help to ensure the smooth running of communal living. Perhaps the best known of these is "Don't kill other people simply for the fun of it," closely followed by "Try not to have sex with members of your close family, or their pets." Even though a minority of people struggle to adhere to these rules, it is obvious why both of them help keep society together. There are, however, several other rules that operate at a more subconscious level but are nevertheless equally vital for group welfare. The notion of reciprocation is perhaps the most important of these.

In order to keep society in one piece, people have to work together and help one another. However, some people will always give more than they take, so how do you know whom to help and whom to ignore? A key part of making this complex decision involves a surprisingly simple rule of thumb: you help those who have helped you. In other words, I scratch your back and you scratch mine. That way, we both have our backs scratched and all is well with the world. If every occasion of reciprocation were this instant and equal, there would be very little room for the exploitation that fascinates those who study the psychology of persuasion. Thankfully, from a researcher's point of view, the real world of back-scratching is a little more complex. If I scratch your back, it says that I like and trust you and that I am a nice person deserving of your help when the time comes. These factors combine to create a potent force that often results in people giving me significantly more than they receive from me. In the art gallery experiment, the bottle of soda was free, but it nevertheless persuaded people to put their hands in their pockets and buy raffle tickets. In the restaurant experiment, the extra candy was worth a few pennies, but it caused people to leave a significantly larger tip.

We like people who help us, and we help people we like. However, for favors, it is surprising how little it takes for us to like a person and how much we give on the basis of so little. It seems that if you want to help yourself, you need to help others first.

IN 59 SECONDS

A large body of research has shown that doing a favor for someone often results in their giving significantly more in return. So does that mean that all favors will result in especially giving and helpful behavior? Additional research has revealed that there are several subtle factors that influence when favors are most effective.

Favors have their strongest effect when they occur between people who don't know each other very well, and when they are small but thoughtful. When people go to a great deal of effort to help someone else, the recipient can often feel an uncomfortable pressure to reciprocate. In a sense, by giving too much at the beginning, one person places the other in a difficult position because the law of reciprocity states that the recipient has to give even more in return. Motivation is also important, as recipients can often experience a drop in self-esteem if they think they are being helped because they are believed not to have the ability to be successful by themselves[35] or if they attribute the favor to an ulterior motive.[36] So, for maximum persuasion, remember: save your favors for strangers, it really is the thought that counts, and the favor has to appear to come from the heart, not the head.

The degree of reciprocity may depend to some extent on cultural factors. In one study by Michael Morris and his colleagues at Columbia Business School, people from different countries were asked about the factors that influenced whether they would assist a colleague who asked for help.[37] Americans were heavily influenced by the reciprocity rule ("Has this person helped me in the past?"), Germans were more concerned about whether their actions would be consistent with company rules, the Spanish were driven more by basic rules of friendship and liking, and the Chinese were swayed by the status of the coworker.

Finally, if you want to get maximum return for your investment, ask for the return favor quickly. Francis Flynn from Stanford University surveyed employees in the customer-service department of a major U.S. airline, and found that favors have their greatest power immediately after they have been granted.[38] It seems that if you leave it too long, people either forget what happened or convince themselves that they didn't really need the help in the first place.

NEVER LOSE YOUR WALLET AGAIN

A few weeks ago I lost my wallet. I panicked, then calmed down, then carefully retraced my steps and failed to find the wallet, then panicked again, then calmed down again, and finally set about canceling my credit cards. Unfortunately, I never saw my wallet again. However, on the upside, I now have a nice new wallet that is far superior to my old worn-out one. I am very eager that my new wallet and I don't permanently part company, so I wondered what I could put into my new wallet to maximize the chances of its being returned if lost.

It turns out that I am not the first person to think about what might encourage someone to return a lost wallet. In the late 1960s and early 1970s, researchers interested in the psychology of helping carried out several studies in which they secretly dropped wallets on busy streets and then monitored the return rates. Perhaps the most prolific of these wallet droppers was psychologist Harvey Hornstein from Columbia University.

Hornstein spent years systematically studying some of the factors that influence the return rates of wallets. In one study, for example, he examined whether people would be more likely to return a wallet if it elicited positive, rather than negative, feelings.[39] Like many of Hornstein's studies, this experiment involved creating a rather unusual scenario giving the impression that the wallet had been lost not once but twice. According to this scenario, the original owner had lost his wallet, and then someone else had found it, attached a short note, and placed it in an envelope addressed to the original owner. However, on the way to the mailbox, the well-intentioned finder had inadvertently dropped the envelope on the street and thus lost the wallet a second time. Those who unknowingly took part in Hornstein's experiment came across an unsealed envelope containing a wallet with a note wrapped around it and had to decide whether to post the envelope back to the original owner. Half of the notes sounded very positive ("It has been a pleasure to help someone . . . and really has been no problem at all"), while the others were far more negative ("I was quite annoyed at having to return it and hope you appreciate the effort I have gone through"). The difference in wording had a significant impact on people's behavior, with almost 40 percent of the wallets with positive notes being returned versus just 12 percent of those with negative notes.

Although Hornstein's finding is interesting, I somehow couldn't see myself permanently wrapping a happy-sounding note around my wallet. Unfortunately, the same applies to much of the academic work into wallet dropping: although it is theoretically sound, it is not especially practical. Unperturbed, I canvassed friends for more useful suggestions about what I might put inside my wallet. Among the ideas were photographs of a baby, a dog, or something that suggested the owner was a thoroughly nice person. To find out which idea was the most effective, I turned back time and conducted a Hornsteinesque study.

I bought 240 wallets and filled them with the same set of everyday items, including raffle tickets, discount vouchers, and fake membership cards. Next, one of four photographs was added to four batches of 40 wallets. The photographs depicted either a smiling baby, a cute puppy, a happy family, or a contented elderly couple. Another 40 wallets contained a card suggesting that the owner had recently made a contribution to charity, while the final batch of 40 acted as a control and contained no additional item. Each extra item was inserted behind a plastic window in each wallet, making it clearly visible when the wallet was opened. All of the wallets were then randomly ordered, and over a period of a couple of weeks were secretly dropped on the streets in areas of high pedestrian traffic but well away from mailboxes, trash containers, vomit, and dog feces.

Within a week 42 percent of the wallets were returned, and a clear pattern emerged. Of the wallets that made their way back, just 6 percent were from the control group, and 8 percent contained the charity card. The results from the wallets containing a photograph of the elderly couple, a cute puppy, or a happy-looking family were slightly more impressive, with return rates of 11 percent, 19 percent, and 21 percent, respectively. However, the winning wallets were those with the photograph of the smiling baby, taking first place with an impressive 35 percent return rate.

Why should the photograph of the baby have performed so well? The answer appears to lie deep within our evolutionary past. Brain-scanning scientists at Oxford University recently examined what was going on in people's heads when they were shown photographs of either baby or adult faces.[40] Even though all of the photographs were matched for attractiveness, activity in the section of the brain directly behind the eyes (officially referred to as the "medial orbitofrontal cortex") kicked in within a seventh of a second after seeing the baby's face but not the adult's. The response happened too fast to be consciously controlled, and the part of the brain involved is associated with people receiving a nice reward, such as a big bar of chocolate or a lottery win. Many scientists think that this "baby-awww" linkage has evolved over thousands of years and promotes the survival of future generations by making people feel good about, and therefore willing to help, vulnerable and defenseless infants. Other research suggests that this caring attitude not only applies to assisting babies but also increases the likelihood of people helping anyone in need. In this view, participants who opened the wallets containing the photograph of the baby couldn't keep their brains from automatically responding to the image of big eyes, broad forehead, and button nose. Within a fraction of a second a deep-seated evolutionary mechanism caused them to rapidly get in touch with their inner parent, become happier and more caring, and thus be more likely to return the wallet.

Whatever the explanation, the practical message is clear: if you want to up the chances of a lost wallet being returned, tuck in a photograph of the cutest, happiest baby you can find and make sure that it is prominently displayed.

motivation

The dark side of visualization,

how to achieve absolutely anything

by creating the ideal plan,

overcoming procrastination,

and employing "doublethink"

THROUGHOUT THE PAST FORTY YEARS, a large number of books, audio products, and training courses have promised to help people look beyond the perils of instant gratification and achieve their long-term goals. From visualization to self-affirmation, from being focused to going with the flow, you pays your money and you takes your choice. There is just one small problem: several scientific studies suggest that many of these exercises don't work. Take, for example, the type of simple visualization exercise that I described at the start of this book. As you may remember, you were asked to close your eyes and imagine the new you—to think how great you would look in those close-fitting jeans, sitting in a huge office at the top of the corporate ladder, or sipping a cocktail as you feel the warm Caribbean sand between your toes. This type of exercise has been promoted by the self-help industry for years, with claims that it can help people lose weight, stop smoking, find their perfect partner, and enjoy increased career success. Unfortunately, a large body of research now suggests that although such exercises might make you feel good, the technique is, at best, ineffective.

In one study, conducted by Lien Pham and Shelley Taylor at the University of California, a group of students was asked to spend a few moments each day visualizing themselves getting a high grade on an important midterm exam that would take place in a few days' time.[1] They were asked to form a clear image in their mind's eye and imagine how great it would feel to make a high grade. The study also involved a control group of students, who went about their business as usual and were not asked to visualize doing especially well on the exams. The experimenters asked the students in both groups to make a note of the number of hours they studied each day, and monitored their final grades. Even though the daydreaming exercise lasted only a few minutes, it had a significant impact on the students' behavior, causing them to study less and make lower grades on the exam. The exercise may have made them feel better about themselves, but it did not help them achieve their goals.

In another experiment, Gabriele Oettingen and Thomas Wadden, at the University of Pennsylvania, followed a group of obese women taking part in a weight-reduction program.[2] During the work, the women were asked to imagine how they might behave in various food-related scenarios, such as going to a friend's house and being tempted with tasty pizza. Each of their responses was categorized on a scale ranging from highly positive (with, for example, someone stating, "I would be a good person and stay well away from the cakes and ice cream") to highly negative ("I would be straight in there, consuming both my own and other people's portions"). After the women were tracked for a year, the results revealed that those with more positive fantasies had lost, on average, twenty-six pounds less than those with negative fantasies.

Oettingen's work has also shown that the same effects happen in many different situations.[3] In yet another study, she worked with a group of students who admitted to having a serious but secret crush on a classmate. She asked them to imagine what would happen in various scenarios, such as arriving early for class, sitting down, then seeing the door open and the apple of their eye enter. Once again, the degree of fantasizing was rated, this time varying between those who seemed to live in a world that would make even the most ardent reader of Harlequin romances blush ("Our eyes meet, and we both know that this is the type of love that happens only once in a lifetime") to more negative scenarios ("We are both free and single. He turns to me, smiles, and asks how I am. For some reason that I still do not fully understand, I explain that I already have a boyfriend"). Five months later, the results revealed that those with positive fantasies were less likely than others to have told the desirable classmate about their crush or made any other overture toward having a relationship with them.

Exactly the same effect applies to career success. Oettingen asked her senior students to note how often they fantasized about getting their dream job after graduating from college. A two-year follow-up revealed that the students who had reported frequently fantasizing about success had submitted fewer job applications, received a lower number of job offers, and commanded significantly smaller salaries than their classmates.

Why should it be so bad for you to imagine yourself achieving your goals? Researchers have speculated that those who fantasize about how wonderful life could be are ill prepared for the setbacks that frequently occur along the rocky road to success, or perhaps they enjoy indulging in escapism and so become reluctant to put in the effort required to achieve their goals. Either way, the message from the research is clear: fantasizing about your perfect world may make you feel better, but it is unlikely to help you transform your dreams into reality.

Fortunately, as this chapter will demonstrate, the results from other research into motivation are not all doom and gloom. A large amount of work has revealed that some techniques do help create permanent and positive changes in people's lives. From weight loss to quitting smoking, changing careers to finding your perfect partner, there are quick and painless techniques that can provide real help. It's all about having the perfect plan, knowing how to beat procrastination, and employing a rather strange form of doublethink.

CREATING THE PERFECT PLAN

Think back to when you have attempted to achieve an important goal or ambition. Perhaps losing some weight, getting a new job, studying for an exam, or preparing for a key interview. What sorts of techniques did you use? Read each of the following statements and then decide whether you tend to use the technique described. Don't spend too long thinking about each statement, and answer as honestly as possible.

When attempting to change an important aspect of my life, I tend to . . .

	YES	NO
1 make a step-by-step plan.		
2 motivate myself by focusing on someone that I admire for achieving so much (e.g., a celebrity role model or great leader).		
3 tell other people about my goal.		
4 think about the bad things that will happen if I don't achieve my goal.		
5 think about the good things that will happen if I achieve my goal.		
6 try to suppress unhelpful thoughts (e.g., avoid thinking about eating unhealthy food or smoking).		

	YES	NO
7 reward myself for making progress toward my goal.		
8 rely on willpower.		
9 record my progress (e.g., in a journal or on a chart).		
10 fantasize about how great my life will be when I achieve my goal.		

Now you need to create two scores. Create Score A by awarding yourself 1 point for each "Yes" answer to questions 1, 3, 5, 7, and 9. Next, create Score B by giving yourself 1 point for each "No" answer to questions 2, 4, 6, 8, and 10. Disregard all other answers. Finally, add Score A and Score B to obtain a number between 0 and 10.

A few years ago I conducted two large-scale scientific studies on the psychology of motivation. The project involved tracking more than five thousand participants from around the world who were attempting to achieve a wide range of aims and ambitions, including losing weight, gaining new qualifications, starting a new relationship, quitting smoking, embarking on a new career, and being more environmentally friendly. One group was followed for six months, the other for one year. At the beginning of the project, the vast majority of participants was confident of doing well. At the end of their allotted time period, everyone was asked to describe the techniques that they had used to try to achieve their goals and to report their level of success. Only about 10 percent reported that they had successfully achieved their aims and ambitions.

The questionnaire above contains the ten techniques that participants used most frequently. Some sound like good common sense, and others frequently appear in self-help books and training courses. However, although the techniques may appear credible, according to our data, only half of them significantly increase your chances of being successful, while the other half are ineffective. The question is, which are which?

In our experiment, participants who endorsed the even-numbered items in the questionnaire were unlikely to achieve their goals. So, for example, those who adopted a celebrity role model, perhaps putting a picture of Cindy Crawford or Bill Gates on their refrigerator door, did not usually drop that all-important clothing size or achieve their business ambitions. Similarly, those relying on willpower, using thought suppression to erase images of cream cakes and chocolate sundaes from their mind, focusing on the bad things that would happen if they didn't achieve their goals, or spending their time daydreaming were also wasting their time. All of these techniques constitute yet more striking examples of the types of motivational myths that prevent people from taking control of their lives.

A different story emerged when we examined the data from the people using the techniques that have an odd number in the questionnaire. Each of these five tools significantly increased the likelihood that people would successfully achieve their aims. Let's look at each in turn.

First, the successful participants in our study had a plan. Author Zig Ziglar once famously remarked that people don't tend to wander around and then suddenly find themselves at the top of Mount Everest. Likewise, those moving aimlessly through life are unlikely to end up suddenly starting a new business or losing a significant amount of weight. Successful participants broke their overall goal into a series of sub-goals and thereby created a step-by-step process that helped remove the fear and hesitation often associated with trying to achieve a major life change. These plans were especially powerful when the sub-goals were concrete, measurable, and time-based. Whereas successful and unsuccessful participants might have stated that their aim was to find a new job, it was the successful people who quickly went on to describe how they intended to rewrite their résumé in week one and then apply for one new job every two weeks for the next six months. Similarly, although many people said that they aimed to enjoy life more, it was the successful ones who explained how they intended to spend two evenings each week with friends and visit one new country each year.

Second, successful participants were far more likely than others to tell their friends, family, and colleagues about their goals. It seems that although keeping your promises to yourself helps ease the fear of failure, it also makes it too easy to avoid changing your life and to drift back to old habits and routines. This is in keeping with several key findings from the psychology literature illustrating that people are more likely to stick to their views and promises if they go public. In one classic experiment, students were asked to estimate the length of some lines that had been drawn on a pad and either make a public commitment to their judgments (by writing them on a slip of paper, signing the paper, and handing it to the experimenter) or keep the estimates to themselves.[4] When the participants were informed that their estimates might be wrong, those who had made a public commitment were far more likely to stand by their opinion than those who had not told anyone. Other work suggests that the greater the public declaration, the more motivated people are to achieve their goals.[5] Telling others about your aims also helps you achieve them, in part because friends and family often provide much-needed support when the going gets tough. In fact, some research suggests that having friends at your side makes life seem easier. In a series of studies carried out by Simone Schnall from the University of Plymouth, people were taken to the bottom of a hill and asked to estimate how steep it was and therefore how difficult it would be to climb.[6] When they were accompanied by a friend, their estimates were about 15 percent lower than when they were on their own, and even just thinking about a friend when looking at the hill made it seem far more surmountable.

Third, those who ended up making and maintaining permanent changes in their lives frequently tended to remind themselves of the benefits associated with achieving their goals. It wasn't a case of imagining their perfect selves but rather of having an objective checklist of how life would be better once they achieved their aim. In contrast, unsuccessful participants tended to focus on how failure to change would result in having to endure the negative aspects of their current situation. For example, when asked to list the benefits of getting a new job, successful participants might reflect on finding more fulfilling and better-paid employment, whereas their unsuccessful counterparts might focus on a failure leaving them trapped and unhappy. When looking at weight loss, successful participants might remark on how good they will look and feel when they drop a dress size, whereas unsuccessful participants might talk about how not losing weight will mean continued unhappiness about their appearance. While the former technique encourages participants to look forward to a more positive future, the latter demotivates by fixating on unsatisfactory events and experiences.

Fourth, there was the issue of reward. As part of their planning, successful participants ensured that each of their subgoals had a reward attached to it. Often it was something small, and it never conflicted with the major goal itself (no going on a binge of chocolate bars to celebrate a week of healthy eating), but nevertheless it gave them something to look forward to and provided a sense of achievement.

Finally, successful participants also tended to make their plans, progress, benefits, and rewards as concrete as possible by expressing them in writing. Many people kept a hand-written journal, some used a computer, and a few even covered their fridge or bulletin board with graphs or pictures. Either way, the act of writing, typing, or drawing significantly boosted their chances of success.

IN 59 SECONDS

To achieve your aims and ambitions, there are four key techniques that will help you succeed: having the right kind of plan, telling your friends and family, focusing on the benefits, and rewarding yourself each step of the way. To help you incorporate these techniques into your life, I have created a unique motivational journal that can be used when you are attempting any form of change.

1. What is your overall goal?
My overall goal is to ...

2. Creating a step-by-step plan

Break your overall goal into a maximum of five smaller steps. Each step should be associated with a goal that is concrete, measurable, realistic, and time-based. Think about how you will achieve each step and the reward that you will give yourself when you do. The rewards can be anything you like, perhaps ice cream, new shoes or clothes, the latest high-tech gadget, a book, dinner out, or a massage. For each of the five sub-goals, complete the following statements in writing.

STEP 1

My first sub-goal is to...

I believe that I can achieve this goal because...

To achieve this sub-goal, I will...

This will be achieved by the following date:

My reward for achieving this will be...

STEP 2
My second sub-goal is to . . .

I believe that I can achieve this goal because . . .

To achieve this sub-goal, I will . . .

This will be achieved by the following date:

My reward for achieving this will be . . .

STEP 3
My third sub-goal is to . . .

I believe that I can achieve this goal because . . .

To achieve this sub-goal, I will . . .

This will be achieved by the following date:

My reward for achieving this will be . . .

STEP 4

My fourth sub-goal is to . . .

I believe that I can achieve this goal because . . .

To achieve this sub-goal, I will . . .

This will be achieved by the following date:

My reward for achieving this will be . . .

STEP 5

My fifth sub-goal is to . . .

I believe that I can achieve this goal because . . .

To achieve this sub-goal, I will . . .

This will be achieved by the following date:

My reward for achieving this will be . . .

3. What are the benefits of achieving your overall goal?

List three important benefits, focusing on how much better life will be for you and those around you. Focus on enjoying the benefits associated with your desired future rather than escaping the negative aspects of your current situation.

-

-

-

4. Going public

Whom are you going to tell about your goal and sub-goals? Perhaps your friends, family, or colleagues. Could you describe it on a blog or display it somewhere prominent in your house or at the office?

PROCRASTINATION AND THE ZEIGARNIK EFFECT

Research suggests that about 20 percent of people identify themselves as chronic procrastinators.[7] Presumably this figure underestimates the scale of the problem, given that it can be based only on people who completed the questionnaires on time. Regardless of the actual figure, it is obvious that procrastination can be a major problem, causing people to fail to pay bills on time, not complete projects by deadlines, and make inadequate preparation for important exams and interviews. Procrastination is a surprisingly complex phenomenon that can stem from a variety of causes, including fear of failure, perfectionism, low levels of self-control, a tendency to see projects as a whole rather than breaking them into smaller parts, being prone to boredom, the feeling that life is too short to worry about seemingly unimportant tasks, and an inability to accurately estimate how long it takes to do things.

However, the good news is that the problem can be overcome using a technique first uncovered during an informal observation of waiters.

According to research lore, in the 1920s a young Russian psychology graduate named Bluma Zeigarnik found herself in a Viennese café, taking tea with her supervisor. Being students of human nature, they were watching how the waiters and customers behaved, and they happened to notice a curious phenomenon. When a customer asked for the check, the waiters could easily remember the food that had been ordered. However, if the customer paid the check and then queried it a few moments later, the waiters had to struggle to remember anything about the order. It seemed that the act of paying for the meal brought a sense of closure as far as the waiters were concerned, and erased the order from their memories.

Zeigarnik was curious, and she returned to the laboratory to test an idea. She asked people to do a number of simple tasks (such as stacking wooden blocks or placing toys in a box), but sometimes she stopped the participants before they had finished the assigned task. At the end of the experiment, the participants were told to describe all of the tasks. As with her observations of waiters, Zeigarnik found that the unfinished tasks stuck in people's minds and so were far easier to remember.[8]

According to Zeigarnik, starting any activity causes your mind to experience a kind of psychic anxiety. Once the activity is completed, your mind breathes an unconscious sigh of relief, and all is forgotten. However, if you are somehow thwarted from completing the activity, your anxious mind quietly nags away until you finish what you started.

What has this got to do with procrastination? Procrastinators frequently put off starting certain activities because they are overwhelmed by the size of the job in front of them. However, if they can be persuaded, or can persuade themselves, to work on the activity for "just a few minutes," they often feel an urge to see it through to completion. Research shows that the "just a few minutes" rule is a highly effective way of beating procrastination and could help people finish the most arduous of tasks.[9] It is also a perfect application of Zeigarnik's work— those few minutes of initial activity create an anxious brain that refuses to rest until the job is finished.

Zeigarnik's work on the psychology of unfinished activity is just one example of her fascinating research. On another occasion she attempted to restore movement to patients paralyzed by hysteria by having a stooge dressed in a military uniform suddenly enter the room and order the patient to stand. Unfortunately, the results of that study have been lost in the mists of time, although one recent Russian biographer noted that it is no longer possible to repeat the study, as it is impossible to find anyone in Russia who holds the required reverent attitude toward either the military or political figures.[10]

DOUBLETHINK

At the beginning of this chapter I described how research conducted by psychologists Lien Pham and Shelley Taylor showed that asking students to visualize themselves doing well on an important exam caused them to study less and make lower grades. In fact, I described only one part of their fascinating study. While one group of participants was busy seeing themselves as A students, another group was asked to spend a few moments each day imagining the *process* of revision by visualizing when, where, and how they intended to study. A third group of students acted as a control, doing no exercises at all. Compared to the control group and to the group who were visualizing themselves as A students, the students who imagined themselves going through the process of studying spent significantly more time revising and eventually earned higher exam grades. According to the researchers, visualizing the process of study proved especially effective at reducing exam-related anxiety and helped students better plan and manage their workload. Subsequent research has shown that the same effect occurs in several different areas, with, for example, tennis players and golfers benefiting far more from imagining themselves training than winning.[11]

Additional work, conducted by Lisa Libby from Ohio State University and her colleagues, suggests that the type of "behavioral commitments" involved in such visualization exercises can be made even more effective by seeing yourself as others see you.[12] In this study, conducted one day before the 2004 American presidential election, more than a hundred voters were asked to imagine themselves going to the polling booth the following day. One group was told to carry out the visualization exercise from a first-person perspective (seeing the world through their own eyes), while another group was instructed to carry out the same task from a third-person perspective (seeing themselves as someone else would see them). Remarkably, 90 percent of those who imagined themselves from a third-person perspective went on to vote, compared with just more than 70 percent of those who employed first-person visualization. Although the explanation for the effect is uncertain, it could be that adopting a third-person perspective requires more mental effort than a first-person one and so results in more significant behavioral changes.

Other researchers have developed "super-strength" visualization tools that aim to combine the motivational effects of imagining yourself doing well with the practical benefits associated with thinking about whatever is required to achieve your aim. Much of this research has been conducted by Gabriele Oettingen at the University of Pennsylvania and involves a little bit of Orwellian doublethink.

In *1984,* George Orwell introduced the concept of "doublethink," describing it as simultaneously holding two opposing beliefs in your mind and yet accepting both. In Orwell's novel, this technique was used by a totalitarian government to continuously rewrite history and thus control the populace. However, recent research has shown that the same type of idea can be used in a more productive way, helping people to achieve their goals and ambitions. Oettingen speculated that one of the most effective states of mind involves people being optimistic about achieving their goal but also realistic about some of the problems that they may encounter. To investigate, she developed a novel procedure that encouraged people to hold both types of thought in mind, and she then carried out a series of studies to assess its effectiveness.

The procedure is simple. People are asked to think about something they want to achieve, such as losing weight, learning a new skill, or changing their drinking habits. Next, they are told to spend a few moments fantasizing about reaching the goal and to note the top two benefits that would flow from such an achievement. After this, they are asked to spend another few moments reflecting on the kinds of barriers and problems that they are likely to encounter if they attempt to fulfill their ambition, and again, make a note of the top two issues. Now comes the doublethink. People are asked to reflect on their first benefit, elaborating on how it would make their life more enjoyable. Immediately afterward, they are asked to think about the biggest hurdle to such success, focusing on what they would do if they encountered the difficulty. Then they repeat the same process for the second positive aspect of achieving their aim and the second potential problem.

In several experiments, Oettingen discovered that this procedure provides the best of both worlds. When people focused on an existing relationship that they wanted to improve, those engaging in doublethink were more successful than those who just fantasized or focused on the negatives.[13] Returning to the theme of romance, she applied the doublethink procedure to students harboring a secret crush. Those who employed the fantasy-reality technique were more successful than those who merely dreamed about their perfect date or dwelled solely on the difficulties of revealing their true feelings.[14] Additional work has used the doublethink procedure to encourage employees to become more involved in training courses; nurses to build better relationships with patients' family members and show greater commitment to best practice; and middle managers to make better decisions, delegate more effectively, and improve their time-management skills.[15]

The research shows that it *is* possible to use visualization to motivate. The solution is a question of balance, interleaving the benefits of achievement with a realistic assessment of the problems that could be encountered. In short, doublethink.

IN 59 SECONDS

The following procedure, based on the doublethink procedure, can be used to motivate you to achieve your goals and persevere in the face of difficulties.

1. What is your goal?

2. Potential benefits and setbacks

QUESTION A
Write down one word that would reflect an important way in which your life would be better if you achieved your goal.

QUESTION B
Write down one word that would reflect a significant barrier that stands in the way of achieving your goal.

QUESTION C
Write down one word that would reflect another important way in which your life would be better if you achieved your goal.

QUESTION D
Write down one word that would reflect another significant barrier that stands in the way of achieving your goal.

3. Elaboration
Elaborate your answer to Question A.
   Imagine all of the benefits that would flow from this achievement and note your ideas in the space below.

Elaborate your answer to Question B.
   Imagine how the obstacle hinders achievement and the steps that you would take to deal with it and note your ideas in the space below.

Elaborate your answer to Question C.

Imagine all of the benefits that would flow from this achievement and note your ideas in the space below.

Elaborate your answer to Question D.

Imagine how the obstacle hinders achievement and the steps that you would take to deal with it and note your ideas in the space below.

DIETING AND DRINKING

Surveys show that most people attempt to diet or to cut down on their drinking at some point in their lives. However, the same surveys also suggest that the vast majority fails, often blaming their downfall on a lack of motivation. Part of the problem is that people do not tend to follow their gut instincts when starting and stopping. Instead, they are unknowingly influenced by a wide range of factors. Brian Wansink at Cornell University has devoted his academic career to understanding some of the factors at work, and his results illustrate just how much irrationality surrounds the dinner table.

In one study Wansink and his colleagues speculated that

people's decisions about whether to continue eating might be unconsciously determined by a surprisingly simple question: "Have I finished my food?"[16] Wansink therefore created a soup bowl with a special bottom, by which he could secretly and continuously refill the bowl via a concealed tube. Groups of participants sat around a table, chatting and tasting soup for twenty minutes, and then gave their opinion about the soup to the experimenters. Without being aware, half of them were taking their soup from a "bottomless bowl" that was being continuously refilled, while the others had normal bowls.

Those with the bottomless bowls consumed more than 75 percent more soup than those with a normal bowl. In addition, those who consumed more weren't aware of how much they had eaten, and said that they were no less hungry than those who had consumed a normal portion.

However, there is some consolation in realizing that by understanding a few of the hidden factors that influence consumption, we can create quick but effective techniques for cutting the extent of our eating and drinking.

IN 59 SECONDS

The Power of Slow

Some research suggests that eating more slowly helps people eat less, perhaps because it fools our brains into thinking that we've eaten more and allows extra time for the body to digest food.[17] In an additional twist on this work, Corby Martin and his colleagues at the Pennington Biomedical Research Center had overweight participants eat a lunchtime meal at three different speeds: (1) their normal rate, (2) half their normal rate, or (3) their normal rate to begin with, followed by half their normal rate.[18] Eating at the slower rate resulted in men, but not women, eating less. However, starting the meal at a normal rate of eating and then dropping to the slower rate caused both men and women to experience a large reduction in their appetite. The normal-slow combination was even more effective than eating slowly all the way through the meal, suggesting that the secret to feeling satisfied is to start at your normal speed but then savor each and every mouthful.

Make Mine a Tall, Thin One

Brian Wansink and Koert van Ittersum, at Cornell University, asked students to pour a single shot of whiskey from a full bottle into a glass.[19] Those given a short, wide glass poured, on average, 30 percent larger shots than those given a tall, narrower glass. It seems that people used the depth of the liquid as an indicator of the amount of liquid in the glass, not noticing that one glass was far wider than the other. The researchers then repeated the experiment with experienced bartenders and discovered that they poured, on average, 20 percent larger shots into the short, wide glass. If you want to reduce your drinking, stay away from short, wide glasses and stick to tall, narrow ones.

Out of Sight, Out of Mind

Research shows that just placing food or drink out of sight or moving it a few feet away can have a big effect on consumption. In a series of studies, experimenters strategically placed jars of chocolates around an office and carefully counted how many were consumed.[20] In one condition, they compared placing the jars on people's desks with moving them just six feet away. In another, they placed the chocolates in either transparent or opaque jars. Placing the chocolates on people's desks resulted in the staff's consuming an average of six more chocolates per person each day, and the chocolates in transparent jars were eaten 46 percent more quickly than those in opaque jars. A similar principle applies to food around the house. In another study (described in the snappily titled paper "When Are Stockpiled Products Consumed Faster? A Convenience-Salience Framework of Post-Purchase Consumption Incidence and Quantity"), researchers stocked people's homes with either large or moderate quantities of ready-to-eat meals and discovered that the food was eaten at twice the rate in the overstocked homes.[21] To cut intake, make sure that tempting foods are out of sight, stored in a place that is difficult to access, such as a high cabinet or the basement.

Focus, Focus, Focus

People eat significantly more when they are distracted at mealtimes and therefore are not paying attention to their food. In one experiment, the amount of attention that moviegoers paid to a film was related to how much popcorn they consumed. Those who were more absorbed by the movie ate significantly larger amounts.[22] In another experiment, people who listened to a detective story during their lunchtime ate 15 percent more food than those who sat in silence.[23] Distractions while eating, such as watching television, reading a magazine, or even chatting with others, encourage people to consume more.

Beware of Large Bowls

Is the amount you eat influenced by the size of bowls and spoons? A few years ago, Brian Wansink invited a group of friends to a party at which he secretly conducted an experiment.[24] Each guest was randomly handed either a 17- or 34-ounce bowl and a 2- or 3-ounce spoon. The guests then helped themselves to ice cream. However, seconds before they took their first mouthful, the researchers snatched the bowls and weighed them. The results revealed that those given the large spoons and large bowls had, on average, taken 14 percent and 31 percent more ice cream than their modestly equipped companions did. Andrew Geier and his colleagues at the University of Pennsylvania demonstrated that the effect is not confined to ice cream and parties.[25] In their study, a bowl of M&M's was left in the hallway of an apartment building, along with a spoon and a sign saying, "Eat your fill: please use the spoon to serve yourself." On some days the experimenters placed a tablespoon-sized scoop next to the bowl, and on others they used a larger scoop. The findings revealed that the larger spoon caused people to take almost twice as many M&M's from the bowl. Try cutting down on your eating by using smaller bowls, plates, and cutlery.

Keep a Food Diary

Research conducted by Kaiser Permanente Center for Health Research suggests that making a note of how much you eat can help you lose weight.[26] During the study, participants who kept daily food records lost twice as much weight as those who kept none. You don't need to turn into a veritable Samuel Pepys to gain the benefits; just scribbling down what you eat on a Post-it note or sending yourself an e-mail has the same effect. According to the theory, becoming aware of what you are eating on a daily basis will help you break old habits and consume less.

Regret and Reflection

Not happy with your body but finding it difficult to motivate yourself to go to the gym? Try harnessing the power of regret and avoiding reflection. Research conducted by Charles Abraham and Paschal Sheeran has shown that just a few moments' thinking about how much you will regret *not* going to the gym will help motivate you to climb off the couch and onto an exercise bike.[27] And once you get there, avoid those imposing floor-to-ceiling mirrors. Other work, by Kathleen Martin Ginis and her colleagues at McMaster University, compared people pedaling on an exercise cycle in front of a mirror to those pedaling in front of a bare wall.

The results revealed that the group who constantly saw themselves in the mirror ended up feeling significantly less revitalized and more exhausted than the group who faced the wall. Researchers believe that the mirrors may encourage people to focus on their less-than-perfect bodies and consequently to do more harm than good.[28]

Use More Energy

Think about how you could burn more calories by making small changes to your everyday routine. It might be something as simple as using wax polish rather than a spray during housework (rubbing is a far more energy-consuming activity than spraying), ensuring that you have to use the stairs more often (e.g., not taking the elevator at work or alternating floors when doing housework), or listening to upbeat music to encourage vigorous movement when you are walking or mowing the lawn.

Mirror, Mirror, on the Kitchen Wall

Work conducted by Stacey Sentyrz and Brad Bushman, at Iowa State University, suggests that placing a mirror in your kitchen may help you shed pounds.[29] In several studies, participants were given the opportunity to eat healthy or unhealthy food. In one study, in a supermarket, almost a thousand shoppers were presented with the option of trying new types of full-fat or no-fat margarine. Half of the time a mirror was strategically placed behind the spreads to ensure that the participants could see their own reflection, and the other half of the time it was removed. The presence of the mirror resulted in a remarkable 32 percent reduction in trying the full-fat margarine. The researchers argued that seeing your own reflection makes you more aware of your body.

The Pitfalls of Diet Packs

Supermarket aisles are full of small-portion "diet packs" of snacks that will help you control your craving and so eat less. But will buying such packs really help you cut down on consumption? To find out, researchers at Tilburg University in the Netherlands gave participants either two bags of potato chips or nine diet packs and asked them to watch TV.[30] Before tucking into their treats and TV, participants were weighed in front of a mirror to create a "dieting mind-set." The results revealed that participants given the diet bags ate twice as many chips as those given the large bags. The researchers speculated that the participants given the diet packs felt they didn't need to exercise so much self-control and thus ended up eating more.

THE BENEFITS OF WRITING YOUR OWN EULOGY

In Charles Dickens's *A Christmas Carol*, Ebenezer Scrooge is visited by three ghostly figures. The first two, the Ghost of Christmas Past and the Ghost of Christmas Present, show how Scrooge's selfishness has made his life lonely and miserable. It is only when the Ghost of Christmas Future appears and leads him to his ill-kept and forgotten grave that Scrooge finally changes his character and becomes a far more giving and compassionate person. Dickens looked at the effect of taking a long-term view and the contemplation of life after death, but a large number of psychologists have done the same, and their findings suggest that Scrooge's fictional transformation can also occur in real life.

In one study, people were stopped in the street and asked to use a 10-point scale to rate how they felt about their favorite charities ("How beneficial is this charity to society?" "How much do you think society needs this charity?" and "How desirable is this charity to you personally?").[31] Some of the people were stopped as they walked past a funeral home, while others were stopped a few blocks later, in front of a nondescript building. When interviewing people in front of the funeral home, researchers positioned themselves so as to ensure that participants were forced to face a large sign reading "Howe's Mortuary." The results revealed a Scrooge-like effect, with those facing up to their own death feeling far more benevolent than those standing in front of the nondescript building.

Christopher Peterson at the University of Michigan believes that encouraging people to consider how they would like to be remembered after their death has various motivational benefits, including helping them to identify their long-term goals and assess the degree to which they are progressing toward making those goals a reality.[32] So, with no further ado, let's evoke your own Ghost of Christmas Future.

Imagine a close friend standing up at your funeral and presenting your ideal eulogy. Write the script for your friend. What would you really like them to say about you? Feel free to avoid any sense of modesty, but keep it realistic. How would you want them to describe your personality, achievements, personal strengths, family life, professional success, and behavior toward others? When you have finished writing, take a long and honest look at the eulogy for your ideal self. Do your present lifestyle and behavior justify the comments, or is there work to be done?

creativity

Exploding the myth of brainstorming,

how to get in touch with your inner Leonardo

merely by glancing at modern art,

lying down, and

putting a plant on your desk

IN THE EARLY 1940s, advertising executive Alex Osborn argued that it was possible to enhance creativity by putting a group of people in a room and having them follow a set of simple rules involving, for example, coming up with as many thoughts as possible, encouraging wild and exaggerated ideas, and not criticizing or evaluating anyone's comments. When selling his approach to businesses, Osborn claimed that "the average person thinks up twice as many ideas when working with a group than when working alone," and, perhaps not surprisingly, his novel approach quickly conquered the world.[1] Over the years, organizations around the globe have encouraged their employees to tackle key problems using this approach.

Researchers have gone to a great deal of trouble to test the effectiveness of group brainstorming. In a typical experiment, participants arrive in a group. Half of them are randomly chosen to be in the "work as a group" condition and are placed in one room. They are given standard brainstorming rules and have to come up with ideas to solve a specific problem (perhaps design a new ad campaign or find ways of easing traffic congestion). The other half of the participants are asked to sit alone in separate rooms, are given exactly the same instructions and tasks, and asked to generate ideas on their own. Researchers then tally the quantity of ideas produced under the different conditions, and experts rate their quality. So do such studies show that group brainstorming is more effective than individuals working alone? Many scientists are far from convinced. For example, Brian Mullen, at the University of Kent at Canterbury, and his colleagues analyzed twenty studies that tested the effectiveness of group brainstorming in this way and were amazed to discover that in the majority of the experiments, the participants working on their own produced a higher quantity and quality of ideas than those working in groups.[2]

Other research suggests that group brainstorming may fail, in part, because of a phenomenon known as "social loafing." In the late 1880s, a French agricultural engineer named Max Ringelmann became obsessed with trying to make workers as efficient as possible.[3] After carrying out hundreds of experiments, he inadvertently stumbled upon an unexpected effect that would inspire a century of psychological research. One of Ringelmann's studies involved asking people to pull on a rope to lift increasingly heavy weights. Perhaps not unreasonably, Ringelmann expected people in groups to work harder than those on their own. But the results revealed the opposite pattern. When working alone, individuals lifted around 185 pounds, but they managed only an average of 140 pounds per person when working as a group. Additional work revealed that the phenomenon, like the "bystander" effect described in the "Persuasion" chapter, is largely the result of a diffusion of responsibility.[4] When people work on their own, their success or failure is entirely the result of their own abilities and hard work. If they do well, the glory is theirs. If they fail, they alone are accountable. However, add other people to the situation, and suddenly everyone stops trying so hard, safe in the knowledge that though individuals will not receive personal praise if the group does well, they can always blame others if it performs badly.

Research shows that this phenomenon occurs in many different situations.[5] Ask people to make as much noise as possible, and they make more on their own than in a group. Ask them to add rows of numbers, and the more people involved, the lower the work rate. Ask them to come up with ideas, and people are more creative away from the crowd. It is a universal phenomenon, emerging in studies conducted around the world, including in America, India, Thailand, and Japan.

In short, a large body of research now suggests that for more than seventy years, people using group brainstorming may have inadvertently been stifling, not stimulating, their creative juices. When working together they aren't as motivated to put in the time and energy needed to generate great ideas, and so they end up spending more time thinking inside the box.

So, when it comes to creativity, is it simply a case of staying away from the pack? No. In fact, other research shows that if you really want to get in touch with your inner Leonardo da Vinci, there are several quick and surprisingly powerful techniques available. All it takes is a glance at the right type of modern art, lying down on the job, doing nothing, or putting a plant on your desk.

TESTING FOR CREATIVITY

Psychologists have developed lots of weird and wonderful ways of testing for creativity. People have been presented with a paper clip and given a few minutes to create as many uses for it as possible. They have been given a pencil and a sheet of paper with a square grid drawn on it and asked to make each square into a different object (e.g., television, fish tank, book, etc.). In both cases, the number of responses would be counted and judged for originality by comparison to the responses from all of those taking part. Researchers also often use various types of visual and verbal lateral-thinking problems. Try the following questions to test this aspect of your creativity:

1. Can you add a single line to the following equation to make it correct? (There is just one rule—you are not allowed to place the line through the equal sign like this: $\neq$, thus converting it into a "not equal" sign.)
   IO IO II = IO:50

2. Joanna and Jackie were born on the same day of the same month of the same year. They have the same mother and father, yet they are not twins. How is that possible?

3. A man has married twenty different women in the same town. All are still alive, and he never divorced any of them. Polygamy is unlawful, yet the man has not broken the law. How is this possible?

4. A man walks into an antiques shop and offers to sell a beautiful bronze coin. One side of the coin contains a wonderful image of a Roman emperor's head, while the other shows the date as 500 B.C. The antiques dealer instantly knows that the coin does not date back to 500 B.C. Why?

Answers

1. This is all about time. By adding a short line over the second "I," you convert the number "IO" into the word "TO,"

and now the equation reads "ten to eleven, which is the
same as ten fifty."

IO TO II = IO:50

2. Joanna and Jackie are part of a set of triplets.

3. The man is a minister and so presided over the wedding
   ceremonies.

4. The year 500 B.C. predates the birth of Christ, and thus a
   coin from that time would not be inscribed with an
   abbreviation for "Before Christ."

LISTENING TO THE QUIET GUY

Surrealist Salvador Dalí would sometimes generate ideas for
his paintings by using an interesting technique. He would lie
on a couch and put a glass on the floor. He would then carefully place one end of a spoon on the edge of the glass and
lightly hold the other end in his hand. As he drifted off to
sleep, he would naturally relax his hand and release the spoon.
The sound of the spoon falling into the glass would wake him
up, and he would immediately sketch the bizarre images that
had just started to drift through his half-asleep, semiconscious
mind. In view of the impractical nature of so many of his ideas
(think lobster telephone), clearly this technique might not be
for everyone, but that is not to say that your unconscious
mind is not a powerhouse of creative thought.

In fact, several studies suggest that when it comes to innovative ways of looking at the world, there may be a lot more
going on in your unconscious mind than you realize. In a simple experimental demonstration of this, Stephen Smith at
Texas A&M University presented volunteers with picture-

word puzzles that suggested common phrases and asked them to solve as many as possible.[6] For example, they might be asked to identify the phrase indicated in the following set of words:

YOU JUST ME

The answer is "just between you and me." Now that you have the general idea, try these three:

SALE SALE SALE SALE

$$\frac{STAND}{I}$$

BRO KEN

The answers are "for sale," "I understand," and "broken in half." In Smith's experiment, if a puzzle was unsolved, the volunteers were told to relax for fifteen minutes and then try the puzzle again. More than a third of the puzzles were solved on the second attempt. While relaxing, the volunteers were not working on the puzzles consciously, but their unconscious thoughts devised new and helpful perspectives on the puzzles.

Recent work suggests that you don't even need to spend as long as fifteen minutes away from a problem. Instead, you can achieve the same results with just a few moments' respite.

Psychologists Ap Dijksterhuis and Teun Meurs at the University of Amsterdam carried out a series of fascinating experiments on creativity and the unconscious.[7]

Their ideas about the nature of the unconscious mind and creativity are simple to understand. Imagine two men in a room. One of them is highly creative but very shy. The other is clever, not as creative, and far more domineering. Now imagine going into the room and asking them to come up with ideas for a campaign to advertise a new type of chocolate bar. True to form, the loud but not especially creative man dominates the conversation. He does not allow his quieter counterpart to contribute, and the ideas produced are good but not very innovative.

Now let's imagine a slightly different scenario. Again, you walk into the room and ask for campaign ideas. However, this time you distract the loud man by getting him to watch a film. Under these circumstances, the quiet man is able to make his voice heard, and you walk away with a completely different, and far more creative, set of ideas. In many ways, this is a good analogy for the relationship between your mind and creativity. The quiet guy represents your unconscious mind. It is capable of wonderful ideas, but they are often difficult to hear. The loud guy represents your conscious mind—clever, not as innovative, but difficult to get out of your head.

Dijksterhuis conducted a series of experiments to find out whether people might become more creative if their conscious minds were distracted. In perhaps the best known of these studies, volunteers were asked to devise new and creative names for pasta. To help them, the experimenters started by presenting five new names, all of which ended with the letter *i* and thus sounded like typical pasta possibilities. Some of the volunteers were then given three minutes to think before listing their ideas. In terms of the "two guys in the room" analogy, these volunteers were listening to the comments of the loud, and not especially creative, guy in their heads. Another group of volunteers was asked to forget about the pasta and instead spend three minutes performing a mentally challenging task—carefully tracking a dot as it moved around a computer screen and clicking the space bar whenever it changed color. In terms of the room analogy, this task was designed to distract the loud guy and give the quiet man a chance to have his voice heard. Only after completing this difficult and attention-sapping task were the participants asked to list some new names for pasta.

The researchers developed a simple, no-nonsense, and ingenious way of deciding whether the pasta names suggested by volunteers should be categorized as creative or uncreative. They worked through all of the suggestions, carefully counting the number of times that a pasta name ending in *i* versus another letter was proposed. Since the five examples given at the start of the experiment all ended with *i,* they concluded that any suggestion also ending in *i* was evidence that people were simply following the crowd and being uncreative, whereas those names ending in another letter were more innovative.

The results were interesting. The volunteers who had been consciously thinking about the task produced more pasta names ending in *i* than did those who had been busy chasing a dot around a computer screen. In contrast, when the more unusual pasta names were examined, the dot-chasing volunteers produced almost twice as many suggestions as those in the other groups.

These startling findings yielded considerable insight into the relationship between creativity and the unconscious. Volunteers in the "follow the dot" condition felt as if all their attention and mental effort were fully engaged in tracking a dot as it moved around a computer screen. However, their unconscious mind was working on the problem at hand. Perhaps more important, it wasn't just reproducing the same work as their conscious mind; it was thinking about things in a very different way. It was being innovative. It was making new connections. It was creating truly original ideas.

Many standard texts on creativity emphasize the value of relaxation. They tell people to take it easy and empty their mind of thoughts. The Dutch research suggests exactly the opposite. Genuine creativity can come from spending just a few moments occupying your conscious mind, thus preventing it from interfering with the important and innovative activity in your unconscious. Everyone can be more creative— it is just a matter of keeping the loud guy in your head busy and giving the quiet guy a chance to speak up.

IN 59 SECONDS

When you next want to come up with a creative solution to a problem, try the following technique and see what pops into your mind. If the word-search puzzle is not for you, try tackling a difficult crossword puzzle, Sudoku, or any other task that fully occupies your conscious mind.

A. What problem are you trying to solve?

B. Find the ten target words inside the grid. The words might run horizontally, vertically, or diagonally and be either forward or backward. There may also be an overlap between the words.

TARGET WORDS

SIXTY

SECONDS

CREATIVITY

BOOST

QUICK

RAPID

THINK

CHANGE

NEW

FRESH

Y	V	S	N	S	H	Y	E	X
T	F	R	E	S	H	E	S	D
I	S	Q	H	D	G	T	I	A
V	E	R	A	N	S	S	F	Y
I	T	E	A	O	Q	E	T	T
T	T	H	O	C	U	X	H	O
A	C	B	E	E	I	C	I	N
E	H	I	Q	S	C	H	N	I
R	A	P	I	D	K	E	K	A
C	S	I	T	Q	W	T	T	B

C. Now, without thinking too much about it, jot down the various thoughts and possible solutions that come to you.

ANSWER

GETTING IN TOUCH WITH YOUR INNER GORILLA

A few years ago I wrote a book about creativity called *Did You Spot the Gorilla?* It outlined four techniques designed to help people think and behave in more flexible and unusual ways. Here are summaries of each of the techniques and some exercises designed to help you implement them.

Priming. Prime your mind by working feverishly on a problem, but then give yourself a release of effort by doing something completely different. During the release period, feed your mind with new and diverse ideas by, for example, visiting a museum or an art gallery, paging through magazines or newspapers, going on a train or car journey, or randomly searching the Internet. But don't push it. Simply immerse yourself in novel ideas and experiences, and leave it up to your brain to find connections and create seemingly serendipitous events.

Perspective. Changing perspective helps produce novel solutions. Try imagining how a child, idiot, friend, artist, or accountant would approach the problem. Alternatively, think about two analogous situations by applying the "is like" rule (e.g., "Attracting more people to my business *is like* a street entertainer trying to attract a crowd"). How is the problem solved in these situations? Can this idea be applied to your problem? Finally, think about doing the exact opposite of every solution you have created so far.

Play. When you are being too serious, your brain becomes constrained. Jump-start your creativity by having some fun. Take a break for fifteen minutes, watch a funny film, or digitally alter a photograph of your colleague so that he or she looks more like an owl.

Perceive. When the world becomes too familiar, your brain reverts to automatic pilot and stops seeing what is right in front of your eyes. Try switching your mind to manual by becoming more curious about the world. Ask yourself an interesting question each week. How do elephants communicate over hundreds of miles? Why do people laugh? Why are bananas yellow? How cmoe yuor bairn is albe to udnertsnad tihs snetence eevn tghouh olny the frist and lsat ltetres of ecah wrod are crreoct? Invest some time and energy in trying to discover possible answers to the question, if only for the fun of it.

NATURE CALLS

In 1948 George de Mestral went for a stroll in the countryside in his native Switzerland. When he returned home he noticed that his clothing was covered in tiny burs. As he set about the annoying task of removing them one by one, he decided to figure out why they stuck to his clothing. Close examination revealed that the burs were covered with tiny hooks that easily attached themselves to the loops in fabric. Inspired by this simple concept, de Mestral wondered whether the same idea could be used to attach other surfaces together, a thought that eventually resulted in his inventing Velcro.

De Mestral's story is frequently cited as evidence for one of the most important principles underlying creativity: the realization that an idea or technique from one situation can be applied to another. This principle certainly appears to account for many famous examples of breakthrough thinking, including, for example, Frank Lloyd Wright's finding inspiration for the design of a church roof by noticing the shape of his hands at prayer. However, there may have been another hidden but equally important factor at work.

A significant amount of research has examined the effects of the natural environment on people's thinking and behavior. The work shows that even a small amount of plant life can have a surprisingly large impact on making the world a better place. The recovery rates of patients in hospitals are significantly improved when they are able to see trees from their ward windows,[8] and prisoners whose cell windows overlook farmlands and forests report fewer medical problems than others.[9] The effects are not just confined to prisoners and patients but extend to everyone. Other studies have examined the relationship between greenery and crime. In perhaps the most ingenious of these, researchers focused their attention on a large public-housing development in Chicago.[10] The development was especially interesting for two reasons. First, some sections contained a relatively large number of shrubs and trees, while other areas resembled the proverbial concrete jungle. Second, previous to the study the residents had been randomly assigned to apartments in the development, thus ensuring that any differences in crime rates in the two types of areas could not be the result of income, background, or any other such factors. The study yielded impressive results. The parts of the development that contained greenery were associated with 48 percent fewer property crimes and 52 percent fewer violent crimes than those that contained nothing but concrete. The researchers speculated that the greenery may have put people in a good mood and therefore made them less likely to commit crimes.

In the same way that greenery seems to reduce antisocial

behavior, it also seems to make people more creative. In a series of experiments, Japanese psychologists Seiji Shibata and Naoto Suzuki asked people to carry out various creativity exercises in carefully controlled office environments. In one study some of the offices contained a potted plant that had been carefully positioned in front of, or to the side of, the participant, while other offices were devoid of any greenery. In another study the researchers carefully analyzed the effect of replacing the plant with a similar-size magazine rack. Time and again the researchers discovered that the addition of the potted plant enhanced people's creativity. The results from these artificial studies appear to stand up to scrutiny in more realistic settings as well. An eight-month study of creativity in the workplace conducted by Robert Ulrich at Texas A&M University showed that adding flowers and plants to an office resulted in a 15 percent increase in ideas from male employees and more flexible solutions to problems from their female counterparts. In another study, researchers discovered that children engage in significantly more creative play when they are in courtyards containing greenery versus comparatively barren outdoor spaces.[11] Why should a little nature have these effects?

According to some theorists, the explanation dates back thousands of years. Evolutionary psychologists attempt to explain behavior on the basis of how it might have helped people thrive and survive through generations, and in their opinion, living amid healthy trees and plants might initiate an ancient feeling of calm because it suggests that there will be an abundance of food nearby and eases the worry about where the next meal is coming from. Such pleasant feelings then make people more helpful, happy, and creative.

So is a long country walk or a well-placed potted plant the minimum needed to get your creative juices flowing? Andrew Elliot and his colleagues at the University of Rochester looked

at the relationship between creativity and the nearly sublimi-
nal presentation of color.[12] The researchers thought that since
the color red is commonly associated with a sense of danger
and error (think red traffic lights and teachers' red pens)
whereas green is associated with positivity and relaxation
(think green traffic lights and nature), the merest suggestion
of such colors might hinder or help creativity. They presented
participants with a booklet containing some standard anagrams, writing the participant's code number in the corner of
each page of the booklet in either red or green ink. They asked
the participants to check that the number on each page was
correct and then told them to work through the booklet.
Remarkably, even though everyone saw the code numbers for
just a few seconds, those who were exposed to the green ink
solved about 30 percent more anagrams than those who saw
the red ink. The evidence suggests that for creativity you are
better off going green.

IN 59 SECONDS

To inspire creative thoughts, place plants and flowers in a room and,
if possible, ensure that windows look out on trees and grass, not
concrete and steel. Don't try to fake it. Pictures of waterfalls do not
aid innovation, and even high-definition screens showing live
camera feeds from natural scenes do not make people feel more
relaxed.[13] So if you really cannot introduce nature into a space, head
for the nearest green spot. Also, when decorating rooms to inspire
creative and innovative thinking, avoid red and go for green. The
same concept applies if you are trying to get creative juices flowing
for others—prime them with the color green (green folders, green
chairs, or even your green clothing).

MUSICAL CHAIRS

There are two schools of thought relating to group dynamics and creativity. One believes in not changing team membership, arguing that people then feel more comfortable with one another and so are happier to suggest the kinds of weird and wonderful ideas that are the hallmark of creativity. In contrast, the other point of view holds that it is better to generate new patterns of thinking by constantly mixing up the membership.

To find out which position is better, Charlan Nemeth and Margaret Ormiston at the University of California conducted a revealing study.[14] In the first part of the experiment, groups of people were asked to think of new ways to solve real problems, such as boosting tourism in the San Francisco Bay Area. Next, the membership of half of those groups was kept constant, while the makeup of the other half of the groups was changed in order to create totally new teams. Those who remained together rated their groups as friendlier and more creative than those that had been asked to move around. However, the newly formed groups generated significantly more ideas, which were later judged to be more creative.

Other work suggests that even one new person can make a difference. In a study conducted by Hoon-Seok Choi and Leigh Thompson, three-person groups were first asked to think of as many uses as possible for a cardboard box.[15] Next, the experimenters kept the membership of half of the groups constant and changed just one person in the other half of the groups. When asked to repeat the cardboard-box task, the groups containing one new member devised significantly more creative uses for the box. Further analysis showed that the newcomer had helped increase the creativity of the two original team members.

So, with respect to group creativity, the message is clear: play musical chairs. Even though a team may have worked well together in the past, you can maximize the potential for new and exciting thoughts by changing members as often as possible.

THE POWER OF SMALL

Can small cues have a surprisingly large impact on the way people think? In studies conducted by Ap Dijksterhuis and Ad van Knippenberg at the University of Nijmegen in the Netherlands, participants jotted down a few sentences describing either a typical football hooligan or a typical professor.[16] When then asked a series of general-knowledge questions, those who had spent time thinking about a typical football hooligan answered 46 percent of the questions correctly, whereas those who had spent a few moments reflecting on a typical professor attained a mark of 60 percent. Other studies have shown that similar types of priming effects occur in many different situations. Put people in front of computer wallpaper showing dollar symbols, and they behave in a more selfish and unfriendly way, giving less money to charity and sitting farther away from others.[17] Give interviewers a cup of iced coffee, and they unknowingly rate interviewees as colder and less pleasant.[18] Add a faint smell of cleaning fluid to the air, and people tidy up more thoroughly.[19] Put a briefcase on a table during a meeting, and people suddenly become more competitive.[20] The evidence points to a little counting for a lot.

Priming can also quickly make people more creative. In a study conducted by psychologist Jens Förster at the International University Bremen in Germany,[21] participants were asked to jot down a few sentences about the behavior, lifestyle, and appearance of a typical punk (chosen because punks were, as the researchers put it, "anarchic and radical"), while others did exactly the same for a typical engineer ("conservative and logical"). Everyone was then given a standard test of creativity. The results revealed that those who had spent just a few seconds thinking about the punk were significantly more creative than those who had put time into thinking about the typical engineer. Without people being aware of it, their ability to be creative was dramatically altered by a few quick and simple thoughts. Interestingly, the effect works only with generic stereotypes, such as punks and engineers. Ask people to spend a few moments thinking about a famous figure, such as Leonardo da Vinci, and more likely than not their creative juices suddenly run dry.[22] It seems that if the bar is set too high, people unconsciously compare their own meager skills to those of a genius, become disheartened, and stop trying.

In 2005 Förster conducted a new type of creativity-priming experiment that has real implications for instant change. He speculated that merely glancing at a piece of modern art designed to provoke a sense of unconventionality would unconsciously inspire viewers to become more creative.

To test his idea, Förster asked participants to take a standard creativity task ("think of as many uses for a brick as possible") while seated in front of one of two specially created art prints. The two prints were each about three feet square, almost identical, and consisted of twelve large crosses against a light green background. In one picture all of the crosses were dark green, while in the other print eleven were dark green and one was yellow. The researchers speculated that the unconscious mind would perceive this single yellow cross as breaking away from its more conservative and conventional green cousins and that this would encourage more radical and creative thinking. The results were astounding. Even though the participants didn't consciously notice the picture, those seated in front of the "creative" picture produced significantly more uses for the brick. A panel of experts judged their responses as far more creative. The message is clear: if you want to fast-track a group or an individual to think more creatively, use the power of visual priming.

But other work suggests that instant creativity is not just about sitting in front of a modern art print. It is also about how you use your body.

There is a strong link between anxiety and creativity. When people feel worried, they become very focused, concentrate on the task at hand, become risk-averse, rely on well-established habits and routines, and see the world through less-creative eyes. In contrast, when people feel at ease in a situation, they are more likely to explore new and unusual ways of thinking and behaving, see the bigger picture, take risks, and think and act more creatively.

In view of this link, it should theoretically be possible to increase people's creativity by making them feel more at ease. Using willing volunteers, researchers have tested a variety of anxiety-reducing procedures, including lengthy relaxation exercises, funny films, and listening to Vivaldi's *Four Seasons*. The good news is that the results suggest that people have more creative and interesting ideas when they feel comfortable in their surroundings, although the relaxation procedures have proven somewhat time-consuming. With speed always of the essence, a few years ago psychologists Ronald Friedman and Jens Förster created a quick technique for making people feel relaxed. A rewarding side effect was the discovery that their technique also enhanced creativity.[23]

When you like an object, you sometimes pull it toward

you. Similarly, when you dislike it, you tend to push it away. You have been executing these simple pull-push behaviors from birth, and you probably repeat them on an almost daily basis. As a result, strong associations have become ingrained in your brain, with the act of pulling being associated with a positive feeling and that of pushing being seen as far more negative. Friedman and Förster wondered whether getting people to perform these actions for just a few moments might be enough to trigger the feelings associated with them and therefore affect people's creative thinking.

They asked willing volunteers to sit at a table and complete standard creativity tasks, such as devising as many uses for everyday objects as possible or solving some classic lateral-thinking puzzles.

Half of the volunteers were asked to place their right hand under the table and gently pull the table toward them, giving their brains a subtle signal that they liked their surroundings. The other half were asked to place their right hand on top of the table and push down, thus unconsciously giving the impression that they felt under threat. The pushes and pulls were gentle enough not to move the table, and none of the volunteers had any idea that pushing and pulling might affect their creativity. While gently pushing or pulling with one hand, they completed the creativity task with the other. Friedman and Förster found that regardless of whether people were generating alternative uses for everyday objects or trying to bring about those all important "aha" moments, those who were pulling scored significantly higher than those who were pushing.

It is a simple but effective technique. It is also not the only piece of research to reveal the strange effects that your body can have on creativity in the brain. Another experiment, conducted by Ronald Friedman and Andrew Elliot at the University of Rochester, involved asking people to tackle difficult anagrams with their arms either crossed or resting on their thighs.[24] In the same way that pushing and pulling is unconsciously associated with liking and disliking, so folding the arms is commonly associated with stubbornness and perseverance. Would this simple act be enough to persuade the participants to spend longer trying to solve the anagrams? Yes. The volunteers with their arms folded struggled nearly twice as long as those with their hands on their thighs. Perhaps more important, because of this they ended up solving significantly more anagrams.

Other work provides scientific justification for perhaps the most popular act of all—lying down on the job. An experiment conducted by Darren Lipnicki and Don Byrne at Australian National University involved asking participants to try to solve a series of five-letter anagrams while either standing up or lying on a mattress.[25] The anagrams were a mixed bunch—some were relatively simple ("gip" into "pig") while others were tough ("nodru" into "round"). Interestingly, the volunteers solved the puzzles about 10 percent faster when horizontal and thus achieved a higher score in the allotted time. What caused the difference?

The answer, according to Lipnicki and Byrne, might have to do with a small section of your brain referred to as the locus coeruleus (Latin for "the blue spot"). When activated, this region produces a stress hormone called noradrenaline that, in turn, increases heart rate, triggers the release of energy, and raises blood flow around the body. When you stand up, gravity draws blood away from the upper body, which subsequently increases activity in the locus coeruleus, whereas lying down decreases its activity. Some researchers think that noradrenaline may also impair the brain's ability to engage in certain types of thinking, including the creativity and flexibility required to solve anagrams. It seems that the act of adopting an upright or supine (Latin for "can't be bothered") position dramatically affects the chemicals racing through your body and causes your brain to operate in quite different ways.

IN 59 SECONDS

Priming

To prime your mind for thinking creatively, spend a few moments describing a typical musician or artist. List their typical behaviors, lifestyle, and appearance. Or, following on from Förster's work in creativity and patterns, use the following designs to help produce original ideas. They can be turned into examples of modern art and used to adorn the walls of boardrooms and meeting spaces. Alternatively, they can be loaded on computers as wallpaper or even used as subtle background designs on the pads that people use to scribble their ideas. Whatever you choose, creating creativity has never been so quick or easy.

Bodywork

The next time you are trying to be creative in a meeting, gently lean forward and pull against the table. When the going gets tough, cross your arms to help perseverance in the face of failure. If that doesn't work, lie down. If anyone accuses you of being lazy, quietly explain that you are employing your locus coeruleus in the war against rigid thinking.

attraction

Why you shouldn't play hard to get,

how the subtle art of seduction involves

the simplest of touches,

roller-coaster rides, and

avoiding artificial Christmas trees

IMAGINE BEING HANDED a jar containing ten cookies and being asked to remove one, take a nibble, and rate it for quality and taste. Now imagine being asked to perform exactly the same task but this time being handed a jar containing just two cookies. It would seem reasonable to think that the initial number of cookies in each jar wouldn't affect your ratings. Reasonable but wrong. According to work conducted by psychologist Stephen Worchel at the University of Hawaii at Hilo, cookies taken from a jar that is almost empty taste significantly better than identical cookies taken from a full jar.[1]

Why should this be the case? How much we desire and treasure an object depends, in part, on how easy it is to obtain. A jar crammed full of cookies suggests that the contents are plentiful. In contrast, a nearly empty jar suggests that the cookies are scarce, and therefore significantly more desirable. In Worchel's experiment, this simple idea unconsciously affected how participants perceived the availability of the cookies and how good they tasted.

Exactly the same effect explains why collectors spend millions on limited editions, people are attracted to books or films that have been banned, and retailers are quick to point out limited stocks. But does it also apply to dating?

It is a question that has taxed some of the world's greatest minds. The classical Greek philosopher Socrates, when advising the prostitute Theodota on the best way to attract men, clearly preferred the "play hard to get" strategy, noting:

> They will appreciate your favors most highly if you wait
> till they ask for them. The sweetest meats, you see, if
> served before they are wanted, seem sour, and to those
> who had enough they are positively nauseating: but even
> poor fare is very welcome when offered to a hungry man.[2]

A few hundred years later the great Roman poet Ovid was
moved to agree:

> Fool. If you feel no need to guard your girl for her own
> sake, guard her for mine, so I may want her more. Easy
> things nobody wants, but what is forbidden is tempt-
> ing . . . Anyone who can love the wife of an indolent
> cuckold, I should suppose, would steal buckets of sand
> from the shore.[3]

The wise words of Socrates and Ovid are echoed in many
modern-day books about dating. Time and again, people are
advised to play it cool and make any potential love of their life
do the running. But does playing hard to get really work?

To find out, Elaine Hatfield from the University of Hawaii
and her colleagues conducted a series of fascinating and, at
times, odd studies.[4] In the first of these, students were shown
photographs and brief biographies of teenage couples and
asked to rate how desirable they found each member of the
couple. The biographies had been carefully constructed to
ensure that some of the teenagers appeared to have fallen for
their partner after only a couple of dates (think "easy") while
others had taken much longer (think "hard to get"). Contrary
to the researchers' expectations, the students gave much
higher ratings to those people who had declared their undying
love within moments of meeting their partner, leading them
to conclude that it appears that "all the world does love
a lover." Undaunted, the researchers undertook a second,
slightly more realistic study.

This time the research team asked a group of women who had signed up with a dating agency to help out. Whenever a man telephoned them for a date, they were asked to respond in one of two ways. On half of the calls they were to accept immediately ("easy"), while the rest of the time they would pause for precisely three seconds before saying yes ("hard to get"). After the call, all of the guys were told that they had taken part in an experiment ("she was faking it") and asked to rate their dates. Once again, the team discovered that playing hard to get did not affect the ratings. The team then wondered whether the experimental three-second pause had been ambiguous. They decided to make things a little more clearcut. In yet another study the women with the dating agency either rapidly accepted any offer of a date ("easy") or paused, explained that they had received countless offers and then rather begrudgingly arranged for just a coffee ("hard to get"). This time, the results revealed absolutely no effect.

Desperate, the researchers did what many people do when the going gets tough in the heady world of dating: they turned to prostitution.[5]

In a bizarre and little-known social psychology experiment, researchers persuaded a group of prostitutes to chat with their clients in one of two ways. While pouring them a drink before getting down to business, they would either say nothing ("easy") or casually explain that they were starting college soon and so would subsequently be seeing only the customers who they liked best ("hard to get"). The research team then monitored how many times each client contacted the prostitute during the following month and, yet again, found no relationship between the prostitute playing hard to get and the return rate.

To discover why playing hard to get should prove to be such a myth, Hatfield and the team asked a group of men whether they would rather date someone who was eager to have a relationship or someone who made others do all of the running. Most said that there were pros and cons for each option. According to the interviewees, "easy" women were relaxing and fun to be with but could be an embarrassment in public. In contrast, hard-to-get women might appear to be a conquest but were often unfriendly, cold, and had a tendency to humiliate you in front of your friends. As a result of the interviews, the researchers speculated that the best strategy would be to give a potential date the impression that in general you were hard to get (and therefore a scarce resource worth having) but really enthusiastic about him or her specifically. They tested this notion by using some of the same techniques (although this time not involving the prostitutes) and found overwhelming evidence to support their hypothesis.

However, being able to attract a mate is not just about conveying the magic "I am choosy, and I have chosen you" impression. Instead, research into the psychology of dating has uncovered a number of equally quick but effective ways of making your attraction to someone a mutual affair. All you need is a simple touch, an afternoon at a theme park, and the confidence to ask people about their favorite pizza topping.

THE POWER OF TOUCH

French psychologist Nicolas Guéguen has spent his career investigating some of the more unusual aspects of everyday life, and perhaps none is more unusual than his groundbreaking work on breasts. For years psychologists have been fascinated by the impact of women's chests on male brains, and they have carried out a series of studies that have scientifically proven that men are attracted to women with large breasts. This work, although not surprising, suffers from one significant drawback. Most of it has been undertaken in the relatively artificial confines of the laboratory and has involved presenting men with photographs of women with breasts of various sizes and asking them to select the one that they find most attractive. As a result, whenever this work was presented at academic conferences, other scientists would ask the same question time and again: "Yes, that's all very well, but does men's preference for large-breasted women actually exist in real life?"

Enter Nicolas Guéguen.

Guéguen decided to conduct two studies investigating breast size and male behavior in more realistic settings. One of these, subsequently described in his paper "Women's Bust Size and Men's Courtship Solicitation," involved systematically changing the apparent size of a young woman's breasts and examining the number of times she was approached by men in a nightclub.[6] The woman (who, according to the experimental report, was selected because she had an A-cup bust size and had been rated by male students as having average physical attractiveness) was asked to sit in a nightclub for an hour and look longingly at the dance floor. Meanwhile, a hidden researcher carefully counted the number of men who asked her to dance. Over the course of twelve weeks, the experimenters used latex inserts to vary the woman's bust size between a B and a C cup. The effect was as dramatic as it was predictable. Without the help of the latex inserts she was approached by men 13 times over the course of a night. When she moved up to an artificial B cup, this frequency rose to 19 times, while the fake C cup resulted in a staggering 44 approaches.

Of course, it could easily be argued that the researchers stacked the deck in their favor. After all, probably most of the men in the nightclub were there to meet women and would have had the time to look at several people before making an approach. What would happen if these factors were removed? What if the context was far less sexual and men had only a few seconds to make up their minds? To find out, Guéguen conducted another experiment, resulting in his article "Bust Size and Hitchhiking: A Field Study."[7]

This time the woman with the highly variable breasts was asked to stand at the side of a busy road and try to thumb a ride. Meanwhile, two researchers sat in a car on the opposite side of the road and secretly counted the number of male and female drivers who drove by and the number who stopped to offer the woman a ride. After a hundred cars had passed, the experimental hitchhiker added or removed latex to alter the size of her breasts. The results from 426 women drivers revealed that bust size had no impact on whether they stopped, with around 9 percent pulling up regardless of whether they had been presented with an A, B, or C cup. In stark contrast, the pattern from 774 male drivers was completely different. Of the men, 15 percent stopped to pick up the women without latex inserts, compared to 18 percent when she transformed into a B cup and 24 percent when confronted with a C cup. The researchers concluded that in the male mind, breast size looms large even when men are not in an overtly sexual setting.

Another aspect of Guéguen's work has examined the power of touch.[8] A large number of studies has shown that touching someone on the upper arm for just a second or two can have a surprisingly significant effect on how much help they then provide. In one experiment American researchers approached people in the street and asked them for a dime. A brief touch on the upper arm increased the likelihood of getting the money by 20 percent. Similar work has shown that the same subtle touch also significantly increases the likelihood that people will sign petitions, leave a tip for waitstaff, participate in a supermarket taste test (which then, in turn, increases the chances that they will buy the product), drink more in a bar, and become involved in charity work. Could it, however, also dramatically increase the chances of success in courtship?

To find out, Guéguen arranged for a twenty-year-old man to approach 120 women in a nightclub during a three-week period. The approaches were carefully controlled to ensure consistency across all 120 women. Each took place when slow songs were being played and involved the man walking up to a woman and saying, "Hello. My name's Antoine. Do you want to dance?" Half of the time the request was accompanied by a light touch on the top of the woman's arm, and the other half of the time the young man kept his hands to himself. If the woman declined, the man said, "Too bad, maybe another time?" and moved nine or ten feet away, then tried his luck with another woman. If the woman accepted, the man explained that she had just taken part in an experiment and handed her a sheet containing additional details about the study. Who says romance is dead?

In a second study by Guéguen, one of three male researchers approached women in the street and attempted to obtain their telephone numbers. Apparently all three of the men had to be good-looking, because according to the report describing the work, "pre-test evaluation showed that it was difficult to obtain the phone number from young women in the street" ("Honestly, it's part of a scientific experiment, officer"). The men approached a total of 240 women, told them that they were really pretty, suggested going for a drink later in the day, and asked for their telephone number. As before, half of the time the men touched the women lightly on the arm as they delivered their chat-up line. The men were then instructed to wait ten seconds, smile, and gaze at the woman. If the woman declined the kind offer, she was allowed to walk away. If she accepted, the researcher quickly explained that the whole thing had been an experiment, handed her an information sheet, and delivered one final scripted line: "Thanks for your participation, and I'm sorry that I have taken up your time. Perhaps we could meet another time. Bye."

The results from both experiments were impressive. In the nightclub, women accepted the offer of a dance 43 percent of the time when not being touched on the arm and 65 percent after even the briefest of touches. In the street, the research team obtained telephone numbers from 10 percent of women with no physical contact and almost 20 percent when touching. In both cases a brief touch dramatically increased success.

Why is a touch so effective when flirting? Many psychologists believe that the answer has to do with sex and status. A large body of research supports the not especially surprising fact that women find high-status men more attractive than their low-status counterparts. From an evolutionary perspective, those men represent ideal mates because they are able to provide for the couple and any potential offspring in times of need. But how do women decide on the status of a stranger within a few moments of meeting him?

The answer, in part, is touch. There is considerable evidence that a gentle touch is perceived as a sign of high status.[9] For example, ask people to look at photographs of one person touching another, and they consistently rate the "toucher" as far more dominant than the "touchee." This is especially true of that all-important male-to-female touch on the upper arm.

Most women don't consciously register the touch, but unconsciously it makes them think more highly of their potential beau.

Women frequently accuse men of being shallow and too easily influenced by a pair of large breasts. Guéguen's adventures with hitchhiking and latex certainly suggest that this is the case. However, his work in the psychology of female seduction shows that women's romantic decision making can also be swayed by physical factors, providing they signal high status. Perhaps the real message is that deep down we are all a tad more shallow than we might like to admit.

IN 59 SECONDS

If you want to get someone to help you out, try the briefest of touches on the upper arm. The same behavior also increases the likelihood that one person will find another person attractive, providing that the touch is short, confined to the upper arm, and delivered at the same time as a compliment or request. Do be careful, however, because it is easy to get this terribly wrong. Touching is a strong social signal, and even a few inches can make all the difference between the recipient inviting you in for coffee or calling the police.

IN 59 SECONDS

More than thirty years of psychological research has revealed that most people adopt one of several very different "loving" styles in their romantic relationships. This style does not tend to change throughout a person's life, and it plays a key role in determining their relationships. Some researchers believe that these styles are determined by people's relationship with their primary caregiver during childhood,[10] and others argue that it is all about brain functioning.[11] Regardless, the following questionnaire will give you an insight into how you score on the three main loving styles.[12]

Take a few moments to read the nine statements that follow, and assign each of them a rating to indicate the degree to which they describe you. Some of the statements refer to a specific relationship, while others refer to your general beliefs. Whenever possible, answer the questions with your current partner in mind or, if you are not in a relationship, answer with your most recent partner in mind. If you have not been in a relationship, answer in a way that is consistent with how you believe you would think and behave. Don't spend too long thinking about each statement—and answer honestly.

Assign each item a rating between 1 ("strongly disagree") and 5 ("strongly agree").

1 I was attracted to my partner within   1 2 3 4 5
   moments of meeting him/her.

2 When it comes to relationships, I find a   1 2 3 4 5
   certain type of person attractive, and
   my partner fits that ideal.

3 My partner and I simply feel like we were meant for each other.   1 2 3 4 5

4 I value loving relationships that grow out of strong friendships.   1 2 3 4 5

5 I cannot say exactly when I fell in love. It seemed to happen over a relatively long period of time.   1 2 3 4 5

6 Love is not a mysterious sensation but rather an extreme form of caring and friendship.   1 2 3 4 5

7 My partner would not be happy if he/she knew some of the things that I get up to.   1 2 3 4 5

8 I like the idea of playing the field with several different partners.   1 2 3 4 5

9 I tend to bounce back from failed love affairs quite easily.   1 2 3 4 5

Scoring

This type of questionnaire measures the three main kinds of loving styles. Based on concepts first proposed by the famous Greek philosopher Plato, these are commonly referred to by psychologists as Eros (Greek for "desire"), Ludus ("game playing"), and Storge ("affection"). To calculate your score for each style, add your scores together for the following statements.

Statements 1, 2, and 3 = Eros
Statements 4, 5, and 6 = Storge
Statements 7, 8, and 9 = Ludus

The highest of the three scores indicates your main loving style.

Eros: These lovers have very strong ideas about the type of physical and psychological characteristics that they desire in a partner. When they encounter a match, they frequently experience love at first sight and, all being well, engage in an emotionally intense relationship. Such relationships tend to survive for a few years but often falter as the love of their life changes over time and no longer matches their strict criteria. When this happens, the passionate Eros lover again sets off in search of the perfect soul mate. Extroverted and giving, passionate lovers feel secure in their relationships and are willing to be emotionally close to others. They tend to become infatuated during the initial stages of any relationship, and while in the grip of passionate love would not dream of infidelity.

Storge: These lovers value trust over lust. Instead of having a perfect partner in mind, they slowly develop a network of friends in the hope that affection will transform into deep commitment and love. Once committed, they are intensely loyal and supportive, and tend to form only one or two long-term romantic relationship(s) throughout their life. Highly altruistic and trusting, they have often been brought up in a large family and feel comfortable with the idea of depending on others for support.

Ludus: These lovers have no ideal type in mind but are instead happy to play the field. They strive for novelty and thrills, are uncomfortable with commitment, and quickly move from one short-term relationship to another. Summed up by the expression "They like the face they face," roving lovers enjoy the thrill of the chase and display little in the way of loyalty or commitment. More neurotic and self-conscious than most, they have little sympathy for the feelings of others. They are risk takers whose loving style is often driven by a fear of being abandoned by a partner—a situation that they avoid by not getting too close to anyone.

THE SCIENCE OF SPEED DATING

Speed dating is not complicated. During the course of an evening you meet a series of complete strangers face-to-face. Each encounter lasts just a few minutes, during which you have to decide whether you ever want to see your "date" again. Apparently invented in the late 1990s by an American rabbi as a way to help Jewish singles find partners, the idea rapidly spread from one community to another, and now it represents one of the most popular ways of meeting potential soul mates. But what is the best way of using these vital few moments (three minutes or less) to impress a possible love of your life? Subtly mention your Ferrari? Bare your soul and hope for the best? According to the latest research into the mysteries of attraction, it's more about pizza toppings, mirroring, avoiding spread betting, and modesty.

A few years ago I teamed up with fellow psychologists James Houran and Caroline Watt to examine the best chat-up lines when speed dating.[13] We assembled fifty single men and fifty single women, randomly paired them, and asked the pairs to spend three minutes chatting. We then told everyone to make quick notes about the lines they had used to impress one another, rate their potential beau for attractiveness, and then try again with another person. To uncover the best chat-up lines, we compared the conversations of participants rated as very desirable by their dates with those seen as especially undesirable.

Those who obtained few dates from the evening tended to employ old standards like "Do you come here often?" or struggled to impress with comments like "I have a Ph.D. in computing." Those more skilled in seduction encouraged their dates to talk about themselves in a fun and offbeat way, with the top-rated male's best line being "If you were on a hit show, who would you be?" while the top-rated female asked, "If you were a pizza topping, what would you be?" These types of lines are successful because at a speed-dating event people frequently feel that they are trapped in Groundhog Day, having the same conversation again and again. Getting people to open up and talk about themselves in a creative, funny, and unusual way promotes a sense of closeness and attraction.

In addition, there is the small matter of "monkey see, monkey do." Research shows that we all have an unconscious tendency to mimic others. Without realizing it, we copy the facial expressions, posture, and speech patterns of the people we meet. Most psychologists think that such mimicry aids communication by helping people think and feel the same way. However, the degree to which a person mirrors our own behaviors also has a surprisingly large influence on how we feel about that person.

The power of this effect was beautifully illustrated in a simple but elegant study by Dutch psychologist Rick van Baaren and his colleagues at the University of Nijmegen.[14] The research team descended on a small restaurant and asked a waitress to help them. After showing customers to their table, the waitress was to take their order in one of two ways.

Half of the time she was to politely listen and be generally positive by using phrases such as "Okay" and "Coming right up." The other half of the time she was to repeat the order to the customers. Repeating the order proved to have a remarkable effect on the tips that customers left when they finished their meal.

Those who had heard their own words repeated left tips that were 70 percent larger than those left by the "polite and positive" group. Another study conducted by the same team showed that mimicry also affects the degree to which we find others attractive.[15] In that experiment an individual posing as a marketing researcher stopped people on the street and asked whether they would be kind enough to take part in a survey. Half of the time the experimenter unobtrusively copied the person's posture and gestures as they answered the questions, and half of the time the researcher behaved normally. When questioned later, the first group subjected to the mirroring reported feeling a much closer emotional bond with the experimenter yet had no idea that their own behavior was being copied. The message here is that to convince people that the chemistry is right, you should mirror their movements. Lean forward when they lean forward, cross your legs when they cross theirs, hold your hands in the same position as they do. Without their realizing it, these small but important movements will help make the object of your affections feel that you share that certain—as the French say—"Je ne sais quoi."

So is a successful speed date simply about pizza toppings and mirroring? No. Other research suggests that it is also about being selective. A few years ago, Paul Eastwick and his colleagues at Northwestern University staged a series of experimental speed-dating sessions involving more than 150 students.[16] After each date the students were asked to rate how attractive they found their partner. The results revealed that people who reported finding a large number of daters desirable tended to be rated as undesirable by others. You might think that this finding was caused by a small group of especially ugly people trying to increase their chances of success by ticking the "yes" box for everyone they met. First, I can't believe that you would be so judgmental, and second, according to the data you would be wrong. The researchers had a group of people rate all of the participants for attractiveness and examined the speed-dating data from the attractive and unattractive people separately. The "if you want to meet lots of people, then I don't want to meet you" pattern emerged in both groups, proving that the original effect was not the outcome from a group of ugly, desperate participants. Instead, it seems that the speed-dating equivalent of spread betting can be picked up by daters within moments and is a big turnoff. In general, liking lots of others usually means that people will like you. In a more romantic context, however, potential dates want to feel special. Research suggests that they are especially skilled at detecting those who are simply out to meet as many people as possible.

Finally, a word of warning for men: be careful not to fall into the "too good to be true" trap. Psychologist Simon Chu at the University of Central Lancashire and his colleagues asked a group of women to look at photographs and brief descriptions of sixty men and rate their attractiveness as possible long-term partners.[17] As part of the description, the researchers systematically varied the men's alleged jobs, deliberately choosing careers that implied either high ("company director"), medium ("travel agent"), or low ("waiter") status. Overall, the good-looking men were rated as more attractive than others. Likewise, those in high-status jobs were generally seen as more desirable than those with smaller paychecks. No great surprise there. However, the important finding was that good-looking men in high-status jobs were seen as relatively unattractive long-term propositions. Chu and his colleagues argue that women might well avoid these types of men because they are likely to prove attractive to many other women and so might be especially likely to be unfaithful. The findings suggest that for speed dating, if you are a good-looking guy, have a great job, a huge bank balance, and a lavish lifestyle, and you are looking for a long-term partner, you should keep at least some of your assets under wraps.

IN 59 SECONDS

In speed dating you have only moments to impress. So to make best use of the short time available, think of lines that get the other person to talk about themselves in a creative, fun, and unusual way. Mimic (within reason) the way they sit, how they use their hands, their speech patterns, their facial expressions. Avoid spread betting. Rather than check the "yes, I would like to see you again" box for lots of people in the hope of obtaining the maximum number of dates, focus on the one or two people who appear to generate genuine chemistry. Finally, some advice specifically for men from Simon Chu's research: if you are good-looking and highly successful, remember that for many your looks and status might make you fall into the "too good to be true" category. Assuming that adding a prosthetic scar or two is out of the question, be prepared to downplay your successes. Of course, for everyone else, the theory represents a great way of coping with rejection—if one person after another turns you down, convince yourself that you are too damn attractive and successful for your own good.

SEX AND SPORT

When attempting to impress women, men often make a special effort to present themselves as especially caring and altruistic creatures. However, research suggests that they may have it all wrong.[18] When women were asked to indicate the traits that they found most desirable in friends, short-term partners, and long-term partners, most placed kindness high on their shopping list. However, each and every time it was trumped by bravery. It seems that when it comes to love, women value courage and a willingness to take risks over kindness and altruism. So instead of men making a special effort to woo women by describing their tireless work for charity, they should perhaps consider mentioning their love of skydiving, the importance of standing up for what you think is right, and following your heart no matter where it leads.

This bravery effect emerged in an online survey that I conducted with fitness expert Sam Murphy to explore the relationship between sport and attraction. Are men more impressed by women who play soccer or climb mountains? Do women go for bodybuilders or yoga fanatics?

More than six thousand people reported which sporting activities would make a member of the opposite sex more attractive. Results revealed that 57 percent of women found climbing attractive, making it the sexiest sport from a female perspective. This was closely followed by extreme sports (56 percent), soccer (52 percent), and hiking (51 percent). At the bottom of the list came aerobics and golf, with just 9 percent and 13 percent of the vote, respectively.

In contrast, men were most attracted to women who did aerobics (70 percent), followed by those who took yoga (65 percent), and those who went to the gym (64 percent). At the bottom of their list came golf (18 percent), rugby (6 percent), and bodybuilding (5 percent).

Women's choices appeared to reflect the type of psychological qualities that they find attractive, such as bravery and a willingness to take on challenges, while men appeared to be looking for a woman who was physically fit without appearing muscle-bound. No one, it seemed, was attracted to golfers.

HOW TO CONSTRUCT
THE PERFECT FIRST DATE

In 1975 Senator William Proxmire created the Golden Fleece award to highlight instances wherein the U.S. government had, in the senator's opinion, frittered away public money on frivolous causes. Proxmire gave his first award to the National Science Foundation for supporting a study on why people fall in love, noting, "I believe that 200 million Americans want to leave some things in life a mystery, and right at the top of the list of things we don't want to know is why a man falls in love with a woman, and vice versa." Fortunately, his opinion was not widely shared in the academic community, and over the years psychologists have investigated many aspects of love and attraction. Some of the most intriguing work examines the psychology lurking behind that all-important initial encounter.

First dates can be a tad tricky. Where is the best place for a romantic encounter? What should you talk about? Should you appear really enthusiastic from the very start or play hard to get? Worry not. Help is at hand. During the past thirty years researchers have tackled these questions and uncovered several quick and easy techniques designed to help Cupid's arrow find its target.

Let us first consider the thorny issue of where best to take a potential partner. You might think that a quiet restaurant or a walk in the countryside are both good bets. According to research conducted by psychologists Donald Dutton and Arthur Aron,[19] however, you would be way off the mark. Prior to their research, several experiments had already confirmed what poets had long suspected: when people find someone attractive, their hearts beat faster. Dutton and Aron thought that the opposite could also be true. In other words, people whose hearts are beating faster might be more likely to find someone attractive.

To find out if this was the case, they arranged for a female experimenter to approach men on one of two very different bridges across the Capilano River in British Columbia. One bridge was swaying precariously in the wind about two hundred feet above the rocks, while the other was much lower and far more solid. After asking a few simple survey questions, the experimenter offered the men her telephone number in case they would like to find out more about her work. Those crossing the precarious bridge had higher heart rates than those on the lower bridge. When approached by the young woman, they unconsciously attributed their increased heart rate to her rather than to the bridge, fooled themselves into thinking that they found her particularly attractive, and were far more likely to make a special effort to call her.

Of course, it is one thing to obtain this effect with strangers on bridges, but does it work with real couples in a more realistic setting? A few years ago psychologists Cindy Meston and Penny Frohlich at the University of Texas decided to find out.[20] They visited two large theme parks in Texas and waited near several roller coasters, armed with little more than a clipboard and photographs of an average-looking man and woman. They interviewed romantically involved couples a few moments before or after the couples had scared themselves silly on the ride. The researchers asked them to assign a number between one and seven to indicate how attractive they found both the person that they were with and the people in the photographs. The experimenters anticipated that those who had finished the ride would have higher heart rates than those preparing for it and, according to the "heart beating faster, person attractive" theory, would give higher attractiveness ratings.

Describing their findings in a paper titled "Love at First Fright," the researchers admitted that only some of their predictions were supported. Those rating the photographs after the ride did find the people in the pictures significantly more attractive than those waiting in line did. However, a different pattern emerged when it came to people rating one another: people found the person they were with slightly less attractive after the ride. When speculating about why this might be the case, the researchers wondered whether these ratings may have been influenced by the potential embarrassment of their partner's finding out that they had just been given a lower than expected attractiveness rating ("You gave me a one?"). They also considered the possibility that people may look less attractive after a roller-coaster ride because of "sweating, messy hair, and post-anxiety expressions." However, similar work, examining whether a similar effect occurs when couples watch exciting films, has provided more clear-cut evidence in support of the theory that we take cues from our own physiology when deciding how attractive we find others.[21] Researchers secretly observed couples leaving different kinds of films and discovered that those who had just seen a suspense thriller were especially likely to be holding hands and touching each other.

Of course, the perfect date is not just about getting your heartbeat racing. There is also the important issue of what you say and when you say it.

A few years ago psychologist Arthur Aron (he of the two bridges) and his colleagues also examined whether it was possible to place people on the fast track to attraction by getting them to chat about certain topics.[22] Obviously, the more couples get to know each other, the more likely they are to disclose personal information. Aron and his team wondered whether the reverse was also true—namely, could the act of disclosing personal information to another person make you feel especially close to that person?

The work involved people who didn't know each other being paired and instructed to chat about increasingly private aspects of their lives. By asking each other a series of preset questions, each couple was given forty-five minutes to play the "sharing game." The list started with normal conversational openings frequently used at dinner parties ("If you could meet anyone in history, who would it be?"), then quickly moved into "drunk with a close friend" territory ("Do you have a hunch about how, and when, you are going to die?"), before finally getting into "young couple trying to be intimate" land ("When did you last cry in front of someone?").

Aron knew that chatting about any subject might promote closeness, so he had other pairs of strangers work their way through a control list of small-talk questions ("What are the advantages and disadvantages of artificial Christmas trees?" "Do you prefer digital clocks or the kind with hands?"). At the end of the sessions, each pair was asked to rate how attractive they found each other. Perhaps not surprisingly, the pairs who had been made to chat about Christmas trees and clocks did not feel that they had developed that all-important sense of chemistry. In contrast, those who had played the sharing game developed the type of intimacy that usually takes months or years to achieve. In fact, the researchers noticed several participants exchanging telephone numbers after the end of the study.

So, when it comes to that all-important first date, go somewhere scary and don't be afraid of intimate conversation. Common sense says that your date may find you a tad strange. Science suggests that you will be irresistible.

IN 59 SECONDS

Beat Fast, My Still Heart

To help promote the chances of a successful date, choose an activity that is likely to get the heart racing. Avoid slow-moving classical music concerts, countryside walks, and wind chimes. Instead, look toward suspense-filled films, theme parks, and cycle rides. The theory is that your date will attribute a racing heart to you rather than to the activity, and so convince themselves that you have that special something.

The Sharing Game

When it comes to playing the sharing game, it is a case of taking one step at a time. However, providing that each stage seems appropriate, research suggests that disclosing personal information about yourself and encouraging your date to do the same can significantly speed up those all-important feelings of intimacy. Here are ten questions based on items from Aron's sharing game to help the process:

1. Imagine hosting the perfect dinner party. You can invite anyone who has ever lived. Whom would you ask?

2. When did you last talk to yourself?

3. Name two ways in which you consider yourself lucky.

4. Name something that you have always wanted to do and explain why you haven't done it yet.

5. Imagine that your house or apartment catches fire. You can save only one object. What would it be?

6. Describe one of the happiest days of your life.

7. Imagine that you are going to become a close friend with your date. What is the most important thing for him or her to know about you?

8. Tell your date two things that you really like about him or her.

9. Describe one of the most embarrassing moments in your life.

10. Describe a personal problem, and ask your date's advice on how best to handle it.

SIX QUICK TIPS FOR DATING

Reflected Glory. Research shows that women rate a man as more attractive after they've seen another woman smiling at him or having a good time in his company.[23] So if you want to impress women in a bar or at a party, ask a good female friend to come along and openly laugh at your jokes, then have her quietly slip away. And swear her to secrecy.

Your Eyes Are Bigger Than Your Stomach. Evolutionary psychologists believe that hungry men should show a preference for bigger women because their size suggests access to food. To test this idea, researchers asked male students entering or leaving a university dining hall to rate the attractiveness of full-length photographs of women of different sizes.[24] Hungry students rated the heavier women as more desirable. So if you are female, traditionally built, and interested in a guy, suggest going for that all-important drink before a meal, not after. Or try meeting a couple of hours before eating and then insist he have only a light salad.

Disagree, Then Agree. You might think that constant praise and head nodding is the way to a person's heart. However, research suggests that this may not be true. People tend to be more attracted to those who start off lukewarm and then become more positive toward the end of the date.[25] So instead of rushing in at a hundred smiles an hour from the very start of the evening, try playing slightly hard to get for the first hour or so and then turn on the charm later. Also, rather than chatting about things that you both like, talk about things that you both dislike. Describing their work in the snappily titled paper "Interpersonal Chemistry Through Negativity: Bonding by Sharing Negative Attitudes About Others," Jennifer Bosson and her colleagues at the University of South Florida discovered that people feel closer to each other when they agree about dislikes rather than likes.[26]

Fake a Genuine Smile. More than a century ago, scientists discovered that although authentic smiles and fake smiles both involve the sides of the mouth being pulled up, only a genuine smile causes crinkling around the eyes. More recent research has started to explore the subtle science of smiling, including trying to identify the signals that make a smile appear especially flirtatious. Initial work suggests that smiles that take longer to spread over a person's face (more than half a second) are seen as very attractive, especially when accompanied with a slight head tilt toward a partner.[27]

Love or Lust. Gian Gonzaga and his colleagues videotaped couples talking about their first date and then asked them to rate whether the discussion was more associated with love or lust.[28] When the couples decided it was about the joys of love, the tape showed they leaned toward each other, nodded, and smiled. But when they thought about lust, they were more likely to stick out their tongues and lick their lips. So if you want to know what your date has on his or her mind, look for these key signals. Whereas nodding and smiling might signal liking and possible love, the occasional licking of the lips suggests that it might be your lucky night.

Previous Partners. It is always a tricky moment on any date. You are getting on well, and then the issue of previous relationships rears its ugly head. Suddenly a whole series of questions runs through your mind: is it better to pretend to be picky and suggest that you have had only one or two sexual partners? Alternatively, should you appear more experienced and go with a much larger number of lovers? According to work conducted by Doug Kenrick at Arizona State University, it is all a question of balance.[29] Kenrick presented college students with profiles of people who had different numbers of partners and had them rate each person's desirability. The results revealed that for women, increasing a man's number of previous partners from zero to two made them more desirable, but anything over two was seen as unattractive. In contrast, for men, women became more and more desirable as their number of previous partners increased from zero to four, but anything over that was a turnoff.

relationships

The **perils** of "active listening,"

why Velcro can help couples **stick together,**

words **speak** louder than actions, and

a single **photograph** can make

all the difference

ACCORDING TO SOME EXPERTS, the bedrock of successful marital relationships involves a form of interaction that has come to be labeled "active listening." This style of communication involves partners' paraphrasing each other's statements of feelings, and then attempting to empathize with each other. Imagine, for example, that during a counseling session, a wife explains that she is furious with her husband because he regularly gets drunk, comes home smelling of alcohol, and sits in front of the television late. According to the tenets of active listening, the husband would put his wife's concerns into his own words and then try his very best to understand why she feels so angry with him. This intuitively pleasing technique is very popular and has given rise to the phrase "I hear what you are saying. . . ." But is active listening really essential to successful relationships, or is this yet another mind myth?

In the 1990s psychologist and world-renowned expert on marital stability John Gottman and his colleagues at the University of Washington were eager to find out, so they conducted a lengthy and elaborate study.[1] They recruited more than a hundred newlywed couples, invited them to the lab, and asked them to sit in front of a camera and chat for fifteen minutes about a topic of ongoing disagreement. The research team then examined every second of the footage, analyzing each comment. Over the next six years, the experimenters periodically contacted the couples to find out if they were still together and, if so, how happy they were in their relationship.

To test the effectiveness of active listening, they looked at every instance when one person on the film expressed any negative emotion or comment, such as "I am unhappy with your behavior" or "I can't stand the way you talk to my parents." The team recorded how the partner responded, looking for the types of comments associated with active listening, such as paraphrases indicating understanding or empathy. By comparing the frequency of such comments from the conversations of couples who had stayed together with those who had divorced and those who were in happy and unhappy relationships, the team could scientifically evaluate the power of active listening.

Gottman and his team were surprised and shocked by their own findings. Instances of active listening were few and far between, and they didn't predict whether a couple would be successful and happy. According to the results of the study, active listening was unrelated to marital bliss.

Amazed by this outcome, the team turned to another set of videotapes for a second opinion. In a previous study they had followed a group of couples for thirteen years, and now they set about doing the same kind of analysis on those tapes. They found a similar pattern in the data, which suggested that even the most successful, long-term, and happy couples rarely engaged in anything that resembled active listening.

According to Gottman, trying to paraphrase and empathize with your partner when he or she is being critical is a bridge too far and requires a kind of "emotional gymnastics" that few can achieve. Although the team's conclusions proved controversial, especially with many relationship counselors who seemed wedded to the notion of active listening, other research also failed to provide evidence that active listening forms the cornerstone of a successful relationship.[2]

So if listening to and responding to a partner's comments is not the best way forward, what is? The Gottman study suggests that couples in long-term and happy heterosexual relationships tend to exhibit a very particular pattern in times of conflict. The female usually raises a difficult issue, presents an analysis of the problem, and suggests some possible solutions. Males who are able to accept some of these ideas, and therefore show a sense of power sharing with their partner, are far more likely to maintain a successful relationship. In contrast, couples in which the males react by stonewalling, or even showing contempt, are especially likely to break up.

Teaching couples to change the way they respond to each other when the going gets tough is possible, but time-consuming and difficult. However, the good news is that there are several techniques that are surprisingly quick to learn and that can also help people live happily ever after. The only requirement is the ability to write a love letter, place a photograph above the fireplace, and turn back the hands of time to your very first date.

IN 59 SECONDS

According to research conducted by John Gottman, the extent to which you know the minutiae of your partner's life is a good predictor of how long your relationship will last. The following fun quiz will help evaluate how well you and your partner know each other. You should answer the questions by trying to guess the answer that your partner will give. Your partner then tells you the actual answer, and you award yourself one point for each correct response. You then swap roles and repeat the process. Finally, add your two scores together, which will result in a total between 0 and 20.

QUESTION	CORRECT?
1. In general, which of the following types of film would your partner most enjoy? Horror Comedy Action Drama	
2. What was your partner's first job?	
3. In general, which of the following types of sport would your partner most enjoy watching on TV? Football Baseball Basketball Auto Racing	
4. Where was your partner born?	
5. Which of the following classic books would your partner most prefer to read? *Moby-Dick* *A Tale of Two Cities* *Pride and Prejudice* *Frankenstein*	
6. What is your partner's shirt-collar size (male) or dress size (female)?	
7. In general, which of the following types of vacation would your partner most prefer? Beach Skiing Camping City	
8. What is the first name of your partner's closest friend (excluding yourself)?	
9. Which of the following world leaders would your partner most like to meet? Adolf Hitler J. F. Kennedy Mahatma Gandhi Winston Churchill	
10. What color are your partner's eyes?	

THE IMPORTANCE OF BONDING

In the late 1980s, researcher James Laird at Clark University in Massachusetts and his colleagues advertised for people to take part in an experiment into the possible existence of extrasensory perception.[3] Male and female participants who didn't know each other were scheduled to arrive at the laboratory at the same time, and when they arrived they were taken through a rather unusual procedure. A researcher explained that it was important that the pair do a rapport-building exercise before taking the telepathy test, and they were asked to spend a few moments looking into each other's eyes. They were then taken to separate rooms, and one of them was presented with a series of simple pictures while the other tried "psychically" to guess the nature of the images.

At the end of the study, Laird looked at his data and discovered no evidence for psychic powers. Was he disappointed? Not at all. In reality, the study had nothing to do with extrasensory perception. The alleged telepathy test was just an elaborate cover story that allowed the team to conduct a groundbreaking study of the psychology of love.

Many people believe that falling in love is a highly complex affair that depends on a complicated mixture of looks, personality, chemistry, and chance. However, Laird had other ideas. He wondered whether this unique and mysterious sensation might be much more straightforward than it first appeared, and whether it was possible to manufacture the feeling in just a few carefully engineered moments.

His hypothesis was simple. It was obvious from everyday life that couples in love spent a significant amount of time looking into each other's eyes. However, Laird wanted to know whether the reverse was also true. Would it be possible to create a feeling of love by having people spend a few moments gazing at each other?

Normally, gazing at strangers is, at best, perceived as peculiar, and at worst, aggressive. Because of this, Laird had to create an artificial but believable reason for prolonged eye contact, and so he eventually designed the telepathy-test cover story. Without realizing it, the participants in his fake ESP experiment were made to look into each other's eyes and were therefore behaving as if they found each other attractive. Laird thought that this would be enough to kick-start feelings of love and affection.

After the fake telepathy study had ended, all of the participants were asked to rate their amorous feelings toward their experimental partner. The data proved Laird right, with participants reporting genuine feelings of affection and attraction for their newfound soul mate.

The study represents an approach to human behavior first advanced by one of the founding fathers of modern-day psychology, William James. According to James, not only do our thoughts and feelings affect the way we act, but the way we act influences our thoughts and feelings.

Laird is not alone in exploring ways in which this approach can help researchers better understand matters of the heart. Another study, carried out by Arthur Aron from the State University of New York at Stony Brook, and his colleagues from various other universities, suggests that the same type of approach can also help bring couples closer together.[4]

The start of any romantic relationship is usually a time of great excitement, with people enjoying the novelty of experiencing life with a new partner. Fast-forward twenty years and often a very different picture emerges. Now the couple know each other very well, and life has become far more routine—the same restaurants, the same vacation destinations, and the same conversations. Although familiarity can be comforting, it can also induce a sense of boredom and is unlikely to make hearts race the way they once did.

Aron wondered whether, in the same way that gazing into another person's eyes induces attraction, getting couples to experience the thrill of courtship could help them rekindle the romance in their relationship. Specifically, would getting them to break the monotony of married life by doing something new and fun result in their finding each other more attractive? In an initial study, Aron placed newspaper advertisements asking for couples who were willing to participate in an experiment exploring the "factors that affect relationships."

When volunteers arrived at the lab, each couple completed a questionnaire about their relationship and was randomly assigned to one of two groups. The experimenters then cleared away the tables and chairs, rolled out some gym mats, and started the next part of the study.

For half of the couples, the researchers produced a roll of Velcro tape and explained that they were about to take part in a game. If the couples' eyes lit up and they exchanged knowing glances, the researchers quickly put the Velcro away and asked them to leave. For everyone else, the team used the Velcro to secure one person's right wrist to the left wrist of their partner, and also to strap their right and left ankles together.

After resisting the temptation to hum Lionel Richie's "Stuck on You," the researchers placed a 3.3-foot-high foam obstacle in the middle of the room and handed each couple a large pillow. Each couple had to get on hands and knees, crawl up to the obstacle, climb over it, crawl to the other side of the room, turn around, scamper back to the obstacle, climb over it again, and return to their starting position. To make things a little more interesting, they were asked to support the pillow between their bodies at all times (no hands, arms, or teeth allowed), and had only sixty seconds to complete the course. So that no one finished disappointed, the research team removed participants' watches ("We don't want them getting scratched during the frivolity") and pretended that everyone completed the task in the allotted time.

The couples in the other group were asked to do something far more mundane. One member of the couple was asked to get on hands and knees and told to roll a ball to a designated spot in the center of the room. Their partner was asked to watch from the side of the room and, when the ball made it to the spot, change places with their partner and roll the ball back to the starting position.

The experimenters assumed that the vast majority of couples did not usually spend very much time crawling over a large foam obstacle, and so the experience of the couples in the first group would be novel, fun, and relatively exciting. It was a chance for them to work together to achieve a goal and an opportunity to see each other from a new and unusual perspective. Conceptually speaking, it was like the type of experience that they used to have when they first met and life was much more exciting. In contrast, those in the second group were acting as a control, performing a task that was far more mundane and didn't involve any joint effort.

At the end of the experiment, all of the couples completed several questionnaires (including the rather unromantically named "Romantic Love Symptom Check List"), rating, for example, the degree to which their partner made them "tingle" and "burst with happiness." As predicted, the couples who had conquered the giant foam obstacle were far more loving toward one another than those who had completed the ball-rolling task. Just a few minutes of a new and fun joint activity appeared to have worked wonders.

Encouraged by these initial results, Aron and his team

repeated the study, this time using another measure of marital satisfaction instead of the post-experiment questionnaire. At the end of the second study, the experimenters filmed each couple chatting about planning their next vacation or how they might make significant home improvements. Another set of researchers then watched the films and carefully counted every instance when one member of the couple demonstrated some form of hostility. The Velcro couples made significantly more positive comments than the ball rollers.

Aron's findings demonstrate yet another way in which our behavior exerts a powerful influence over how we think and feel. In the same way that gazing into the eyes of a complete stranger can induce feelings of mutual attraction, participating in activities associated with early courtship can help rekindle past passions.

According to this work, any relationship can be helped along by a roll of Velcro tape, a large foam obstacle, and an open mind.

IN 59 SECONDS

Aron's work suggests that long-term couples will feel more attracted to each other when they regularly engage in novel and exciting joint activities that involve working together to achieve a goal. This finding is supported by the results of several surveys showing that long-term couples who are happy in their relationships are more likely to take part in leisure activities that involve both partners and are relatively unpredictable, exciting, and active rather than passive.

So regardless of whether it is playing a sport, amateur dramatics, rock climbing, visiting new places, learning a new dance, or traveling to novel vacation destinations, couples who face life's foam obstacles together stick together.

ROMANCE MADE SIMPLE

I recently conducted a large-scale online survey examining the psychology of romantic gestures. Working with writer Rachel Armstrong, I produced a questionnaire containing descriptions of a wide variety of romantic gestures, including, for example, running your partner a relaxing bath after they have had a bad day at work, offering them your coat when they are cold, and whisking your partner away somewhere exciting for the weekend. More than 1,500 people from the United Kingdom and the United States completed the survey, and the results help reveal the secret psychology underlying romance. Women frequently complain that men are not the most romantic of creatures. But did the survey confirm their suspicions?

Women were asked to look at the list and indicate how frequently their own partner had made each of the romantic gestures. The findings amounted to depressing reading. For example, 55 percent of women said that their partners had never run them a bath after a hard day at work, 45 percent had not been offered a coat when cold, and 53 percent had never been whisked away for an exciting weekend—objective evidence to support long-standing female complaints about unromantic men. But what might the underlying reason be for this poor showing?

In another part of the survey, male respondents were asked to look at the list of romantic gestures and, using a 10-point scale, rate how romantic they thought a woman would find it if her partner carried out each of the gestures. In contrast, female respondents were asked to use the same scale to indicate how romantic they thought it would be if their partner carried out each of the romantic acts. The results revealed that men severely underestimate the romantic value of even the simplest act.

For example, only 11 percent of men, compared with 25 percent of women, awarded the maximum score to the item "Tell her that she is the most wonderful woman that you have ever met." Likewise, 8 percent of men, but 22 percent of women, assigned 10 out of 10 points to "run her a relaxing bath after she has had a bad day at work." The same pattern emerged with almost the entire list, suggesting that men's reluctance to carry out a romantic gesture or two may not stem from laziness or a lack of caring but from underestimating how romantic behavior is perceived by women.

Finally, the survey findings also lent a helping hand to those men who wanted to engage in some heartfelt wooing, by identifying the gestures that women view as most, and least, romantic. The top-ten list of gestures is shown below, along with the percentage of women who assigned each gesture maximum marks on the "how romantic is this" scale.

1. Cover her eyes and lead her to a lovely surprise—**40 percent**
2. Whisk her away somewhere exciting for the weekend—**40 percent**
3. Write a song or poem about her—**28 percent**
4. Tell her that she is the most wonderful woman that you have ever met—**25 percent**
5. Run her a relaxing bath after she has had a bad day at work—**22 percent**
6. Send her a romantic text or e-mail, or leave a note around the house—**22 percent**

7. Wake her up with breakfast in bed—**22 percent**
8. Offer her a coat when she is cold—**18 percent**
9. Send her a large bouquet of flowers or a box of chocolates at her workplace—**16 percent**
10. Make her a mix CD of her favorite music—**12 percent**

Interestingly, it seems that gestures that reflect a form of escapism and surprise top the list, followed by those that reflect thoughtfulness, with blatant acts of materialism trailing in last place—scientific evidence, perhaps, that when it comes to romance, it really is the thought that counts.

FIVE TO ONE: WHEN WORDS SPEAK LOUDER
THAN ACTIONS

Try to spot the unhappy face in the diagram below.

For most people, the task is surprisingly easy, with the unhappy face seeming to jump out from the crowd. Research shows that, conceptually speaking, the same effect influences many aspects of our everyday lives. Negative events and experiences are far more noticeable and have a greater impact on the way we think and behave than their positive counterparts.[5] Put people in a bad mood, and they can easily remember negative life events, such as the end of a relationship or being laid off, but cheer them up, and they find it far harder to recall their first kiss or their best vacation. A single act of lying or dishonesty often has a disproportionate effect on a person's reputation and can quickly undo the years of hard work that have gone into building up a positive image.

American humorist Helen Rowland once noted, "A woman's flattery may inflate a man's head a little, but her criticism goes straight to his heart, and contracts it so that it can never again hold quite so much love for her." This seems to make intuitive sense, but are these assertions supported by findings from modern-day science?

As discussed earlier, psychologist John Gottman has spent more than thirty years exploring the key factors that predict whether a couple will stick together or drift apart.[6] Much of his work has involved examining the comments made by couples when they chat with each other about their relationship. Over the years he has become especially interested in the role played by positive comments (reflecting, for example, agreement, understanding, or forgiveness) and negative ones (involving hostility, criticism, or contempt). By carefully recording the frequency of these, and then tracking the success of the relationship, Gottman was able to figure out the ratio of positive to negative comments that predicted the downfall of a partnership. His findings make fascinating reading and firmly endorse the thoughts of Dale Carnegie. For a relationship to succeed, the frequency of positive comments has to outweigh negative remarks by about five to one. In other words, it takes five instances of agreement and support to undo the harm caused by a single criticism.

Unfortunately, Gottman's work also revealed that the much-needed positive comments are surprisingly thin on the ground. Why should this be the case? Once again, a detailed analysis of couples' conversations revealed the answer. When one person made a supportive remark ("Nice tie"), their partner *tended* to respond with a positive comment of their own

("Thanks. Nice dress"). However, the pattern was far from reliable, and an entire succession of positive remarks ("Nice tie, and really like your shirt, and lovely sweater, too") often failed to produce a single pleasant reply. In contrast, the response to negative comments was far more predictable, with the smallest of criticisms ("Are you sure about that tie?") often provoking a hail of negativity ("Well, I like it even if you don't. And why should I care what you think about my tie? It's not as if you have the best dress sense in the world. I mean, take that dress. You look like a scarecrow that has let itself go. That's it, I am out of here").

Gottman's work shows that relationships thrive and survive on mutual support and agreement, and that even the briefest of bitter asides needs to be sweetened with a great deal of love and attention. Unfortunately, conversational conventions do not encourage these much-needed compliments and supportive comments.

Having partners monitor and modify the language that they use when they speak to each other is difficult and would require a relatively large amount of time and effort. However, the good news is that researchers have discovered quick, but nevertheless effective, ways of using words to improve relationships.

Take, for example, work by psychologists Richard Slatcher and James Pennebaker at the University of Texas at Austin.[7] Slatcher and Pennebaker knew that previous research suggested that having people who have experienced a traumatic event write about their thoughts and feelings helped prevent the onset of depression and enhanced their immune system. They wondered if it could also improve the quality of people's relationships. To find out, they recruited more than eighty newly formed couples and randomly assigned one member of each couple to one of two groups. Those in one group were asked to spend twenty minutes a day for three consecutive days writing about their thoughts and feelings concerning their current relationship. In contrast, those in the other group were asked to spend the same amount of time writing about what they had been up to that day. Three months later the researchers contacted all of the participants and asked them whether their relationship was still ongoing. Remarkably, the simple act of having one member of the relationship write about their feelings for their partner had had a significant effect. Of those who had engaged in such "expressive" writing, 77 percent were still dating their partners, compared to just 52 percent of those who had written about their daily activities.

To explore what lay behind this dramatic difference, the researchers collected and analyzed the text messages that the couples had sent to each other during the three-month assessment period. By carefully counting all of the positive and negative words in the messages, they discovered that the texts from those who had carried out the expressive writing exercise contained significantly more positive words than the messages from those who had written about their daily lives. In short, the results demonstrated how a seemingly small activity can have a surprisingly large impact. Spending just twenty minutes a day for three days writing about their relationship had a long-term impact, both on the language that they used to communicate with their partner and on the likelihood that they would stick together.

Other research has suggested that it doesn't even take twenty minutes a day for three days to improve the health of your relationship. Take a look at the following illustration.

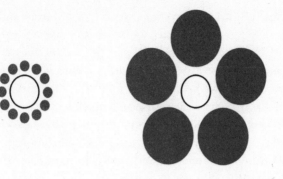

The white circle on the left appears to be larger than the white circle on the right. In fact, the two circles are identical, but they appear to be different sizes because our brains automatically compare each of the circles to their surroundings. The left circle is surrounded by small circles and so, in comparison, appears to be relatively large. In contrast, the right circle is surrounded by large circles and therefore appears to be relatively small.

Bram Buunk, at the University of Groningen and his colleagues from other universities, wondered whether the same type of "comparative thinking" could be used to enhance the way people viewed their relationships.[8] To find out, Buunk recruited participants who were in long-term relationships and asked them to think about their partner in one of two ways. One group was simply asked to jot down a few words explaining why they thought their relationship was good. In contrast, a second group was asked to first think about other relationships that they believed were not as good as their own and then write why theirs was better. Conceptually, the second group's task was similar to the situation on the left side of the illustration. As predicted, by mentally surrounding their relationship with smaller circles, participants felt far more positive about their partner.

Finally, work by psychologists Sandra Murray and John Holmes suggests that even one word can make all the difference.[9] In their study, people were interviewed about their partner's most positive and negative qualities. The research team then followed participants for a year, monitoring which relationships stayed the course and which fell by the wayside. They next examined the different types of language that the people in the successful and unsuccessful relationships had used during the interview. Perhaps the most important difference came down to just one word—"but." When talking about their partner's greatest faults, those in successful relationships tended to qualify any criticism. Her husband was lazy, but that gave the two of them reason to laugh. His wife was a terrible cook, but as a result they ate out a lot. He was introverted, but he expressed his love in other ways. She was sometimes thoughtless, but that was due to a rather difficult childhood. That one simple word was able to help reduce the negative effect of their partner's alleged faults and keep the relationship on an even keel.

IN 59 SECONDS

The following three-day task is similar to those used in experimental studies showing that spending time writing about a relationship has several physical and psychological benefits and can help improve the longevity of the relationship.

DAY 1

Spend ten minutes writing about your deepest feelings about your current romantic relationship. Feel free to explore your emotions and thoughts.

DAY 2

Think about someone that you know who is in a relationship that is in some way inferior to your own. Write three important reasons why your relationship is better than theirs.

DAY 3

Write one important positive quality that your partner has, and explain why this quality means so much to you.

Now write something that you consider to be a fault with your partner (perhaps something about his or her personality, habits, or behavior), and then list one way in which this fault could be considered redeeming or endearing.

A ROOM WITH A CUE

Imagine that you have just walked into the living room of a complete stranger. You know nothing about the person and have just a few moments to look around and try to understand something about their personality. Take a look at those art prints on the walls and the photographs above the fireplace. Notice how books and CDs are scattered all over the place— what does that tell you? Do you think that the person living here is an extrovert or an introvert? An anxious person or someone who is more relaxed about life? Are they in a relationship and, if so, are they genuinely happy with their partner? Okay, time to leave. The fictitious owner is coming back soon, and if they find you here they will be furious.

Psychologists have recently started to take a serious interest in whether it is possible to tell something about a person's personality and relationships from their homes and offices. For example, a few years ago, Sam Gosling at the University of Texas at Austin arranged for people to complete standard personality questionnaires. Then he sent a team of trained observers to carefully record many aspects of their living and work spaces.[10] Were the rooms cluttered or well organized? What kinds of posters did they have on the wall? Did they have potted plants and, if so, how many? The research showed that, for example, the bedrooms of creative people did not have any more books and magazines than the bedrooms of others, but their reading matter was drawn from a greater variety of genres. Likewise, when it came to the workplace, extroverts' offices were judged as warmer and more inviting than those of their introverted colleagues. Gosling concluded that many aspects of people's personality were reflected in their surroundings.

Other work has examined what you can tell about a person's relationship from their surroundings. Time for another exercise. This one really works only if you are currently in a relationship, so you will have to sit it out if you are single. Sorry about that. On the plus side, it is quite quick, so you won't have long to wait.

First, decide which room in your house you tend to use to entertain guests. Okay, now imagine sitting in the middle of that room and looking around (of course, if you happen to be in the room, simply look around). On a piece of paper, make a list of your five favorite objects in the room. This can include posters, art prints, tables, chairs, sculptures, potted plants, toys, gadgets—anything that really appeals to you. Next, think about how you acquired each object on the list. If your partner bought the object, or it was a joint purchase, place a checkmark beside it. You should end up with a list of five objects and between zero and five checkmarks.

What does the number of checkmarks say about your relationship? According to psychologist Andrew Lohmann, at Claremont Graduate University, and his colleagues, a great deal.[11] Lohmann recruited more than a hundred couples and asked them to complete the "check the joint objects in the room" task and also to assess how close they felt to their partner. The results revealed that a large number of checkmarks was associated with a closer and healthier relationship, a tendency to view the relationship as a long-term partnership, and a greater willingness to expend time and effort it make it work. So next time you pop over to a friend's house, you might want to ask about how they came to own some of the most prominent objects in the room—it may reveal more about their relationship than they realize.

The presence of objects that remind a person of their relationship may, for example, bring back happy memories, and so make them feel good. Or such objects might remind them of a particularly emotional or amusing episode in their relationship. However, according to some recent research, they might be doing far more.

In an ingenious study exploring the power of love, Jon Maner at Florida State University, and his colleagues from various other universities, recruited more than a hundred students who were in committed relationships and asked them to look at photographs of members of the opposite sex and choose the one who they thought was the most physically attractive.[12] One group was then asked to write an essay about a time when they felt a strong sense of love for their partner, while a control group was allowed to write about anything they chose.

While producing their essays, all of the students were told to forget about the photograph of the attractive person that they had selected earlier. In addition, they were told that if the image happened to pop into their minds, they were to place a checkmark in the margin of their essay. Asking people not to think about something usually encourages them to dwell on it, and this was certainly the case with the control group, who averaged four checkmarks per page. However, people thinking about being in love found it much easier to push the attractive image out of their mind, resulting in an average of only one tick every two pages.

Later in the experiment, everyone was asked to remember as much as possible about their chosen photograph. Those in the "love" group tended to remember the more general aspects of the image, such as the color of a person's dress or the location of the shot, and tended to forget the features related to physical attractiveness, such as having bedroom eyes or a wonderful smile. In fact, the students in love remembered, on average, only about two-thirds as many attractive features as the control group did.

These findings suggest that spending even a few minutes thinking about the love that you feel for a partner drastically reduces the appeal of attractive members of the opposite sex. According to the research team, this may be a mechanism that has evolved over thousands of years to help keep couples together. On a more practical level, it suggests that any object that reminds you of your partner may be having an important psychological effect. From photos to a wedding ring or a necklace bought on that fun trip abroad, it is all about helping you prefer your partner to the competition.

IN 59 SECONDS

Surrounding yourself with objects that remind you of your partner is good for your relationship. It could be something that you wear, such as a ring, pendant, or necklace. Or perhaps keep a gift from your partner on display in the home or office. Or maybe place a photograph of the two of you in a prominent location, or in a wallet or purse. Either way, remember that these objects are more than mere tokens of love; they also serve an important psychological function. Not only do they usually evoke happy memories and positive thoughts, but they also activate a deep-seated evolutionary mechanism that helps make temptation far less tempting.

stress

Why not to kick and scream,

how to reduce resentment in seconds,

harness the power of a four-legged friend,

and think your way to low blood pressure

THE FAMOUS PSYCHOANALYST Sigmund Freud believed that the psyche is composed of three main components: id, ego, and superego. The "id" is the animalistic portion of your mind that is impulsive and driven by basic instincts, the "superego" represents the more moral side of things, and the "ego" attempts to arbitrate between these two opposing forces. Most of the time, the three parts agree with one another, and all is fine and dandy. However, once in a while, a major disagreement breaks out, and, as is so often the case in life, it usually comes down to sex and violence.

To fully appreciate Freud's idea, imagine locking a horny teenage boy (think id), a priest (superego), and an accountant (ego) in a room with a pornographic magazine. The teenager, representing the animalistic side, would jump on the magazine, while the priest would attempt to rip it out of his immoral grasp and dispose of it. The accountant would then face an uphill struggle getting them to agree on the best way forward. Eventually, all three would calm down, discuss the issue, and perhaps decide that it would be best to pretend that the magazine didn't exist. That way, the teenager wouldn't be tempted to look at the naughty photographs, and the priest wouldn't have to lecture constantly about the importance of morality. Happy with the clever compromise, the three hide the magazine under the carpet and try to forget about it. Unfortunately, that is easier said than done. Day after day the teenager would be tempted to take a peek, but every time he lifted the carpet, the priest would wag his finger. Eventually the tension would build, making everyone feel more and more anxious.

According to Freud, we are frequently caught up in struggles between our inner teenager and priest, with one arguing for what we want to do and the other for what we ought to do. The teenager wants to have an extramarital affair, and the priest points out the importance of marriage vows. The teenager wants to strike out at someone who has upset him, and the priest votes in favor of forgiveness. The teenager wants to go ahead with a shady business deal, and the priest emphasizes the need to be a good law-abiding citizen. Most of the time we end up pretending that these problems don't exist and try to bury them deep within the unconscious. However, the mental stress caused by having to keep our conceptual pornographic magazines hidden under the carpet builds and can eventually make us feel frustrated, anxious, and angry.

Many psychologists have argued that the best solution is to release these repressed feelings in a safe and socially acceptable way. Punch a pillow. Shout and scream. Stamp your feet. Anything to calm down your inner teenager before he kicks in the door. This cathartic approach to anger management has gained wide acceptance—but was Freud correct?

For several years, psychologists have examined the effects of putting people under stress and then encouraging them to shout and scream. A few years ago, Brad Bushman at Iowa State University carried out an experiment in which six hundred students were asked to produce an essay describing their views on abortion.[1] These essays were then taken away and allegedly given to another student for evaluation. In reality, the experimenters evaluated all of the essays themselves and made sure that the students received bad marks, negative feedback, and a handwritten note saying, "This is one of the worst essays I have read." Perhaps not surprisingly, the students were annoyed with the way their essays had been evaluated and were furious with the fictitious evaluator.

Some of the students were then given an opportunity to get their aggressive feelings out of their system. They were given a pair of boxing gloves, shown a photograph of the person that had allegedly marked their essay, and told to think about that person while they hit a seventy-pound punching bag. Although the students were left alone with the bag while venting their aggression, an intercom system allowed the experimenters to count secretly the number of times they hit the bag. In contrast, another group of students was not introduced to the boxing gloves and punching bag but was asked instead to sit in a quiet room for two minutes.

Afterward, everyone completed a standard mood questionnaire that measured, among other things, how angry, annoyed, and frustrated they felt. Finally, games were played between pairs, with the victor winning the right to administer a loud blast of noise in the face of the loser. The winner decided how long and how loud each blast would be, and a computer carefully recorded the choices.

Did the people who punched the bag feel less aggressive than those who had sat quietly in the room? Did the "punchers" feel more inclined to generate louder blasts?

Those who had donned the boxing gloves and punched as hard as they could felt far more aggressive afterward and administered longer and louder blasts of noise in the faces of their fellow participants. The results revealed large differences in the final mood, and blasting behavior, between the two groups, and this pattern has been proven frequently. The venting of anger does not extinguish the flame. In fact, as Brad Bushman remarks in his paper, it is far more likely to pour gasoline onto the fire.

If punching and screaming do not help to quell feelings of stress and frustration, what does? And what can be done to create a more relaxed view of life? Are lengthy anger-management courses or hours of deep meditation the answer? In fact, there are some simple and fast solutions, which include being able to find benefits, doing nothing, and harnessing the positive power of a four-legged friend.

IN SEARCH OF BENEFITS

Everyone will experience negative events at some point in their lives. Perhaps you will contract an illness, have to face the breakup of a long-term relationship, discover that your partner has had an affair, or endure hurtful gossip spread about you by a close friend. Quite understandably, such events usually cause people to feel anxious, upset, and depressed. People often reflect on the past, wishing that things could be different. If another person is responsible for their suffering, thoughts might turn to revenge and retribution. Oftentimes, such experiences lead to feelings of anger, bitterness, and aggression. Given that putting on boxing gloves and hitting a punching bag is likely to make the situation worse rather than better, what is the best way of dealing with such emotions?

One possibility is simply to behave in a way that is incompatible with being angry. Watch a funny film, go to a party, play with a puppy, or tackle a difficult crossword puzzle. Alternatively, you could distract yourself by exercising, creating an art project, or spending an evening with friends or family. However, although such behavior may help reduce feelings of stress caused by relatively minor hassles, it is unlikely to provide a lasting solution to more serious sources of long-term frustration. The good news is that a more effective solution does not require lengthy sessions with a therapist or hours talking about the issues with those around you. It actually takes minutes, not months, and has been shown to help people who have lost their possessions in a fire, suffered bereavement, experienced a heart attack, been the victims of disaster, or been diagnosed with rheumatoid arthritis.[2] It is called "benefit finding."

The procedure can be illustrated by research conducted by Michael McCullough and his colleagues at the University of Miami.[3] More than three hundred undergraduates were asked to choose an incident in their lives in which someone had hurt or offended them. From infidelity to insults, rejection to abandonment, the students all came up with something that had been eating away at them.

One-third of the participants were then asked to spend a few minutes describing the event in detail, focusing on how angry they felt and how the experience had had a negative effect on their lives. A second group was asked to do the same thing, except they were to focus on the benefits that flowed from the experience, including, for example, becoming a stronger or wiser person. The final group was simply asked to describe the plans that they had for the following day.

At the end of the study, everyone was asked to complete a questionnaire that measured their thoughts and feelings toward the person who had upset and hurt them. The results revealed that just a few minutes of focusing on the benefits that were derived from the seemingly hurtful experience helped participants deal with the anger and upset caused by the situation. They felt significantly more forgiving toward those who had hurt them and were less likely to seek revenge or avoid them.

Finding the benefits that resulted flowed from negative life events may seem like wishful thinking, but there is some evidence that such benefits may be genuine. For example, research shows that certain positive character traits, such as gratitude, hope, kindness, leadership, and teamwork, increased in Americans following the 9/11 terrorist attacks.[4] In addition, other work has shown that having a serious physical illness can result in increased levels of bravery, curiosity, fairness, humor, and appreciation of beauty.[5]

When it comes to anger management, putting on the boxing gloves or punching a pillow is far more likely to increase, not decrease, feelings of aggression. Instead, it is possible to significantly reduce such feelings by focusing on the benefits that emerged from the seemingly negative events underlying your anger.

IN 59 SECONDS

When you experience an event that has the potential to make you feel angry, try the following exercise to ease the pain and help you move on.

Spend a few moments thinking about the positive aspects of the event that you found hurtful. For example, did the event help you . . .

- grow stronger or become aware of personal strengths that you didn't realize you had?
- appreciate certain aspects of your life more than before?
- become a wiser person?
- enhance important relationships or end bad ones?
- become more skilled at communicating your feelings?
- bolster your confidence?
- develop into a more compassionate or forgiving person?
- repair and strengthen your relationship with a person who hurt you?

- identify any of your own shortcomings that may stand in the way of your happiness?

Write down how you have benefited from the experience and how your life is better as a result of what happened. Do not withhold anything and be as honest as possible.

FOUR 15-SECOND TIPS FOR CONQUERING STRESS

When you sense danger, your body gears up for action as you prepare either to run away or stand your ground. Unfortunately, the stress of modern-day life can result in this system's being triggered constantly. Whether it stems from not being able to find a parking space or an argument with the kids, most people hit the "fight or flight" button on an all too regular basis. Although mild amounts of stress may help some people focus on the task at hand, constant problems can take their toll, eventually sending the stress meter rocketing and causing increased blood pressure, concentration difficulties, worry, weight gain, and a weakening of the immune system. However, there are several quick and easy ways of bringing your blood pressure back down to earth.

Help Yourself by Praying for Others. Research conducted by Neal Krause at the University of Michigan suggests that praying for others might be good for your health.[6] After interviewing more than a thousand people about the nature of their prayers, finances, and health, Krause discovered that praying for others helped reduce the financial stresses and strains of the person doing the praying and improved their own well-being. Interestingly, praying for material things, such as a new car or a better house, offered no such protection.

Study the Classics. Sky Chafin at the University of California, San Diego, and colleagues at other universities examined which music best reduces blood pressure after a stressful event.[7] Their work involved making people anxious by having them count down aloud from 2,397 in sets of 13, i.e., 2397, 2384, et cetera. To make matters worse, every thirty seconds the experimenter harassed the participants with negative feedback ("Come on, get a move on") and urged them to speed up. Afterward, some of the participants were left alone to recover in silence, while others were played either classical music (Pachelbel's *Canon* and Vivaldi's *Four Seasons: Spring*, movement 1), jazz (including "Flamenco Sketches" by Miles Davis), or pop music (Sarah McLachlan's "Angel" and the Dave Matthews Band's "Crash into Me"). Blood pressure readings revealed that listening to pop or jazz music had the same restorative effect as total silence. In contrast, those who listened to Pachelbel and Vivaldi relaxed much more quickly, and so their blood pressure dropped back to the normal level in far less time.

Here Comes the Sun. Work conducted by Matthew Keller at the Virginia Institute for Psychiatric and Behavioral Genetics, and outside colleagues, looked at the relationship between the sun and emotion.[8] The team discovered that hot weather, indicated by higher temperatures and barometric pressure, caused people to be in a better mood and improved their memory, but only if they had spent more than thirty minutes outside. People who had spent less than the magic half hour in the sun were actually in a poorer mood than usual. Perhaps, as the authors suggested, people resent being cooped up when the weather is pleasant.

Get in Touch with Your Inner Clown. Laugh and the whole world laughs with you, cry and you increase your chances of a heart attack. Well, at least that is the general conclusion from research examining the psychology of humor and stress. People who spontaneously use humor to cope with stress have especially healthy immune systems, are 40 percent less likely to suffer a heart attack or stroke, experience less pain during dental surgery, and live four and a half years longer than average.[9] In 2005 Michael Miller and his colleagues at the University of Maryland showed people scenes from films that were likely to make them feel anxious (such as the opening thirty minutes of *Saving Private Ryan*) or make them laugh (such as the "orgasm" scene from *When Harry Met Sally*). Participants' blood flow dropped by about 35 percent after watching the stress-inducing films, but rose by 22 percent following the more humorous material. On the basis of the results, the researchers recommended that people laugh for at least fifteen minutes each day.

PAWS FOR THOUGHT

There are many ways in which a dog can make you feel better. Scientists have conducted numerous studies that examine how you might benefit from having a four-legged friend.

Some of the best-known research, run by Erika Friedmann at the University of Maryland, and outside colleagues, investigated the possible relationship between dog ownership and cardiovascular functioning.[10] After carefully following the recovery rates of patients who had suffered a heart attack, Friedmann discovered that those who were dog owners, compared to those without a canine pal, were almost nine times more likely to be alive twelve months later. This remarkable result encouraged scientists to explore other possible benefits of canine companionship, resulting in studies showing that dog owners coped well with everyday stress, were relaxed about life, had high self-esteem, and were less likely to be diagnosed with depression.[11]

The magnitude of these benefits should not be underestimated. One study measured the blood pressure and heart rate of dog owners as they carried out two stressful tasks (counting backward by threes from a four-digit number and holding their hand in a bucket of ice water) while in the presence of their pet or spouse.[12] The participants had lower heart rates and blood pressure and made far fewer errors on the counting task in the presence of their dog than they did if their partner was present—scientific evidence, if any is needed, that your dog is better for your health than your husband or wife is.

Interestingly, the same cannot be said for cats. Some studies show that living with a cat may help alleviate negative moods but is unlikely to make you feel especially good,[13] and others suggest that cat owners may actually be more likely than others to die in the twelve months following a heart attack.[14]

Promising as they may seem, such studies do have one huge problem. Although dog ownership is related to a more relaxed attitude toward life and a healthier cardiovascular system, that doesn't necessarily mean that having a dog is the cause of these benefits. People who own a dog may have a certain type of personality, and it could be that which is responsible for their longer and less stressful lives.

To help separate correlation from causation, Karen Allen at the State University of New York at Buffalo conducted a much-needed study.[15] She assembled a group of city stockbrokers who suffered from hypertension, randomly divided them into two groups, and gave each person in one group a dog to look after. Both groups had their blood pressure monitored over a six-month period. The results revealed that the stockbrokers with dogs were significantly more relaxed than those in the control group. In fact, when it came to alleviating the effects of mental stress, the dogs proved more effective than one of the most commonly used drugs to treat hypertension. More important, as the people were randomly assigned to the "dog" and "no dog" condition, there was no difference in personality between the groups, and so that factor could not account for the findings. In addition to feeling less stressed, the hard-nosed city types had become emotionally attached to their animals, and none of them accepted the opportunity of returning their newfound friends at the end of the study.

Several theories have been proposed to explain why owning a dog should be good for you. It could be that the exercise associated with daily walking benefits your physical and psychological health. Others have argued that dogs act as the ultimate "nonjudgmental friend," patiently listening to your innermost thoughts and never passing your secrets on to others. Seen in this way, dogs are like a devoted therapist, albeit one with woolly ears, a wet nose, and low fees. An alternative theory is that simply touching or stroking a dog could have a calming and beneficial effect (evidence shows that even a nurse holding a patient's hand significantly lowers the patient's heart rate).[16]

However, most researchers acknowledge that one of the most important factors centers on the social benefits of owning a dog. Spend time in a park frequented by people out walking their dogs and you will quickly see how man's best friend encourages strangers to talk to one another ("Aw, how cute. . . . What breed is he?" "What a lovely dog . . . How old is she?" "Look at what I've just stepped in . . . Did he do that?"). A large body of research has demonstrated that spending time with other people is a major source of happiness and health, and dogs' inadvertent but effective ability to bring people together is likely to play a major role in promoting the well-being of their owners.

But just how good are dogs at initiating such meetings, and what kind of dog is best for networking? To find out, animal psychologist Deborah Wells from Queen's University Belfast arranged for a researcher to give up several lunch hours in order to walk back and forth along the same stretch of road with a variety of dogs. Each walk continued until the researcher had passed three hundred people coming in the opposite direction. Another experimenter, walking a few paces behind, secretly noted whether each passerby looked at the researcher, smiled at her, or stopped to talk. For three of the trips the researcher was accompanied by a yellow Labrador puppy, an adult Labrador, or an adult Rottweiler. As a control experiment, on three other days she walked alone, carrying a twenty-inch brown teddy bear (chosen to have attention-grabbing big brown eyes, short limbs, and a high forehead) or a yucca plant.

Finally, 1,800 passersby and 211 conversations later, the results revealed that the teddy bear and the plant initiated lots of looking but did not result in very much smiling and resulted in almost no chatting. In contrast, the dogs caused people to look, smile, and chat. The Rottweiler produced a very low chat rate, presumably because people associated the breed with aggression and liked the idea of keeping their throats intact and fully functional. In contrast, around one in ten people stopped to chat to the researcher when she was with the adult or puppy Labrador.[17]

This study is not the only one to support the notion that people talk to those with animals. Previous work found that a female experimenter sitting on a park bench received more attention from passersby when she had a pet rabbit or turtle at her side than when she sat alone blowing bubbles or next to a working television set.[18]

IN 59 SECONDS

There are two key messages from this research. First, owning a dog helps to relieve the stresses and strains of everyday life, in part because it promotes social contact. Second, to maximize the chances of such meetings, choose a Labrador rather than a Rottweiler, teddy bear, yucca plant, television set, or bubble mixture.

However, if your lifestyle is incompatible with owning a dog, there are still two things that you can do to gain the benefits of a four-legged friend.

i-dog

You could consider getting a robotic dog, rather than a real one. Recent research by Marian Banks and her colleagues at the Saint Louis University School of Medicine examined the effects of robot dogs and real dogs on patient loneliness in long-term-care facilities.[19] The research team took a living dog or a Sony AIBO to each facility on a weekly basis, spending about thirty minutes with patients on each visit. During the course of eight weeks, patients formed the same strength of emotional bond with both types of dog, and both helped to alleviate feelings of loneliness to the same extent.

Tune in to Animal TV.

In an innovative study, Deborah Wells examined whether merely looking at a video of an animal can have the same type of calming and restorative effects as those created by being in its company.[20] She created three short videotapes (ten fish swimming in a plant-filled aquarium, ten parakeets in an aviary, or ten monkeys sitting in trees) and took participants' blood pressure before and after they watched the videos. In one control condition, Wells organized another group of people to watch a videotape of a well-known soap opera, and still another to watch a blank television screen. Two main findings emerged. First, physiologically speaking, watching the soap opera was almost identical to staring at a blank television screen. Second, compared to the two control conditions, all three animal videos made the participants feel much more relaxed. To help reduce your heart rate and blood pressure in less than a minute, go online and watch a video of a cute animal.

LOWER YOUR BLOOD PRESSURE BY DOING NOTHING

A few years ago I conducted an experiment into the psychology of alcohol consumption as part of a television program. The study involved a group of students spending an evening in a bar with their friends. It was easy to persuade people to participate because the drinks were on the house. The only downside was that throughout the course of the evening our guinea pigs were asked to take a few short tests. On the night of the experiment, everyone arrived and the first round of testing began. Each student was presented with a list of numbers and asked to remember as many as possible, walk along a line marked on the floor, and undergo a reaction-time test that involved the experimenter's dropping a ruler from between her first finger and thumb and asking the students to catch it the moment they saw it move.

Having completed the initial tests, we quickly moved on to the desirable part of the evening—drinking. Each student was randomly assigned to a blue group or a red group, given an appropriate badge, and told that they were more than welcome to make good use of the free bar. There was, however, just one rule—each person had to go to the bar and order their own drink, and no one was to get any drinks for friends. Throughout the evening, we frequently interrupted the flow of conversation, pulling people away for testing and having them perform the same memory, balance, and reaction tests as before.

As the amount of alcohol flowing through their veins increased, people became much louder, significantly happier, and far more flirtatious. The test results provided an objective measure of change, and by the end of the evening most people had to struggle to recall any list of numbers that contained more than one digit, consistently failed even to find the line marked on the floor, and closed their fingers a good sixty seconds after the ruler had clattered to the ground. Okay, so I am exaggerating for comic effect, but you get the idea. By far the most fascinating result, however, was the similarity in scores between those wearing red badges and those wearing blue, because both groups had been deliberately duped.

Both groups seemed to suffer significant memory impairment, experience increased difficulty balancing on the line, and constantly let the ruler slip through their fingers.

But what the students in the blue group didn't know was that they hadn't touched a drop of alcohol throughout the entire evening. Before the experiment started, we had secretly stocked half of the bar with drinks that contained no alcohol but nevertheless looked, smelled, and tasted like the real thing. The bar staff had been under strict instructions to look at the color of each person's badge and provide those in the red group with genuine alcohol and those in the blue group with the nonalcoholic fakes. Despite the fact that not a single drop of liquor had passed their lips, those with blue badges managed to produce all of the symptoms commonly associated with having a few too many. Were they faking their reactions? No. Instead, they were convinced that they had been drinking, and that thought was enough to convince their brains and bodies to think and behave in a "drunk" way. At the end of the evening we explained the ruse to the blue group. They laughed, instantly sobered up, and left the bar in an orderly and amused fashion.

This simple experiment demonstrates the power of the placebo. Our participants believed that they were drunk, and so they thought and acted in a way that was consistent with their beliefs. Exactly the same type of effect has emerged in medical experiments when people exposed to fake poison ivy developed genuine rashes, those given caffeine-free coffee became more alert, and patients who underwent a fake knee operation reported reduced pain from their "healed" tendons. In fact, experiments comparing the effects of genuine drugs as compared to those of sugar pills show that between 60 percent and 90 percent of drugs depend, to some extent, on the placebo effect for their effectiveness.[21]

Exercise is an effective way to reduce blood pressure, but how much of this relationship is just in the mind? In a groundbreaking and innovative study, Alia Crum and Ellen Langer at Harvard University enlisted the help of more than eighty hotel room attendants selected from seven hotels.[22] They knew that the attendants were a physically active lot. They cleaned and serviced an average of fifteen rooms each day, with each room taking about twenty-five minutes, and they were constantly engaging in the type of lifting, carrying, and climbing that would make even the most dedicated gym-goer green with envy. However, Crum and Langer speculated that even though their attendants were leading an active life, they might not realize that this was the case; the researchers wondered what would happen if the attendants were told how physically beneficial their job was for them. Would they come to believe that they were fit people, and could this belief cause significant changes in their weight and blood pressure?

The research team randomly allocated the attendants in each hotel to one of two groups. Those in one group were informed about the upside of exercise and told the number of calories they burned during a day. The experimenters had done their homework, and so they could tell the attendants that a fifteen-minute sheet-changing session consumed 40 calories, that the same amount of time vacuuming used 50, and that a quarter of an hour scrubbing a bathroom used 60 more calories. So that the information would stick in their minds, everyone in the group was given a handout containing the important facts and figures, and the researchers placed a poster with the same information on a bulletin board in the staff lounge. The control group of attendants was also given the general information about the benefits of exercise, but they were not told about the calories they themselves burned. Everyone then completed a questionnaire about how much they tended to exercise outside of work, their diet, and drinking and smoking habits. They also took a series of health tests.

A month later the researchers returned. The hotel managers confirmed that the workloads of the attendants in the "wow, your job involves lots of exercise" group and the control group had remained constant. The experimenters then asked everyone to complete the same questionnaires and health tests as before, and set about analyzing the data.

The two groups had not taken additional exercise outside of work, and neither had they changed their eating, smoking, or drinking habits. As a result, there were no actual changes in their lifestyle that would suggest that one group should have become fitter than the other.

The researchers turned their attention to the health tests. Remarkably, those who had been told how many calories they burned on a daily basis had lost a significant amount of weight, lowered their body mass index and waist-to-hip ratio, and experienced a decrease in blood pressure. The control group attendants showed no similar improvements.

So what caused this health boost? Crum and Langer believe that it is all connected to the power of the placebo. By reminding the attendants of the amount of exercise that they were getting on a daily basis, the researchers altered the attendants' beliefs about themselves, and their bodies responded to make these beliefs a reality. It seems that in the same way people slur their words when they think they are drunk, or develop a rash when they think they are ill, so merely thinking about their normal daily exercise can make them healthier.

Whatever the explanation for this mysterious effect, when it comes to improving your health, you may already be putting in the necessary effort. It is just a case of realizing that.

IN 59 SECONDS

Crum and Langer's research is controversial but, if valid, suggests that being conscious of the fuel-burning activities that you engage in every day is good for you. The following chart gives an approximate number of calories burned by someone of average weight carrying out a range of normal activities (people with higher or lower weight will burn proportionately more or fewer calories). Use the chart to calculate the approximate number of calories you burn each day.

Keep the chart handy to remind yourself of the "invisible" exercise that you get each day of your life, and according to the theory, you should see your stress level drop by doing nothing.

ACTIVITY	A Calories burned per minute	B Do you carry out this activity during a typical week?	C If so, for roughly how many minutes each week?	D Total number of calories burned (column A x column B)
Normal walking	3			
Brisk walking	6			
Cycling	5			
Light housework	4			
Ironing	3			
Washing dishes	3			
Mowing the lawn	5.5			
Washing the car	5.5			
Mopping the floor	5.5			
Gardening	5			
Reading a book	1.5			
Shopping	3			
Sitting at a desk	1.5			
Watching TV	1.5			
Sexual intercourse	2			
Driving	1.5			
Sleeping	1			
Talking on the telephone	1			
Eating	.5			
Taking a shower	5			
Standing up	1.5			
Walking up and down stairs	8			
Playing with kids	4			
			TOTAL	

decision making

Why two heads are no better than one,

how never to regret a decision again,

protect yourself against

hidden persuaders,

and tell when someone is lying to you

WHEN PEOPLE HAVE an important decision to make in the workplace, they often arrange to discuss the issues with a group of well-informed and levelheaded colleagues. On the face of it, that seems a reasonable plan. After all, when you're making up your mind, it is easy to imagine that consulting people with a variety of backgrounds and expertise could provide a more considered and balanced perspective. But are several heads really better than one? Psychologists have conducted hundreds of experiments on this issue, and their findings have surprised even the most ardent supporters of group consultations.

Perhaps the best-known strand of this work was initiated in the early 1960s by MIT graduate James Stoner, who examined the important issue of risk taking.[1] It will come as no great surprise that research shows that some people like to live life on the edge, while others are more risk averse. However, Stoner wondered whether people tended to make more (or less) risky decisions when they were part of a group. To find out, he devised a simple but brilliant experiment.

In the first part of his study, Stoner asked people to play the role of a life coach. Presented with various scenarios in which someone faced a dilemma, they were asked to choose which of several options offered the best way forward. Stoner had carefully constructed the options to ensure that each represented a different level of risk. For example, one scenario was about a writer named Helen who earned her living writing cheap thrillers. Helen had recently had an idea for a novel, but to pursue the idea she would have to put her cheap thrillers on the back burner and face a decline in income. On the positive side, the novel might be her big break, for which she could earn a large amount of money. On the downside, the novel might be a complete flop, and she would have wasted a great deal of time and effort. Participants were asked to think about Helen's dilemma and then indicate how certain she should be that the novel was going to be a success before she gave up her regular income from the cheap thrillers.

If a participant was very conservative, they might indicate that Helen needed to be almost 100 percent certain. If the participant felt much more positive about risk, they might indicate that even a 10 percent likelihood of success was acceptable.

Stoner then placed participants in small groups of about five people each. The groups were told to discuss the scenarios and reach a consensus. His results clearly showed that the decisions made by groups tended to be far riskier than those made by individuals. Time and again, the groups would advise Helen to drop everything and start work on the novel, while individuals would urge her to stick with writing thrillers. Hundreds of further studies have shown that this effect is not so much about making riskier decisions per se but about polarization. In Stoner's classic studies, various factors caused the group to make riskier decisions, but in other experiments groups have become more conservative than individuals alone. In short, being in a group exaggerates people's opinions, causing them to make a more extreme decision than they would on their own. Depending on the initial inclinations of individuals in the group, the final decision can be extremely risky or extremely conservative.

This curious phenomenon has emerged in many different situations, often with worrisome consequences. Gather a group of racially prejudiced people, and they will make even more extreme decisions about racially charged issues.[2] Arrange a meeting of businesspeople who are open to investing in failing projects, and they will become even more likely to throw good money after bad.[3] Have aggressive teenagers hang out together, and the gang will be far more likely to act violently. Allow those with strong religious or political ideologies to spend time in one another's company, and they will develop more extreme, and often violent, viewpoints. The effect even emerges on the Internet, with individuals who participate in discussion lists and chat rooms voicing more extreme opinions and attitudes than they normally would.

What causes this strange but highly consistent phenomenon? Teaming up with people who share your attitudes and opinions reinforces your existing beliefs in several ways. You hear new arguments and find yourself openly expressing a position that you may have only vaguely considered before. You may have been secretly harboring thoughts that you believed to be unusual, extreme, or socially unacceptable. However, when you are surrounded by other like-minded people, these secret thoughts often find a way of bubbling to the surface, which in turn encourages others to share their extreme feelings with you.

Polarization is not the only phenomenon of "groupthink" that can influence the hearts and minds of individuals when they get together.[4] Other studies have shown that compared to individuals, groups tend to be more dogmatic, better able to justify irrational actions, more likely to see their actions as highly moral, and more apt to form stereotypical views of outsiders. In addition, when strong-willed people lead group discussions, they can pressure others into conforming, can encourage self-censorship, and can create an illusion of unanimity.

Two heads are not necessarily better than one. More than

fifty years of research suggests that irrational thinking occurs when people try to reach decisions in groups, and this can lead to a polarization of opinions and a highly biased assessment of a situation.

If groups are not the answer, what is the best way of making up your mind? According to the research, it is a question of avoiding the various errors and pitfalls that often cloud our thinking. The difficulty is that many of the techniques that underlie rational decision making involve a thorough understanding of probability and logic. However, some of these techniques can be learned in just a few moments. Take, for example, how to guard against the most common tricks used by salespeople, how to decide whether someone is lying, and how to ensure that you never, ever regret a decision again.

GETTING YOUR FOOT IN THE DOOR AND THE DOOR IN YOUR FACE

Let's start with a simple question: Imagine being offered two jobs. In terms of working hours, duties, location, and career prospects, Job A is absolutely identical to Job B. In fact, the only difference between the two positions is the disparity between your salary and that of your future coworkers. In Job A your annual pay will be $50,000 and your colleagues will be earning $30,000. In Job B you will be earning $60,000 and your fellow employees will be earning $80,000. Would you be tempted by Job A or Job B? Surveys show that the majority of people choose Job A.[5]

Viewed in purely financial terms, the decision is completely irrational because Job B pays $10,000 more. However, if the scientific study of human nature tells us anything, it is that we are far from being rational creatures. Instead, we are social animals easily persuaded by a whole host of factors, including how we feel, how we see ourselves, and how we appear to others. Although, objectively speaking, Job B pays more than Job A, in Job A we are earning $20,000 more than our fellow employees, and the feeling of superiority evoked by the pay difference proves more than enough to compensate for the absence of the extra earnings that would come with Job B.

This subtle and often unconscious effect can also influence our buying behavior.

I can still remember the very first time I saw a salesman working in a large department store. I was eight years old and my parents had taken me to London. We had wandered into the store, and I had become mesmerized by the man enthusiastically demonstrating the latest breakthrough in kitchen-knife technology. This wonderful piece of equipment was able to do everything you could possibly want from a knife, and several things you probably didn't want, including the ability to cut an empty cola can in half. Toward the end of the pitch, the nice man calmly informed us that the knife retailed for $20.

But then something strange happened. Right before our very eyes, he suddenly transformed into a man who could not stop himself from offering an amazing deal. Actually, the knife was going to be just $16—no, $10. And then, because we had been such a great crowd, he was prepared to sell it to us for just $6. Just when we couldn't believe our good fortune, like the end of a carefully choreographed fireworks display, the real explosions started. He was going to give us a second identical knife for no extra cost, throw in five smaller knives for free, and put them all in a leatherette case that usually retailed for more than $20. Each amazingly generous step surprised and delighted the crowd. More important, it persuaded the majority of people, including my parents, to purchase some knives that they had had no intention of buying when they first walked into the store. Still, it was a lesson learned. When we got home, I attempted to use the wonder knife to cut through an empty cola can, and the handle fell off.

My parents and I had been fooled by a technique that researchers refer to as "that's not all." Without prompting, the salesperson keeps making the deal better and better until it becomes totally irresistible. Even the smallest of reductions or the tiniest of additions is effective. In one study, 40 percent of people bought a cupcake and two cookies together for 75 cents, but 73 percent put their hands in their pockets when the cost of the cupcake was advertised as 75 cents and the two cookies were suddenly added for "free."[6]

In addition to examining these frequently used principles of persuasion, psychologists have also explored other more unusual, but nevertheless still highly effective, techniques. There is, for example, the so-called pique technique, in which a strange request makes people pay more attention and increases the likelihood of compliance. In one study, by Michael Santos at the University of California and his colleagues, a beggar (actually a researcher) asked passersby if they could spare a quarter or 37 cents.[7] Significantly more people gave away their money when confronted with the unusual request.

Related to this is the "disrupt, then reframe" technique, in which you momentarily surprise a person to shake them out of autopilot and then present a normal request. In a series of studies, experimenters went from door to door selling pads of paper for charity.[8] In one condition they stated, "They sell for $3. It's a bargain." In the "disrupt and then reframe" condition they said, "They sell for 300 pennies—that's $3. It's a bargain." This strange, and surprising, change almost doubled sales.

Much of the work in quick but effective techniques has focused on two principles: getting your foot in the door and the door in your face.

In the early 1960s Stanford psychologists Jonathan Freedman and Scott Fraser conducted a groundbreaking experiment in persuasion.[9] The research team started by randomly telephoning more than 150 women and pretending to be from the California Consumers' Group. The researcher asked if they would mind taking part in a survey about their use of household products for a publication called *The Guide*. Unlike its competitors, *The Guide* liked to really get to the bottom of things. So, would it be possible, asked the researcher, for a team of six men to come and spend a couple of hours rooting through their cupboards? The search was going to be thorough and would involve going into every storage area to catalog all of the soap, dishwashing liquid, cleaning fluid, and bleach that they could get their hands on. Perhaps not surprisingly, less than a quarter of the women agreed to this forensic-style search. However, this was only part of the experiment. Another group of women received a similar call, but instead of requesting access to all areas, the researcher asked if they would mind taking part in a quick telephone survey about the household products they preferred. Almost everyone agreed. Three days later, they received a second call, asking if they would mind if the six-man search team investigated their cupboards. Under these circumstances, more than half of the women agreed.

In a follow-up experiment, the same team wanted to see if they could *persuade* people to place a very large sign proclaiming "Drive Carefully" in their front yard. Even though the sign was apparently designed to help cut speeding in the area, almost no residents agreed to display it. The researchers then approached a second group of residents and asked them to display a much smaller sign that was just three inches square, and almost everyone accepted. Two weeks later, the researchers returned and asked whether the residents would now mind replacing the small sign with the large placard. An amazing 76 percent had no objections.

These experiments demonstrate the power of the "foot in the door" technique. People are far more likely to agree to a big request if they have already agreed to a small one.

More than forty years of research has shown that the technique works in many different situations.[10] Get people to make modest donations to charity, and larger ones will follow. Get employees to agree to little changes in working conditions, and bigger ones are accepted more readily. Get them to change normal lightbulbs for low-energy ones and the likelihood of far more significant energy-efficient lifestyle changes increases.

Finally, when researchers are not getting their foot in the door, they are encouraging people to slam it in their faces. Whereas the foot in the door is about starting low and gradually working up, this technique involves beginning with an outrageous request, receiving a firm no, and then getting people to agree to a much more modest offer. Perhaps the best-known work on the principle was carried out by Robert Cialdini at Arizona State University and his colleagues.[11] In his classic study, a research team posing as members of the county youth counseling program asked students whether they would mind taking a group of juvenile delinquents to the zoo for the day. They were not surprised to discover that fewer than 20 percent of the students accepted the offer of a day out with the animals.

Unperturbed, the research team adopted a different tack. This time they approached another group of people with a much larger request, asking whether, for the next two years, they would mind donating two hours of their time each week to help counsel the juvenile delinquents. Once again, their request met with widespread refusal. However, after people turned them down, the research team returned with a far more modest request. Yes, you guessed it—how would they feel about just taking the juvenile delinquents for a day out at the zoo? Under these circumstances, more than half of the students agreed.

In another example, French researchers arranged for a young woman to continuously find herself without any money in a restaurant, so she would have to ask other customers to help cover her bill.[12] When she asked for just a few francs, only 10 percent of those approached offered the money. However, when she started by asking them to cover the entire bill and then moved on to requesting just a few francs, 75 percent of people reached for their money. Once again, this technique is effective in many different situations. From negotiating about house prices to working hours, salary to overdraft limits, it pays to start high.

Persuasion is all about getting your foot in the door, the door in your face, surprising people with an unusual request, and offering an endless stream of bargains. More important, research shows that these techniques can be learned in exactly forty-seven seconds. Actually, thirty seconds tops. And that includes a free set of smaller knives.

IN 59 SECONDS

We are not the rational creatures that we like to think we are. We can easily be influenced by a variety of quick and effective techniques. Beware of people using the "that's not all" principle, offering unprompted discounts and bargains to get you to part with your money. Likewise, be wary of those who start small and build up or start big and quickly back down to a more "reasonable" offer. Of course, it is also possible to use exactly the same techniques to influence others yourself. That's fine, but as Obi-Wan Kenobi famously noted, your newfound Force can have a strong influence on the weak-minded, so do be careful to use it only for good.

NEVER REGRET A DECISION AGAIN

> When making a decision of minor importance, I have always found it advantageous to consider all the pros and cons. In vital matters, however . . . the decision should come from the unconscious, from somewhere within.
>
> —SIGMUND FREUD

Imagine your boss telling you that she thinks her office looks a little uncultured and asking if you would be good enough to buy an expensive-looking modern art print to liven up the walls. You put on your coat and drive to the local gallery, only to find that it has only the following four prints in stock.

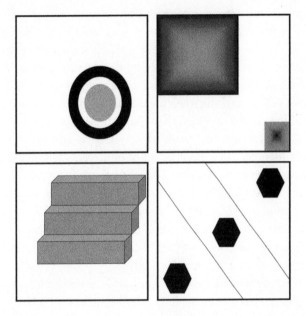

How do you make up your mind? One possibility is to think about the pros and cons of each piece in terms of your boss's personality, the company's image, and the existing office decor. Alternatively, you could just trust your gut instinct and choose the print that "feels" right. Or you could rely on a different technique that, according to recent research, is significantly more likely to result in a good decision.

A few years ago, psychologists Ap Dijksterhuis and Zeger van Olden carried out an experiment using the same type of poster-choosing procedure.[13] In their study, participants were asked to come to the lab, look at five posters, and use one of three techniques to choose the poster that they liked best. One group was asked to study each of the posters for about a minute and a half, list some key reasons why they liked or disliked each one, carefully analyze their thoughts, and then select the winning poster. A second group merely glanced at all five posters and then chose the one that they liked best. Those in the third group were quickly shown the posters, asked to spend five minutes solving difficult anagrams, briefly looked at the posters a second time, and then made their choice. After making their decisions, all of the participants rated the degree to which they liked all five posters.

After everyone had made their selection and ratings, the experimenters carried out an act of unprecedented generosity, giving them their favorite poster as a free gift for taking part in the study. Finally, just as each person left the laboratory clutching their rolled-up booty, the experimenter casually remarked that it would be good to have their telephone number, just in case there was any problem with the data storage and they needed to rerun the study.

Now, if you take part in a study and the researchers explain that they need your telephone number in case of a hard-disk failure, they are up to something. The most likely scenario is that the experiment is far from over and they intend to call you at a future date. The call may take a number of forms. Your telephone might ring in the dead of night, and a market researcher might ask if you would mind taking part in a survey about soap. Alternatively, you might get a call from an alleged long-lost friend wondering if you want to meet. Or, as happened here, one of the team might call to say hello and ask how you are getting on with your poster.

About a month after the experiment, the researchers contacted the participants and asked them how satisfied they were with their posters and how many euros they would be prepared to sell them for. When they had originally chosen their posters in the laboratory, the participants who had been asked to carefully consider the pros and cons of each print were confident that they had made the right choice. In fact, they were far more confident than those who had made their choice within moments of seeing the posters or those who had been asked to solve anagrams and then decide. However, four weeks later a very different picture emerged. The participants who had spent time solving anagrams before chosing their posters were the happiest with their choices and wanted significantly more money in order to part with their cherished print.

You might argue that the choices made in such studies are unlike the complicated choices that people have to make in real life. In fact, the researchers have obtained the same curious effect again and again.[14] Whether it is deciding which apartment to rent, which car to buy, or which stocks to invest in, people who are shown the options but then kept busy working on a difficult mental activity make better decisions than others do.

Why should this be the case? Dijksterhuis believes that just as the power of the unconscious mind can be harnessed to help people become more creative (see the "Creativity" chapter), it can also be used to encourage better decisions. When having to decide between options that differ in only one or two ways, your conscious mind is very good at studying the situation in a rational, levelheaded way and deciding the best course of action. However, when the going gets complex, the mind has only a limited ability to juggle a small number of facts and figures at any one time, and so the result is not so good. Instead of looking at the situation as a whole, the conscious mind tends to focus on the most obvious elements and, in doing so, can miss the bigger picture. In contrast, your unconscious mind is much better at dealing with the complex decisions that pervade many aspects of our lives. Given time, it slowly works through all of the factors and eventually reaches a more balanced decision. Dijksterhuis and Van Olden's explanation for the effect, referred to as the "unconscious thought theory," argues for a kind of middle ground when making complex decisions. Thinking too hard about an issue is in many ways as bad as making an instant choice. Instead, it is all a question of knowing what needs to be decided, then distracting your conscious mind and allowing your unconscious to work away on the issue. And how do you get your unconscious mind to work on a problem? Well, just as we saw in the section on boosting creativity, one technique involves keeping the conscious mind busy with a distracting but difficult task, such as solving anagrams or counting backward by threes.

Solving anagrams before making an important decision is, of course, not the only way of helping to ensure that you won't regret the decision. In fact, according to other research, there is an even quicker way of minimizing the likelihood of regretting a decision.

Thomas Gilovich, at Cornell University, has been studying the psychology of regret for more than a decade. His findings make fascinating reading.[15] Much of his work has involved asking people to look back over their lives and describe their biggest regret. About 75 percent of respondents regret not doing something, with the top three slots taken by not studying hard enough at school, not taking advantage of an important opportunity, and not spending enough time with friends and family. In contrast, only 25 percent of people regret doing something, such as making a bad career decision, marrying someone they didn't love, or having a child at the wrong point in their lives.

It seems that part of the problem is it's relatively easy to see the negative consequences of something that happened. You made a poor career decision, and so you were stuck in a job that you didn't enjoy. You had kids when you were very young, and so you couldn't go out with friends. You married the wrong person, and found that you constantly argued. The negative consequences are known, and so although the potential for regret may still be substantial, it is limited. However, the situation is completely different when it comes to things that didn't happen. Suddenly the possible positive benefits seem almost endless. What would have happened if you had accepted that job offer, been brave enough to ask the love of your life on a date, or spent more time at school studying? Under these circumstances, you are limited only by the power of your imagination.

Gilovich's fascinating work provides scientific support for the words of the nineteenth-century American poet John Greenleaf Whittier, who once noted, "For of all sad words of tongue or pen, the saddest are these: It might have been."

IN 59 SECONDS

Anagrams and the Unconscious Mind

When making straightforward decisions, stick with the conscious mind by thinking about the pros and cons and assessing the situation in a rational, levelheaded way. However, for more complex choices, try giving your conscious mind a rest and letting your unconscious work. The following exercise, based on the research of Dijksterhuis and Van Olden, is designed to aid the decision-making process.

A. What decisions do you have to make?

B. Work through as many of these anagrams as possible in five minutes. If you get stuck, don't struggle for too long. Instead, move on to the next one.

ANAGRAM	CLUE	YOUR ANSWER
1. Open change	European city	
2. A motto	Well-known fruit	
3. Past eight	Popular in Italy	
4. Noon leap	European general	
5. Ring late	Three sides	
6. Tail north	Swimming, cycling, and running	
7. Did train	Island vacation spot	
8. Eat	Time for . . .	
9. Loaded inn	Flower	
10. Cool cheat	Better than diamonds for many women	
11. Neat grain	South American country	
12. Lob aloft	Game of four quarters	
13. Groan	Popular in churches	
14. Mini rat	Alcoholic drink	
15. Cheap	Soft fruit	

C. Now, without thinking too much about the problem, write down your decision here.

ANAGRAM ANSWERS
1. Copenhagen. 2. Tomato. 3. Spaghetti. 4. Napoleon. 5. Triangle.
6. Triathlon. 7. Trinidad. 8. Tea. 9. Dandelion. 10. Chocolate.
11. Argentina. 12. Football. 13. Organ. 14. Martini. 15. Peach.

Containing Regret

Research shows that when most people look back on their lives, they tend to regret things that they didn't do. Once you understand this, there are quick and effective techniques that you can use to avoid feelings of regret.

First, to prevent regret in the first place, adopt a "will do" attitude toward opportunity. As writer Max Lucado once suggested, "Go to the effort. Invest the time. Write the letter. Make the apology. Take the trip. Purchase the gift. Do it. The seized opportunity renders joy. The neglected brings regret."

Second, if you do regret not doing something, see if there is anything you can do to remedy the situation. Write the letter, make that telephone call, spend more time with the family, mend broken relationships, go back to college and get the grades. Use the regret as a wake-up call, a way of motivating yourself.

Finally, if it really isn't possible to do anything to make things better, make a mental picture of a fence around the imaginary "what might have been" benefits that might otherwise occupy your thoughts. Instead of dwelling on the positive things that might have happened, spend time thinking about three benefits of your current situation and three negative consequences that could have occurred had you made the decision that's causing the regret.

ARE YOU A "MAXIMIZER" OR A "SATISFICER"?

Take a few moments to read the following ten statements and assign each a rating to indicate the degree to which it describes you.[16] Don't spend too long thinking about each statement, and answer honestly.

Assign each item a rating between 1 ("strongly disagree") and 5 ("strongly agree").

1   When watching television, I tend to channel-   1 2 3 4 5
    hop rather than stick with just one program.

2   I tend to find shopping difficult because   1 2 3 4 5
    I won't buy something unless it is exactly
    what I want.

3   I take a long time to choose a rental video or   1 2 3 4 5
    DVD because I like to consider lots of
    possible films.

4   I sometimes think about the opportunities   1 2 3 4 5
    that have passed me by in life.

5   I like to consider all of the different options   1 2 3 4 5
    before making a decision.

6   I don't like making decisions that are   1 2 3 4 5
    irreversible.

7   When I have made a decision, I often   1 2 3 4 5
    wonder how things would have worked out
    if I had made a different choice.

8 I find it difficult to settle for second best.   1 2 3 4 5

9 When on the Internet, I tend to surf,   1 2 3 4 5
quickly skipping from one site to another.

10 I rarely feel happy with what I have because   1 2 3 4 5
I find it easy to imagine getting
something better.

To score the questionnaire, add your ratings. Low scores run between 10 and 20, medium scores between 21 and 39, and high scores between 40 and 50.

Research suggests that people often approach many aspects of their lives using one of two fundamental strategies—maximizing or satisficing. "Maximizers" tend to obtain high scores on the questionnaire, and "satisficers" tend to obtain low scores. Extreme maximizers constantly check all available options to make sure that they have picked the best one. In contrast, extreme satisficers look only until they have found something that fulfills their needs. As a result, maximizers objectively achieve more but take longer to find what they want and may be less happy because of a tendency to dwell on how things could have been.

For example, in one study of job hunting, researchers categorized more than five hundred students from eleven universities as maximizers or satisficers and then tracked them as they tried to find employment.[17] The maximizers ended up with salaries that were, on average, 20 percent higher than those of the satisficers, but they were also less satisfied with their job search and more prone to regret, pessimism, anxiety, and depression.

If you are a maximizer and find yourself wasting too much

time searching for the perfect product, you might find it helpful to limit the resources that you put into some activities (e.g.,
give yourself only thirty minutes to find your friend a birthday
card) or make certain decisions irreversible (for example, by
throwing away receipts).[18]

There is an old adage that happiness is about wanting
what you have, not having what you want. It seems that when
maximizers get what they want, they may not always want
what they get.

HOW TO DECIDE WHETHER PEOPLE ARE TELLING YOU THE TRUTH, THE WHOLE TRUTH, AND NOTHING BUT THE TRUTH

How do you think people tend to behave when they lie to
you? Take a look at the list of behaviors in the table below and
place a checkmark in either the "True" or the "False" column
after each statement.

TRUE   FALSE

When people lie, they tend to . . .

—avoid eye contact.

—smile more.

—squirm in their seats or, if they are standing up,
    shift from foot to foot.

—develop sweaty hands and faces.

—cover their mouth with their hands.

TRUE FALSE

—give long and rambling answers to questions.

—give answers that sound unstructured and jumbled.

—nod their head more.

—gesture more.

—grow longer noses.

People are often surprisingly economical with the truth. In a survey that I conducted with the *Daily Telegraph,* a quarter of the respondents claimed to have told a lie within the last twenty-four hours. Other work suggests that an impressive 90 percent of people say that they have lied on a date and that about 40 percent of the population are happy to lie to their friends. Deception is also a major problem in the workplace, with surveys suggesting that around 80 percent of people have lied during a job interview, and almost 50 percent of employees have told their boss at least one important lie.[19]

In view of the prevalence of lying, it is not surprising that all sorts of techniques have been developed in an attempt to detect such fibbery. In ancient times, for example, there was the ever popular "red-hot poker" test. In a procedure that could reasonably be described as hell on earth, a poker would be placed into a fierce fire, removed, and the accused forced to lick it three times. The theory was that the innocent person would have a sufficient amount of saliva on the tongue to prevent burning, whereas a guilty party would have a much drier tongue that would thus become somewhat attached to the poker.

According to the history books, a similar but less barbaric technique was used during the Spanish Inquisition. The accused would be made to eat some barley bread and cheese, while those around prayed that the Angel Gabriel would prevent the person from successfully swallowing the food if they had lied. To my knowledge, neither of these techniques has been subjected to proper scientific testing, in part, I am guessing, because it would be tricky to obtain the necessary informed consent from participants and the Angel Gabriel. However, if such studies were to be carried out, any positive findings would support one of the most commonly held theories about lying—the Anxiety Hypothesis.

This idea holds that people become very nervous when they lie, and so they develop a variety of anxiety-related symptoms, including a drying of the mouth, which could cause them to become stuck to red-hot pokers and find it difficult to swallow barley bread.

Although the theory is intuitively appealing, obtaining reliable proof for it has proven far from easy, with some research suggesting that liars are no more stressed than those who tell the truth.

In a recent study, for example, conducted by Richard Gramzow at the University of Southampton, and outside colleagues, students were first connected to machinery that measured their heart rate and then interviewed about their recent exam performance.[20] The interview involved the students' describing the grades that they had obtained over the years and comparing their own skills and abilities with those of classmates. What the students didn't know was that after the interview the experimenters were going to obtain their actual exam results and so would be able to identify which students had been telling the truth and which had been exaggerating. Interestingly, the results revealed that nearly half of the students had exaggerated their academic achievements. Even more interestingly, the heart-rate data showed that those who had raised their grades for the occasion were no more stressed than their honest colleagues were. If anything, they were slightly more relaxed.

The results from studies using high-tech anxiety-measuring machinery are, at best, mixed. However, that hasn't stopped the public from accepting the idea that people become terribly tense when they are being economical with the truth. Perhaps driven by the countless films and television programs that show liars with sweaty palms and racing hearts, most believe that the best signs of deceit are those popularly associated with increased anxiety.

Teams of researchers have spent hours carefully comparing films of known liars and truth tellers, with trained observers coding every smile, blink, and gesture. Each minute of footage takes about an hour to analyze, but the resulting data allow researchers to compare the behavior associated with a lie and with truth, and thus uncover even the subtlest of differences. The findings are fascinating. Honestly.

Take a look at the questionnaire at the beginning of this section. How many checkmarks did you put in the "True" column? All of the behaviors listed in the questionnaire are things that people do when they become nervous. They avoid eye contact, squirm in their seats, sweat, and start to garble their words. According to the researchers who have spent hours coding the behavior of liars and truth tellers, not one of the items in the table is reliably associated with lying. In fact, liars are just as likely to look you in the eye as truth tellers are, they don't move their hands nervously, and they don't shift about in their seats.

However, because most people hold these mind myths in their heads, they are terrible at deciding whether someone is lying. Present them with videotapes of people lying and telling the truth and ask them to spot the liar, and they perform little better than chance. Show adults films of children describing a true event and a fictitious one, and the adults are unable to tell which is which.[21] Ask someone to convince their long-term partner that they found a photograph of an attractive person unattractive, and they are surprisingly successful.[22] Even groups of lawyers, police officers, psychologists, and social workers have been unable to reliably detect deception.[23]

So what really gives away a liar? Although lying does not always make people stressed, it usually taxes their minds. Lying involves having to think about what other people already know or could find out, what is plausible, and what fits in with what you have said before. Because of this, liars tend to do the things that correspond to thinking hard about a problem or issue. They tend not to move their arms and legs so much, cut down on gesturing, repeat the same phrases, give shorter and less detailed answers, take longer before they start to answer, and pause and hesitate more. In addition, there is also evidence that they distance themselves from the lie, causing their language to become more impersonal. As a result, liars often reduce the number of times that they say words such as "I," "me," and "mine," and use "him" and "her" rather than people's names. Finally, there is increased evasiveness, as liars tend to avoid answering the question completely, perhaps by switching topics or by asking a question of their own.

To detect deception, forget about looking for signs of tension, nervousness, and anxiety. Instead, a liar is likely to look as though they are thinking hard for no good reason, conversing in a strangely impersonal tone, and incorporating an evasiveness that would make even a politician or a used-car salesman blush.

IN 59 SECONDS

Body Language

For successful lie detection, jettison the behavioral myths surrounding the Anxiety Hypothesis and look for signs more commonly associated with having to think hard. Forget the idea that liars have sweaty palms, fidget, and avoid eye contact. Instead, look for a person suddenly becoming more static and cutting down on their gestures. Also, learn to listen. Be on guard for a sudden decrease in detail, an increase in pauses and hesitations, and an avoidance of the words "me," "mine," and "I" but an increase in "her" and "him." If someone suddenly becomes very evasive, press for a straight answer.[24]

To spot possible shifts, try to establish what researchers have referred to as an "honest baseline." Before asking questions that are likely to elicit deceptive answers, start with those that are far more likely to make the person respond in an honest way. During these initial answers, develop an understanding of how they behave when they are telling the truth by looking at their body language and listening to the words they say. Then, during the answers to the trickier questions, watch for the behavioral shifts outlined above.

Also, remember that even if you do see these signals, they are not an absolute guarantee of a lie. Unlike taxes and death, nothing is that certain when it comes to lying. Instead, such clues are simply an indication that all is perhaps not as it should be—a good reason to dig deeper.

E-mail Me

Communication expert Jeff Hancock and his colleagues at Cornell University asked students to spend a week making notes of all of their significant face-to-face conversations, telephone chats, texts, and e-mails, and then work through the list, indicating which ones contained lies.[25] The results revealed that people lied in 14 percent of e-mails, 21 percent of texts, 27 percent of face-to-face conversations, and 37 percent of telephone calls. According to Hancock, people are reluctant to lie in e-mails because their words are recorded and what they say can come back to haunt them. So if you want to minimize the risk of a lie, ask others to e-mail you.

DECIDING HOW LONG SOMETHING WILL TAKE

In an insightful study of time management, Roger Buehler at Wilfrid Laurier University asked students to indicate when they expected to finish an important term paper.[26] The students believed that they would hand in their work, on average, ten days before the deadline. They were, however, being far too optimistic; in reality, they tended to finish the papers just one day before the deadline. This effect, known as the "planning fallacy," is not limited to students trying to finish their term papers on time. Research shows that people have a strong tendency to underestimate how long a project will take and that people working in groups are especially likely to have unrealistic expectations.[27] Even when they are trying to be realistic, people tend to imagine that everything will go according to plan, and they do not consider the inevitable unexpected delays and unforeseen problems.

However, Buehler's work has also suggested a quick and effective way of overcoming the problem. When his students were told to think about when they had managed to finish similar tasks in the past, their answers for meeting future deadlines proved much more accurate. It seems that to get an accurate estimate of the time needed to complete a project, you can look at how long it took to finish broadly similar projects in the past.

If that doesn't work, you could always try a technique investigated by Justin Kruger and Matt Evans at the University of Illinois at Urbana-Champaign.[28] In their studies, participants estimated how long it would take to carry out a relatively complicated activity, such as getting ready for a date. One group was asked simply to make their estimates, while another group was encouraged to "unpack" the activity into its constituent parts (showering, changing clothes, panicking) before deciding on a time frame. Those who did the mental unpacking exercise produced estimates that proved far more accurate than those of other participants. So to find out how long it really will take you to do something, isolate all of the steps involved and then make your time estimate.

parenting

The Mozart myth,

how to choose the best name for a baby,

instantly divine a child's destiny using

just three marshmallows, and

effectively praise young minds

WOLFGANG AMADEUS MOZART was born in 1756, composed some of the world's greatest classical music, and died, probably of acute rheumatic fever, in 1791. He was a genius. However, some believe that his music is able to reach parts of the brain that other compositions can't and that it can make you more intelligent. Moreover, they seem convinced that this effect is especially powerful for young, impressionable minds, recommending that babies be exposed to a daily dose of Mozart for maximum impact. Their message has spread far and wide—but is it really possible to boost a youngster's brainpower using the magic of Mozart?

In 1993 researcher Frances Rauscher and her colleagues at the University of California published a scientific paper that changed the world.[1] They had taken a group of thirty-six college students, randomly placed them in one of three groups, and asked each group to carry out a different ten-minute exercise. One group was asked to listen to Mozart's Sonata for Two Pianos in D Major, the second group heard a standard relaxation tape, and the third group sat in complete silence. After the exercise, everyone completed a standard test designed to measure one aspect of intelligence, namely the ability to manipulate spatial information mentally (see illustration on the following page). The results revealed that those who had listened to Mozart scored significantly higher than those who heard the relaxation tape or sat in complete silence. The

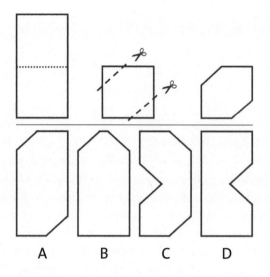

The type of item that might appear in a test measuring the ability to manipulate spatial information mentally. The top row shows a piece of paper being folded in half and then having two pieces cut away. Participants are asked to look at the four shapes on the bottom row and choose the shape they would see when they unfolded the cut paper.

authors also noted that the effect was only temporary, lasting between ten and fifteen minutes.

Two years later, the same researchers followed up their initial study with a second experiment that involved a larger group of students and took place over the course of several days.[2] The students were again randomly placed in one of three groups. In the first part of the experiment, one group listened to Mozart, another group sat in silence, and a third heard a Philip Glass track ("Music with Changing Parts"). Again, strong differences emerged, with those who listened to Mozart outperforming the other two groups in a further test of mental paper folding. On later days, the Philip Glass track was replaced with an audiotaped story and trance music. Now, the Mozart and the silence groups obtained almost identical scores, while those who listened to the story or the trance music trailed in third place. The evidence suggested that Mozart's music might have a small, short-term effect on one aspect of intelligence.

Journalists soon started to report the findings. *New York Times* music critic Alex Ross suggested (no doubt with his tongue firmly in his cheek) that they had scientifically proven that Mozart was a better composer than Beethoven. However, some writers soon started to exaggerate the results, declaring that just a few minutes of Mozart resulted in a substantial and long-term increase in intelligence.

The idea spread like wildfire, and during the latter half of the 1990s the story mutated even further from the original research. Up to that point, not a single study had examined the effect of Mozart's music on the intelligence of babies. However, some journalists, unwilling to let the facts get in the way of a good headline, reported that babies became brighter after listening to Mozart. These articles were not isolated examples of sloppy journalism. About 40 percent of the media reports on the alleged "Mozart" effect published toward the end of the 1990s mentioned this alleged benefit to babies.[3] The continued popular media coverage of what was now being labeled the "Mozart" effect even impinged on social policy. In 1998 the State of Georgia supported the distribution of free CDs containing classical music to mothers of newborns, and the state of Florida passed a bill requiring state-funded day-care centers to play classical music on a daily basis.

The alleged "Mozart" effect had been transformed into an urban legend, and a significant slice of the population incorrectly believed that listening to Mozart's music could help boost all aspects of intelligence, that the effects were long-lasting, and that even babies could benefit. However, as the 1990s turned into the twenty-first century, the situation went from bad to worse.

First, Christopher Chabris at Harvard University collected the findings from all of the studies that had attempted to replicate Rauscher's original results and concluded that the effect, if it existed at all, was much smaller than had originally been thought.[4]

Then other work suggested that even if it did exist, the effect may have nothing to do with the special properties of Mozart's Sonata for Two Pianos in D Major, and could in fact be associated with the general feelings of happiness produced by this type of classical music. For example, in one study researchers compared the effects of Mozart's music with those of a much sadder piece (Albinoni's Adagio in G Minor for Organ and Strings), and found evidence that, once again, Mozart had more of an effect than the alternative.[5] However, when the research team conducted a control experiment about how happy and excited the music made participants feel, the alleged "Mozart" effect suddenly vanished. In another study, psychologists compared the effect of listening to Mozart with that of hearing an audiotape of Stephen King's short story "The Last Rung on the Ladder."[6] When participants preferred Mozart to King, their performance on the mental manipulation task was better than when listening to the piano concerto. However, when they preferred King to Mozart, they performed better after they had heard his story.

The public's belief about the alleged "Mozart" effect is a mind myth. There is almost no convincing scientific evidence to suggest that playing his piano concertos for babies will have any long-term or meaningful impact on their intelligence. Would it be fair to conclude that there is no way of using music to boost children's intelligence? Actually, no. In fact, evidence for the benefits of music exists, but it involves throwing away the Mozart CDs and adopting a more hands-on attitude.

Some research has shown that children who attend music lessons tend to be brighter than their classmates. However, it is difficult to separate correlation from causation. It could be that having music lessons makes you brighter, or it could be that brighter or more privileged children are more likely to take music lessons. A few years ago, psychologist Glenn Schellenberg decided to carry out a study to help settle the matter.[7]

Schellenberg started by placing an advertisement in a local newspaper, offering free weekly arts lessons to six-year-old children. The parents of more than 140 children replied, and each child was randomly assigned to one of four groups. Three of the groups were given lessons over the course of several months at the Royal Conservatory of Music in Toronto, while the fourth group acted as a control group and didn't receive lessons until after the study had ended. Of those who attended the lessons, one-third were taught keyboard skills, another third were given voice training, and the final third went to drama classes. Before and after their lessons, all of the children completed a standard intelligence test.

The results showed clear IQ improvements in children who had been taught keyboard skills and given voice lessons, whereas those given drama lessons were no different than the control group. Why should this be the case? Well, Schellenberg believes that learning music involves several key skills that help children's self-discipline and thinking, including long periods of focused attention, practicing, and memorization.

Whatever the explanation, if you want to boost the brainpower of your offspring, perhaps it is time to take that Mozart CD out of the player and get the kids to start tickling the ivories themselves.

PLAYING THE NAME GAME

Parents often find it surprisingly difficult to decide what to call their baby, in the knowledge that their child is going to spend his or her entire life living with the consequences of their choice. Research suggests that they are right to give the issue careful thought; a large body of work shows that people's names can have a sometimes powerful effect.

For example, in one of my previous books, *Quirkology,* I described work suggesting that when it comes to where people choose to live, there is an overrepresentation of people called Florence living in Florida, George in Georgia, Kenneth in Kentucky, and Virgil in Virginia.[8] Also, in terms of marriage partners, research has revealed that more couples share the same letter of their family name than is predicted by chance. It is even possible that people's political views are, to some extent, shaped by their names. Research on the 2000 presidential campaign indicated that people whose surnames began with the letter *B* were especially likely to make contributions to the Bush campaign, whereas those whose surnames began with the letter *G* were more likely to contribute to the Gore campaign.

Since then, I have conducted additional work that has uncovered other ways in which your surname might influence your life. I recently teamed up with Roger Highfield, then science editor of the *Daily Telegraph,* to discover whether people who had a surname that began with a letter toward the start of the alphabet were more successful in life than those with names starting with letters toward the end. In other words, are the Abbotts and Adamses of the world likely to be more successful than the Youngs and the Yorks?

There was good reason to think that there may indeed be a link. In 2006 American economists Liran Einav and Leeat Yariv analyzed the surnames of academics working in economics departments at U.S. universities and found that those whose initials came early in the alphabet were more likely to be in the best-rated departments, become fellows of the Econometric Society, and win a Nobel Prize.[9] Publishing their remarkable findings in the *Journal of Economic Perspectives,* they argued that "alphabetical discrimination" probably resulted from the typical practice of alphabetizing the names of authors of papers published in academic journals, which meant that those with names toward the beginning of the alphabet appeared more prominent than their alphabetically challenged peers.

I wondered whether the same effect might apply outside the world of economics. After all, whether on a school register, at a job interview, or in the exam hall, those whose surnames fall toward the start of the alphabet are accustomed to being put first. We also often associate the top of a list with winners and the bottom with losers. Could all of these small experiences accumulate to make a long-term impact?

Everyone participating in the experiment stated their sex, age, and surname, then rated how successful they had been in various aspects of their life. The results revealed that those with surnames that started with letters toward the beginning of the alphabet rated themselves more successful than those whose names started with later letters. The effect was especially pronounced in career success, suggesting that alphabetical discrimination is alive and well in the workplace.

What could account for this strange effect? One pattern in

the data provided an important clue. The surname effect increased with age, giving the impression that it was not the result of childhood experiences but a gradual increase over the years. It seems that the constant exposure to the consequences of being at the top or bottom of the alphabet league slowly makes a difference in the way in which people see themselves. So should these results give those whose surname initial falls toward the end of the alphabet cause for concern? As a Wiseman, and therefore someone with a lifetime's experience of being near the end of alphabetical lists, I take some comfort from the fact that the effect is theoretically fascinating but, in practical terms, very small.

The choice of a first name can matter too. Even after drawing up a short list of possible names for their offspring, and asking friends and family for advice, some people still struggle. Is it better to go with a traditional name or a modern one? Is naming a child after a celebrity a good idea? Is it more important to have a name that rolls off the tongue or one that stands out from the crowd? Psychology can lend a helping hand.

Previous work has shown that people with names that have positive associations do especially well in life. For example, teachers tend to award higher essay grades to children who they believe have more likeable names (Rose, for instance),[10] college students whose names have undesirable associations experience high levels of social isolation, and those whose surnames happen to have negative connotations (such as Short, Little, or Bent) are especially likely to suffer feelings of inferiority.[11]

I teamed up with the Edinburgh International Science Festival to help discover which first names were seen as especially successful and attractive in the twenty-first century. This study involved more than six thousand people going online and indicating whether they thought some of the most popular first names in the United Kingdom seemed successful and attractive. Strong trends emerged. Traditional names with royal associations (such as James and Elizabeth) were viewed as highly successful and intelligent. In contrast, the most attractive female names tended to be soft-sounding ones that end with the *ee* sound (such as Lucy and Sophie), whereas the sexiest male names were short and often rugged-sounding (such as Jack and Ryan). At the other end of the spectrum, Lisa and Brian were seen as the least successful, and Ann and George as the most unattractive.

There is also the issue of initials. As noted in *Quirkology,* research by Nicholas Christenfeld and his coworkers at the University of California suggests that a person's initials may become an issue of life or death.[12] After analyzing a huge computerized database containing millions of Californian death certificates, they discovered that men with positive initials (such as A.C.E., H.U.G., and J.O.Y.) lived about four and a half years longer than average, whereas those with negative initials (such as P.I.G., B.U.M., and D.I.E.) died about three years early. Women with positive initials lived an extra three years, although there was no detrimental effect for those with negative initials.

New research, conducted in 2007 by Leif Nelson and Joseph Simmons, indicates that these effects are not just limited to the relatively small number of people whose initials happen to make especially positive or negative words.[13] Instead, according to their work, even the hint of initial-based positivity or negativity is enough to exert a major influence on people's lives.

In certain situations, single letters are associated with success or failure. Perhaps the best-known, and in many ways most important, example of this occurs during the grading of exams. In most forms of testing, those who have done well are awarded As and Bs, whereas those toward the bottom of the class tend to receive Cs and Ds. Nelson and Simmons wondered whether people whose first or last initials matched one of the two top grades might be unconsciously motivated to perform well on exams, whereas those whose names start with either *C* or *D* might not try to achieve such high marks. To find out if this bold hypothesis was true, the duo analyzed fifteen years of students' grade point averages from a large American university. Remarkable as it may seem, the results revealed that students with first or last names starting with an *A* or a *B* had obtained significantly higher grade point averages than those beginning with the letters *C* or *D.*

Excited by their initial success, Nelson and Simmons turned their attention to the impact that this effect might have on people's lives. They thought that if students whose names began with *A* or *B* obtained higher exam marks than those whose names began with *C* or *D,* the former group might find it easier to get into better graduate schools and so have more successful careers. To test their hypothesis, they needed to find a large, searchable database containing students' initials and the graduate school that they had attended. After much searching, they eventually found the perfect resource—the online database of the American Bar Association. The research team created a computer program capable of scanning the online information for the number of people with the key initials in each of the 170 law schools listed. After designating the quality of the schools by using information from *U.S. News & World Report* rankings and comparing this with the data from almost four hundred thousand lawyers, Nelson and Simmons had their answer. As the quality of law schools declined, so too did the proportion of graduates from those law schools who had the initials *A* or *B.* As they note at the end of their report, "It seems that people with names like Adlai and Bill tend to go to better law schools than do those with names like Chester and Dwight."

IN 59 SECONDS

Research shows that people with surnames that begin with a letter toward the beginning of the alphabet are more successful in life than those whose names begin with letters toward the end. Obviously, the potential for choosing a successful surname is limited, unless you are prepared to change your name or, if you are female, to marry a man whose surname falls toward the start of the alphabet. However, with respect to choosing a child's first name, other research can provide a helping hand. Names with positive connotations, royal associations, or those that sound especially attractive are all good bets. Finally, do not underestimate the power of initials. Avoid creating a set of initials that make a word with negative associations, and help to ensure exam success by going for names starting with the letter *A* or *B*.

PRAISE BE!

Almost every manual on good parenting promotes the power of praise, with some self-help gurus suggesting that the single best thing you can do for your children is to build up their self-esteem by constantly giving compliments. Tell your children how intelligent they are when they pass an exam. Congratulate them on their artistic streak when they produce a nice drawing. Celebrate their athletic abilities when they score a goal or win a race. According to this approach, negativity should be banished and the focus instead firmly placed on even the smallest of successes.

The idea has enormous intuitive appeal. Always tell the little ones that they are wonderful, and surely they will grow up to be confident and happy people. So far, so good. There is, however, just one small problem with this rather utopian view of the human psyche. Research suggests that telling children that they are bright and talented is a terrible thing to do.

In the late 1990s Claudia Mueller and Carol Dweck at Columbia University conducted a large-scale program of research on the psychology of praise.[14] Their experiments involved more than four hundred children between 10 and 12 years of age, who were drawn from a variety of ethnic and socioeconomic backgrounds. In a typical study, the children were presented with an intelligence test in which they were asked to look at rows of shapes and, using logic alone, work out which shape should come next in each series. After they had worked through the problems, the experimenters took away their workbooks and calculated the scores but provided each child with false feedback. They explained that each child had done really well, solving 80 percent of the problems correctly.

In addition to this feedback, one group of the children was told that they must be really bright to have solved so many puzzles, while another group was greeted with stony silence. According to the self-help gurus who promote the positive power of praise, just spending a few seconds complimenting a child's ability can have a dramatic effect. The results revealed that they are right, but perhaps not quite in the way they had anticipated.

In the next stage of the experiment, the researchers told the children that they could choose to try one of two tasks. One of the tasks would be quite difficult and so they might not succeed, but they would be challenged and learn even if they failed. In contrast, the other task was much easier, and so they were likely to do well but learn little. About 65 percent of the children who had been told they were intelligent opted for the easy task, compared to just 45 percent of those who had not been praised. The children who had been told they were intelligent were far more likely to avoid challenging situations, and instead stick to the easy stuff. This is not exactly good news for the "praise be" approach to parenting. However, worse was yet to come.

In the next phase of the experiment, the researchers gave the children some more puzzles. This time the puzzles were much harder than the first set, and so most of the children did not perform especially well. Afterward, all of the children were asked how much they had enjoyed the puzzles and whether they would continue working on them at home. Dramatic differences between the groups emerged. The children who had received just a single sentence praising their intelligence found the difficult puzzles far less enjoyable than their classmates did, and so they were far less likely to work on them on their own time.

Even more bad news for the advocates of praise emerged in the third and final part of the study. After the children had struggled on the difficult puzzles, the experimenters asked them to try one final test. This last set of puzzles was just as easy as the one that the children had encountered at the start of the study. Even though the two groups of children had obtained roughly the same scores at the beginning of the experiment, their performances on the final test were very different. The pattern of results was exactly the opposite of that predicted by many self-help gurus. The children who had been told they were intelligent obtained far lower scores than the others.

Why should praise have counterintuitive and counterproductive effects? According to Mueller and Dweck, several factors are at work. Telling a child that they are intelligent might make them feel good, but it can also induce a fear of failure, causing the child to avoid challenging situations because they might look bad if they are not successful. In addition, telling a child that they are intelligent suggests that they do not need to work hard to perform well. Because of this, children may be less motivated to make the required effort, and so be more likely to fail. Unfortunately, if they subsequently obtain a low mark, it is also more likely that their motivation will collapse and a sense of helplessness will set in. After all, low marks suggest that they are not as bright as they were told and that there is nothing they can do about it. The psychological impact of poor results should not be underestimated. At one point in the Mueller and Dweck studies, all of the children were asked to tell their classmates how well they had performed on the test involving the difficult puzzles. Almost 40 percent of the children who had been praised lied about their grade, compared to about 10 percent of those who had not been praised.

Does this mean that all praise is bad praise? So far, I have described only the results from two of the three groups of children involved in the Mueller and Dweck experiment. After getting their initial "Well done, you made 80 percent" feedback, a third group also received a single sentence of praise. However, this time the experimenters praised effort, not ability, noting that they must have tried really hard to have achieved such a high mark. These children behaved very differently from those in the two other groups. When it came to choosing between a challenging task and an easy one, only about 10 percent of them selected the easy option. Compared to the children who had been told that they were intelligent or who received no praise at all, those in the "You must have tried very hard" group found the hard problems more enjoyable and were more likely to try to solve them on their own time. Finally, when given another set of easy problems at the end of the experiment, those in this third group solved significantly more than they did the first time around.

The results clearly showed that being praised for effort was very different from being praised for ability. According to Mueller and Dweck, the children praised for effort were encouraged to try regardless of the consequences, therefore sidestepping any fear of failure. As a result, the possibility for learning outweighed the fear of obtaining a low mark, and they preferred taking the challenging task to the easy option. Also, by definition, these children were more motivated to try hard on future tests, and so were more likely to succeed. And even if they did fail in the future, they could easily attribute their low marks to not trying hard enough, which avoided the sense of helplessness that could set in when poor results were seen as an indication of an innate inability to think.

Although the Mueller and Dweck studies were conducted in middle schools, other research has obtained the same type of findings among younger children and high school students.[15] The consensus is that all praise is not created equal. Some praise can have devastating effects on a child's motivation, and other praise can help the child achieve the very best. Telling children that they possess a certain trait, such as being bright or talented, is not good for their psychological health because it encourages them to avoid challenging situations, not to try so hard, and quickly to become demotivated when the going gets tough. In contrast, praising effort encourages people to stretch themselves, work hard, and persist in the face of difficulties.

IN 59 SECONDS

It is easy to fall into the trap of trying to make children feel good by praising their abilities and talents. However, research shows that such compliments can have a detrimental effect and that it is far better to focus on the children's effort, concentration, and organizational skills. So, for example, when your daughter gets a good exam grade, recognize how hard she must have studied, how well she organized her homework time, and how good she must have been at performing under pressure. Similarly, when your son wins a place on the school football team, praise his ability to train hard and work well with others. This kind of praise encourages effort, resilience, and persistence in the face of failure. To help children focus further, consider asking reflective questions about the techniques and strategies that they used ("What parts of that did you enjoy the most?" or "How did you deal with any problems that came up?"), and try to make the praise as specific as possible ("You played well at football today," rather than "You are good at football").[16]

THE SECRET SCIENCE OF SELF-DISCIPLINE

Let's start with a quick thought experiment. Imagine that you have decided to spend an hour or so in an upmarket coffee shop. You walk in and are presented with a long and tempting list of cakes and pastries. The portions are very small, but the quality is incredible. In your mind's eye, look down the list and choose your favorite item—perhaps a wonderful cheesecake, an amazing cookie, or a tasty piece of pie. Next, imagine giving your order and the waiter bringing a tiny but perfectly formed portion of your dream dessert. Visualize the dessert sitting in front of you right now, looking irresistibly mouth-watering. Then, just as you are about to dig in, the waiter explains that today the coffee shop is running a special offer. You can eat a single portion of the dessert right now, or you can wait thirty minutes and have a double portion for the same price. What would you do? Could you wait and get more, or would you demolish the dessert before the waiter even finishes describing the offer?

In the late 1960s Stanford University psychologist Walter Mischel carried out an amazing experiment involving a real-life version of the imagery scenario described above.[17] Mischel and his team armed themselves with a large bag of marshmal-lows and a bell, went to a local school, and presented four–year-old children with a dilemma. An experimenter invited the children into a room one at a time and showed them to a table on which were a single marshmallow, a bell, and then two more marshmallows. It was explained to the child that the experimenter had to go out of the room for a few minutes, but that if the child could keep their hands off all the goodies on the table until the experimenter came back, he or she could eat the two marshmallows. The experimenter also explained that the child could ring the bell at any point and the experi-menter would return, but that if this happened the child would be allowed to eat only the single marshmallow.

Each child was presented with a slightly less-glamorous version of the dessert-based dilemma that you faced a few moments ago. Ring the bell early and get a single marshmal-low, or wait a while and get twice the prize. This deceptively simple test provided an accurate measure of each child's level of self-discipline. About one-third of the children grabbed the single marshmallow right away, another third took a little longer before ringing the bell, and a final third waited for the experimenter to return and therefore enjoyed two marshmallows.

However, Mischel was not interested only in discovering the percentage of children who were able to resist temptation. Instead, just like the children who obtained the two marshmallows by waiting, he was eager to carry out a truly impressive piece of work by thinking long-term. Ten years later, Mischel contacted the parents of as many of the children as possible. He asked about their children, who by then were adolescents. How well were they coping with life? Did they usually plan ahead? Was there a tendency for them to give up when the going got tough? The few moments spent in the company of three marshmallows and a bell many years before proved to be amazingly predictive. The children who had waited for the experimenter to return before eating their two marshmallows tended to develop into self-motivating and organized adults who were good at coping with difficulties and persisted in the face of failure. In contrast, those who immediately grabbed the single marshmallow grew up to be easily distracted, less motivated, and highly disorganized. Mischel's results also suggest that this ability is formed early in life and continues unchanged into adulthood, as well as that a very large percentage of children prefer to gobble down one marshmallow right away, rather than two in a few minutes' time, and so they struggle to get what they want out of life.

Whereas the marshmallow test measures impulsiveness, other researchers have focused on the kind of self-discipline that children need in order to listen to instructions, pay attention, and do what is required of them rather than the first thing that comes into their head. Some of this work, conducted by Megan McClelland at Oregon State University and her colleagues, has involved asking hundreds of children, between four and five years of age, to play a game called "head to toes."[18] During the game, the experimenter says the phrase "Touch your head" or "Touch your toes." The children have to touch their toes when they hear "Touch your head" and touch their head when they hear "Touch your toes." In the same way that the marshmallow test predicts some aspects of long-term success, so the "head to toes" game provides a good indicator of the level of self-discipline needed for achieving important aims and ambitions. Research shows, for example, that school pupils' level of self-discipline provides a better predictor of their future academic success than their scores on intelligence tests.[19] Outside the classroom, dieters who are able to resist that mouthwatering slice of cake quickly lose weight, students who endure the hardship of homework achieve better exam grades, and athletes who are prepared to spend hours training win more medals.

If you happen to find yourself in the company of a child who is struggling with such skills, what is the best way of helping them control their impulses and behave themselves? Is it better, for example, to play good cop ("Would you be a little darling and please spend only thirty minutes on the computer?") or to adopt a more threatening approach ("If you don't get off the computer now, that optical mouse is going right up your USB port"). In the mid-1960s, Jonathan Freedman from Stanford University conducted an experiment on this issue.[20]

His study involved a group of about forty boys, between seven and ten years of age, who were attending one of two local schools in California. One at a time, the boys were invited into a room and asked to rate the degree to which they liked five toys by assigning each one a number between 0 ("very, very bad toy") and 100 ("very, very good toy"). Four of the toys were fairly mundane: a cheap plastic submarine, a child's baseball glove, a toy tractor, and a Dick Tracy toy rifle.

In contrast, the fifth toy was far more expensive and exciting. This was a toy among toys, a battery-controlled robot that represented the very height of 1960s technological wonder.

After the boy completed the ratings, the researcher explained that he had an errand to run and so would have to leave the room for a few minutes. He told the boy that he was free to play with four of the toys but was not to touch the robot. Half of the boys were clearly told that bad things would happen if they disobeyed the experimenter ("If you play with the robot, I'll be very angry and will have to do something about it"), while the other half were subjected to a more "softly, softly" approach ("Do not play with the robot. It is wrong to play with the robot"). The experimenter then left, leaving the boy staring longingly at the robot and its "come and play with me" flashing eyes. About five minutes later, the experimenter returned, thanked the boy for taking part, and allowed him to leave.

Did the boys succumb to temptation? To find out, the researchers had fitted the robot with a secret device that measured whether the toy had been turned on. The data revealed that only two of the boys had the self-control to leave the robot alone. One of the boys came from the group that had been given stern instructions not to play with the robot, while the other was from the group that had been subjected to the "softly, softly" approach. When the experimenter was not present to enforce the instruction not to play with the robot, both approaches proved equally ineffective.

However, Freedman hadn't expected any real difference in the short term. He was far more interested in differences that might emerge over a long period of time. About six weeks later, he sent a female experimenter back to the schools, apparently to conduct a different study with the same boys. Each boy was invited into the room and asked to make a drawing.

Exactly the same collection of toys had been placed in the corner of the room, and when the children had finished their drawings, the experimenter explained that they could now spend a few minutes playing with any of the toys. This time, none of the toys were designated out of bounds, and so all of them were up for grabs. A big difference emerged between the two groups. Of those in the "I'll be really angry and will have to do something about it" group, 77 percent played with the robot, compared to just 33 percent of those in the "softly, softly" group. Remarkably, just a slight change from the experimenter's instructions of several weeks earlier had had a significant impact on the boys' subsequent behavior, with the softer wording producing far more compliance.

Why the big difference? There are several possible explanations. According to some researchers, it has to do with people's response to threats. Normally, people need to be threatened only when someone does not want them to do something that they want to do. And the more they want to do something, the bigger the threat needs to be to prevent them from doing it. According to this approach, the children who heard the stronger threats would have unconsciously thought, "Wow, people only give out big threats like that when I really want to do something that they don't want me to do, so I must really want to play with the robot." Using the same logic, a quiet request to the other boys that they not play with the robot resulted in their convincing themselves that they didn't really want to play with the toy.

Other researchers argue that the threat instantly elevated the robot to the status of forbidden fruit and elicited the age-old tendency to want to do something because it is not permitted. Although academic arguments rage about whether this tendency is driven by a sense of curiosity, stubbornness, or rebellion, everyone agrees that the effect is powerful and reliable, and explains why attempts to ban teenage smoking, drinking, and fast driving frequently backfire.[21]

In the secret science of self-discipline, the truth is that some children have an almost innate ability to control their impulses, whereas others find it difficult to resist instant gratification. And to instill self-discipline in those who grab the single marshmallow rather than waiting for two later, it's clear that the smaller the threat you make, the bigger the impact.

IN 59 SECONDS

The Marshmallow Test

It is easy to do the marshmallow test with your own children and friends. Find a food that they like and offer them the option of a small portion now or a larger portion if they sit and wait for about ten minutes. If you are going to do this quick and fun assessment, make sure that your guinea pigs can see the small and large portions of food throughout the test. Mischel's research suggests that the experiment is most effective when people are continuously tempted by the sight of their favorite food!

Heads and Toes

During this game, children have to touch their toes when they hear the phrase "Touch your head," and touch their head when they hear the phrase "Touch your toes." To play, explain the rules to your child and give them a couple of practice sessions. Then randomly say the phrase "Touch your head" or "Touch your toes" and award 2 points if the child makes the correct response without hesitation, 1 point when they start to make the incorrect response and then correct themselves, and 0 points for an incorrect response. Try a list of ten commands and see how they score. On average, three-year-old children tend to obtain 3 points, four-year-olds score about 10, and five-year-olds get about 14 correct. If your child does not score within this range, don't panic! It is perfectly normal for children to get a range of scores, but a low score may indicate that he or she could benefit from some of the games described below.

Focusing on Focus

Studies suggest that playing certain types of games can help children learn to pay attention, follow directions, and develop self-control.[22] In the "freeze game," tell your child to dance to music and then freeze when the music stops. In the first part of the game, your child has to dance slowly to slow songs and quickly to fast songs. However, once they have mastered this stage, ask them to do the opposite, dancing quickly to the slow songs and slowly to the fast songs. In a similar exercise, called "conducting the orchestra," give your child any musical instrument and conduct their music using a makeshift baton. In the first part of the game, ask them to play when you wave the baton but stop when you put it down. Next, ask them to play quickly when you move the baton quickly and slowly when you move the baton slowly. Finally, ask your child to do the opposite, playing quickly when you put the baton down and slowly when you wave it around.

There are several other techniques that can help children understand, value, and develop the power of self-discipline. Have them write their name with their nondominant hand, repeat the months of the year or days of the week in reverse order, or name as many objects in a certain category (e.g., vegetables, pets, countries) as they can in thirty seconds. Also, when you see your child concentrating very hard on something, encourage them to reflect on their behavior by, for example, asking them how long they thought they'd been concentrating (point out that time flies when you are focused) or how it felt when someone interrupted them (point out the value of being able to get back into a task after someone interrupts you).

Avoiding Threats

Threats work well in the short term but can actually prove counterproductive over longer periods of time. By pointing out all of the terrible things that will happen if your child follows a course of action, you may be making that activity more attractive in their minds. Instead, try the "softly, softly" approach used in the toy robot experiment. State that you do not want them to do something and leave it there. If they really do insist on knowing why you are stopping them, try to get them to identify some possible reasons themselves.

personality

Why not to trust graphology,

how to gain an apparently magical insight

into other people's personality

from their fingers and thumbs,

their pets, and the time they go to bed

IN 2005 WORLD LEADERS gathered at a major economic forum in Switzerland to discuss some of the biggest problems facing Planet Earth. From poverty to privatization, and capitalism to climate change, nothing escaped their eagle eyes and influential minds. Despite the enormity of the issues, however, much of the media coverage of the event focused on a single sheet of paper that had been carelessly left by one of the attendees at a press conference.

The newspapers had managed to get hold of a page of scribbled notes and doodles apparently made by Tony Blair during the event. They asked various graphologists to make a psychological assessment of the British prime minister on the basis of his handwriting and drawings. The graphologists quickly rose to the challenge, noting how, for example, his disconnected letters, right-sloping writing, and strange way of writing *d* showed the "Blair flair at work" and revealed that he was struggling to keep control of a confusing world, was a daydreamer hoping for the best, was unable to complete tasks, and possessed an unconscious death wish toward his political career.

At the time, Blair was trying to deal with various political problems and scandals, including a forthcoming election with the smallest of majorities, and so the observations seemed to present an accurate insight into his personality. However, a few days later things did not look so rosy: Downing Street pointed out that the page did not belong to Blair but had instead been produced by fellow attendee Bill Gates, founder of Microsoft and one of the world's most successful businessmen.

According to the proponents of graphology, the Blair-Gates mix-up is just a small blot on their copybook. In general, they say, a person's handwriting can reveal amazingly accurate insight into their personality, intelligence, health, and even criminal intent. These claims are taken seriously by many personnel departments, with surveys revealing that between 5 percent and 10 percent of U.S. and UK businesses regularly use graphology to eliminate unsuitable candidates in their recruitment procedures.[1]

But is there really anything to it, or is graphology just another mind myth? Researcher Geoffrey Dean has devoted a great deal of time to examining the topic, gathering hundreds of scientific studies and using them to examine the claims made by the proponents of this ancient art form. The results make for chilling reading.

In one analysis, Dean collated the findings from sixteen academic papers that had examined graphology in the workplace. He compared graphologists' predictions of employee performance with supervisors' ratings of success during job training. The results revealed that there was little relationship between graphologists' predictions and the ratings of job success. In fact, the graphologists were about as accurate as a control group of untrained laypeople who had no experience in graphology at all.

In another analysis, Dean examined studies in which researchers had compared graphologists' attempts to determine a person's character with that person's scores on scientifically validated personality tests. Dean collected the journal articles (this time fifty-three of them) and analyzed the results.

Not only was the graphologists' accuracy poor, but control groups of people with absolutely no training or background in assessing personality from handwriting scored just as well as the so-called experts.

When it comes to obtaining a graphology-based insight into the personality of others, the writing is on the wall. The Blair-Gates slipup does not represent a momentary slip of the pen but is symbolic of the findings of scientific studies that have investigated graphology. Contrary to the claims made by proponents, research suggests that graphology does not provide an amazingly accurate and reliable insight into personality and should not be seen as a useful way to predict employee performance.

So if you cannot understand someone's personality on the basis of their handwriting, how can you gain insight into their real character? The answer involves a concept known as the "Big Five," the eighteenth-century womanizer Giacomo Casanova, and the bumper stickers that people place on their cars.

THE BIG FIVE

Some of the world's greatest thinkers have attempted to understand the complexities of human personality. Freud believed that people were best categorized according to the bodily orifice from which they derived the greatest pleasure, maverick Victorian scientist Sir Francis Galton examined bumps on the skull, and Jung was convinced that personalities were determined by the position of the stars at the moment of birth.

Other scientists, such as Gordon Allport and Hans Eysenck,

pursued a more levelheaded, and ultimately productive, approach.[2] These researchers believed that the secret structure of the human psyche was buried deep within language. They speculated that the words people use to describe themselves and others were created because they accurately reflect fundamental dimensions of personality. They thought that if this was the case, it should be possible to discover the fundamental structure of personality by carefully collecting and collating all of the words that could be used to describe a person.

The enterprise began in the 1930s, with a group of dedicated researchers carefully poring over each page of an unabridged dictionary. They selected each and every word that could be used to describe personality. From "amusing" to "abhorrent," "benign" to "belligerent," the team eventually compiled a list of more than eighteen thousand words. They then worked through the list and identified four thousand words that described relatively stable and central traits. In the 1940s another group of researchers continued the effort and subjected this shortened list to an early form of computerized analysis that reduced it to a set of about two hundred words. Over the next forty years or so, thousands of people were asked to rate themselves and others on various subsets of these adjectives, and researchers employed increasingly sophisticated statistical techniques to analyze the data in an attempt to identify the key dimensions on which people differed. Consensus finally emerged in the early 1990s, when several large-scale studies from many different countries and cultures confirmed the existence of five fundamental dimensions of personality.[3]

Together these factors, collectively referred to as the "Big Five," represent the holy grail of personality research. The five dimensions have been given different labels over the years, but are commonly referred to as openness, conscientiousness, extroversion, agreeableness, and neuroticism (easily remembered by using the acronym OCEAN). Each dimension is seen as a continuum that runs from high to low, and everyone can be described by five scores that indicate where they sit on each scale. Additional work has shown that the dimensions are determined by a combination of genes and childhood experiences and they tend to remain unchanged throughout a person's life, and thus influence almost every aspect of behavior including relationships, performance in the workplace, leisure activities, consumer choice, religious and political beliefs, creativity, sense of humor, and health.

So what lies at the heart of these five dimensions, and what does it mean to obtain a high or low score on each of them?

Openness represents the degree to which a person seeks and appreciates new, interesting, and unusual experiences. High scorers are curious and broad-minded. They get bored easily, but are especially good at tolerating ambiguity and so are skilled at seeing situations and problems from many different perspectives. They are creative, original, wise, funny, imaginative, and unconventional. They have a rich inner life, like new ideas, tend to remember their dreams, and make good hypnotic subjects. In contrast, low scorers tend to be more conventional, down-to-earth, and better able to focus on the practical side of things. They are more comfortable with familiar places and food, and tend to work through problems on a step-by-step basis.

Conscientiousness reflects the degree of organization, persistence, and self-discipline to achieve goals. High scorers are very organized, reliable, hardworking, persevering, and able to forgo short-term rewards for long-term success. They tend to do especially well in the workplace, keep their New Year's resolutions, and be highly punctual. They also tend to live significantly longer than others because they don't usually engage in high-risk behaviors, such as reckless driving, and are far more likely to exercise, eat a balanced diet, and have regular medical checkups. Low scorers tend to be less reliable and more easygoing and hedonistic. They are harder to motivate and more easily distracted, but can show greater flexibility in the face of changing circumstances.

Extroversion reflects the need for stimulation from the outside world and other people. Those who obtain high scores on this dimension are fun to be with, impulsive, optimistic, happy, enjoy the company of others, and have a wide circle of friends and acquaintances. They prefer to lead rather than follow, enjoy aggressive and sexually explicit humor, drink more, are skilled at multitasking, strive for instant gratification, have more sexual partners than others, and are more likely to cheat on their partner. Low scorers tend to be far more considered, controlled, and reserved. Their social life revolves around a relatively small number of very close friends, and they prefer reading a good book to a night out on the town. They are more sensitive to pain, good at focusing on a single task, prefer more intellectual forms of humor, such as puns, and like to work in closed offices with few distractions.

Agreeableness is the degree to which a person cares about others. High scorers are trustworthy, altruistic, kind, affectionate, and, perhaps most important of all, likeable. They are less likely to divorce, are perceived much more favorably in job interviews, and are more likely to be promoted at work. Low scorers tend to be far more aggressive, hostile, and uncooperative. They tend to see things from their own point of view, value being right over caring about other people's thoughts and feelings, perform better in situations that require tough-mindedness, and are less likely to be taken advantage of by others.

The fifth and final dimension, *Neuroticism,* reflects the degree to which a person is emotionally stable and able to cope with potentially stressful situations. High scorers are far more prone to worry, have low self-esteem, set unrealistic aspirations, and frequently experience a range of negative emotions, including distress, hostility, and envy. Their strong need to be loved, coupled with low self-esteem, can lead to forming overly possessive and dependent relationships. Low scorers tend to be calm, relaxed, resilient in the face of failure, and emotionally secure. They are unfazed by negative life events, skilled at using humor to reduce anxiety in themselves and others, able to cope well with misfortune, and sometimes even thrive on stress.

Most psychologists now believe that the apparent complexity of human personality is an illusion. In reality, people vary on just five fundamental dimensions. Understand these dimensions and you gain important insights into your behavior and thinking. Likewise, being able to quickly understand the personality of those around you will help you to understand their actions and how best to communicate with them. Modern-day research suggests that Freud, Galton, and Jung were wrong and that the secret to understanding personality lies in the five fundamental factors that are embedded deep within our language and lives.

IN 59 SECONDS

Psychologists have created several questionnaires to carefully measure people's responses on each of the Big Five dimensions. Unfortunately, they tend to involve a large number of questions, and so take a considerable amount of time to complete. However, some researchers have created a quick and easy version that will help you discover your position on each of the five main dimensions.[4] It does not provide a perfect description but is a useful guide to the fundamental forces that make up your personality.

To complete the questionnaire, please use the rating scale that follows and check a box to describe how accurately each statement describes *you*. Describe yourself as you generally are now, not as you wish to be in the future. Describe yourself as you honestly see yourself, in relation to other people you know who are the same sex as you are and roughly your age. At this point, ignore the numbers in the top-right corner of each box.

I SEE MYSELF AS ...	DISAGREE STRONGLY	DISAGREE MODERATELY	DISAGREE A LITTLE	NEITHER AGREE NOR DISAGREE	AGREE A LITTLE	AGREE MODERATELY	AGREE STRONGLY
1. the life of the party	1	2	3	4	5	6	7
2. feeling little concern for others	7	6	5	4	3	2	1
3. always prepared	1	2	3	4	5	6	7
4. getting stressed-out easily	1	2	3	4	5	6	7
5. having excellent ideas	1	2	3	4	5	6	7
6. not talking a lot	7	6	5	4	3	2	1
7. interested in people	1	2	3	4	5	6	7
8. often forgetting to put things back in their proper place	7	6	5	4	3	2	1
9. relaxed most of the time	7	6	5	4	3	2	1
10. having difficulty understanding abstract ideas	7	6	5	4	3	2	1

SCORING

Look at the numbers in the top-right corner of the boxes that you have checked in statements 5 ("having excellent ideas") and 10 ("having difficulty understanding abstract ideas"). Add these two numbers to find your score on the Openness dimension. If your score is 10 or less, then you should see yourself as a low scorer, whereas if your score is above 10, you should see yourself as a high scorer. Write your total on the line below, and check either the Low or the High score line.

OPENNESS
Total of statements 5 and 10: _____

_____ Low (10 and below)   _____ High (above 10)

Now repeat this process for the remaining four dimensions:

CONSCIENTIOUSNESS
Total of statements 3 and 8: _____

_____ Low (11 and below)   _____ High (above 11)

EXTROVERSION
Total of statements 1 and 6: _____

_____ Low (9 and below)   _____ High (above 9)

AGREEABLENESS
Total of statements 2 and 7: _____

_____ Low (10 and below)   _____ High (above 10)

NEUROTICISM
Total of statements 4 and 9: _____

_____ Low (9 and below)   _____ High (above 9)

A Quick Analysis, and a Few Handy Hints, Based on Your Scores

Openness. High scorers tend to be imaginative and creative but also prone to boredom, and so strive to continually feed their mind with new ideas and experiences. Low scorers are more down-to-earth, and so tend to seek out situations in which they have to turn an existing idea into reality, take small steps rather than initiate radical change, and follow well-established patterns and rules.

Conscientiousness. High scorers are methodical, well organized, and dutiful, and perform best in highly structured and predictable environments where there is a place for everything and everything is in its place. Low scorers are far more laid-back and find it easy to enjoy life, but may well need a helping hand when it comes to self-discipline.

Extroversion. High scorers are energized by the company of others, are evening types, and are motivated more by carrots than sticks. In contrast, low scorers tend to be happiest working alone and in quiet surroundings, are most alert in the morning, and are motivated more by fear of punishment than promise of rewards.

Agreeableness. High scorers tend to be trusting, friendly, and cooperative, but have to be careful to avoid situations in which others might take advantage of their overly giving nature. Low scorers tend to be more aggressive and competitive, and bloom in situations that require tough thinking and straight talking.

Neuroticism. High scorers are prone to insecurity and emotional distress, and avoid situations that they find upsetting because those negative feelings take some time to fade away. Low scorers tend to be more relaxed, less emotional and less prone to distress, and they operate well in situations that others find stressful.

BEHIND THE BIG FIVE

Differences in brain function and upbringing may account for differences in the fundamental dimensions of personality.

For example, a relationship exists between extroversion and brain activation. If you open the top of someone's skull and look in, you will see the wrinkled mass of tissue that is their cortex. This large lump of meat makes up about 80 percent of the weight of a brain and contains an amazing 100 billion neurons. Every cortex has a different pre-set level of arousal. Brain scans have revealed that people scoring low on extroversion have a high pre-set level of arousal. As a result, they avoid situations that further arouse their stimulated brains and are most comfortable when they are engaged in quiet, predictable activities. The exact opposite is true of those who score high on extroversion. Their brains have a much lower pre-set level of arousal, so they have a need for continuous stimulation. Because of this, they enjoy being with other people, risk taking, and impulsive behavior.

Other work has focused more on the relationship between personality and upbringing. For example, University of California psychologist Frank Sulloway believes that levels of openness are determined, at least to some extent, by birth order.[5] According to Sulloway's theory, because younger children haven't developed the abilities and skills that their older siblings have, they explore novel ways to get their parents' love and attention, and this, in turn, causes them to develop into more open, creative, unconventional, adventurous, and rebellious people. To test his theory, Sulloway analyzed the biographies of more than six thousand well-known people from many different walks of life, and he claims that the evidence is overwhelming. He notes that the vast majority of American presidents (including Jimmy Carter, George W. Bush, and Bill Clinton) were firstborns, whereas leaders of revolutions, such as Jefferson, Marx, and Castro, were later in their families' birth order. Likewise, when it comes to science, Sulloway argues that firstborns tend to be members of the scientific establishment, whereas younger siblings, such as Darwin and Copernicus, are the ones who propose radically new ideas. It is a controversial idea,[6] but if correct, it provides a striking illustration of how subtle differences in childhood experience may have a surprisingly dramatic effect on personality.

THE CASANOVA EFFECT

Imagine deciding to quit your job and embark on a new career as a professional palmist. You invest in the requisite purple caftan, set up a small booth on the busy promenade in the nearest seaside town, and nervously await your first customer. A few moments later, a man walks in, sits down, and crosses your palm with silver. You carefully look at the stranger's hand and try to spot any telltale clues that might give you a magical insight into his life. Is his soft skin a sign of office work? Do his chewed nails signal a recent job loss? Is his calloused palm suggestive of too much time at the gym—or does it reflect a strong need to find a love interest? According to some psychologists, you would be much better off ignoring his soft skin, chewed nails, and calloused palm, instead shifting your attention to the length of his index and ring fingers. Their argument is a curious one, which links the famous eighteenth-century womanizer Giacomo Casanova with some of Britain's most famous soccer players.

According to his colorful autobiography, Casanova enjoyed the company of many European kings, cardinals, poets, and artists.[7] At one point he describes how he spent time with the eminent German painter Anton Raphael Mengs. After a while, they started to argue, with Mengs berating Casanova for not observing his religious duties and Casanova accusing Mengs of being a child-beating alcoholic. As the situation moved from bad to worse, Casanova took it upon himself to criticize one of Mengs's paintings. He pointed out that the index finger of a principal male character was longer than the ring finger and was therefore anatomically incorrect, as men's ring fingers were longer than their index fingers. Mengs defended his work by showing that his own index finger was longer than his ring finger. Casanova stuck to his argument, showing that his ring finger was longer than his index finger, claiming that this was true of most men and arguing that his hands were thus "like that of all the children descended from Adam." Affronted, Mengs asked Casanova, "Then from whom do you suppose I am descended?" Casanova replied, "I have no idea; but it is certain that you are not of my species." As the argument escalated, they raised a bet of one hundred pistoles on the issue and promptly rounded up the painter's servants to discover who was right. A quick perusal of the servants' hands revealed that Casanova was correct, but Mengs quickly saved face by rejoicing in the fact that he could now boast of being unique in something.

Evolutionary psychologist John Manning, at the University of Central Lancashire, has dedicated much of his professional life to studying the differences in finger lengths described by Casanova. He argues that they reveal an important insight into the human psyche.[8] Manning and his colleagues measure the length of people's index and ring fingers, and then divide the first length by the second to obtain what is commonly referred to as the "2D:4D" (second digit to fourth digit) ratio. If the ring and index fingers are exactly the same length, then the 2D:4D ratio will be 1.00. If, however, the ring finger is longer than the index finger, then the 2D:4D ratio will be less than 1.00, and conversely, if the index finger is longer than the ring finger, then the 2D:4D ratio will be greater than 1.00.

The research has conclusively revealed that the finger-length pattern described by Casanova tends to be associated far more with men than with women, with the average 2D:4D ratio for men being about .98, while the corresponding figure for women hovers around 1.00. In short, men's ring fingers tend to be longer than their index fingers, whereas women's fingers tend to be about the same length.

Why should this be the case? According to Manning, the explanation dates back to the very start of a person's life and is closely linked to testosterone levels in the womb. After about six weeks or so, the level of testosterone in the womb changes, and those fetuses that are exposed to large amounts of the hormone develop more male characteristics, while those exposed to much smaller levels develop more female attributes. Manning argues that testosterone also plays a key role in determining the length of a person's index and ring fingers, with high levels resulting in a relatively long ring finger. If Manning's theory is right, a person's 2D:4D ratio is related to the amount of testosterone that they were exposed to in the womb and should provide a good indication of the degree to which they possess psychological and physical traits commonly associated with either masculinity or femininity. According to this theory, people with low 2D:4D ratios will be more likely than others to exhibit masculine characteristics, while those with high 2D:4D ratios will be significantly more likely to be in touch with their feminine side.

It is a controversial idea and one that has attracted its fair share of criticism.[9] However, proponents argue that a large body of research now supports the theory, including work examining physical strength and sporting success. In one study, a group of men had their finger lengths measured and were then asked to complete various strength tests, including shoulder, overhead, and bench presses.[10] The results revealed the expected relationships. Men who had lower 2D:4D ratios were able to lift heavier weights than those with higher ratios. Often the differences were far from trivial. For example, for overhead presses, those with 2D:4D ratios of .91 lifted twenty-four pounds more than those with ratios of more than 1.00. In another study, researchers turned their attention to student sprinters and found that their times in the 100-meter, 800-meter, and 1,500-meter races were all related to 2D:4D ratios, with the faster runners having lower ratios.[11] In another experiment, Manning and his team managed to measure the finger lengths of some of the best-known and most highly skilled soccer players in Britain.[12] Attending a centenary celebration designed to mark the end of the 100th English League Championship, the researchers persuaded more than three hundred players to have their hands photocopied, and then compared their finger lengths to those of a control group of more than five hundred men who had never ventured onto a soccer field. The 2D:4D ratio of the players was significantly lower than that of the controls. Strong differences also emerged among the different groups of players, with high-performing "legends" and those who had played at an international level having especially low ratios.

Other work suggests that the 2D:4D effect may also extend to certain psychological traits. A great deal of research has shown that men tend to outperform women in tests that involve the mental manipulation of spatial information (perhaps explaining the alleged fondness of women for turning maps around when navigating). In line with this finding, Manning believes that his research suggests that men with low 2D:4D ratios (who therefore, according to his theory, possess more "masculine" brains) tend to outperform others on these tasks.[13] Similarly, he cites other work suggesting that when it comes to personality, women with lower 2D:4D ratios tend to exhibit traits that the researchers believe to be more male-oriented, including being more assertive and risk taking.[14]

According to Manning, the effect even extends to making music. Noting that there are about ten times as many male professional musicians as females, Manning argues that musical ability is associated more with a masculine brain than a feminine brain and that therefore highly skilled performers should have an especially low 2D:4D ratio. To test this idea, he measured the 2D:4D ratio of fifty-four male members of a well-known British symphony orchestra. Several sections of the orchestra were organized in a hierarchical way, with more highly skilled musicians taking key positions. Manning discovered that performers in these key positions did indeed have significantly lower 2D:4D ratios than their fellow musicians.[15]

In order to obtain a mysterious insight into yourself and others, it may well be better to forget traditional palmistry and instead focus your attention on the apparently important relative lengths of the index finger and the ring finger.

IN 59 SECONDS

Some researchers believe that the relative length of your first and third fingers provides considerable insight into your psychological and physical abilities. To quickly assess yourself, hold your left hand palm up in front of you and look at the length of your first (index) and third (ring) fingers.

Your first finger may be slightly longer than your third finger, and so your hand will tend to resemble the illustration below.

Alternatively, your third finger may be slightly longer than your first finger, and so your hand would be more like the illustration below.

According to the theory, a relatively long third finger is indicative of a more "masculine" brain and body and is associated with, for example, high levels of performance in sports, greater assertiveness, increased emotional stability, and enhanced musical ability.

To carry out a slightly more accurate version of the exercise, hold your right palm up in front of you and look at where your first finger joins the palm of your hand. There will be several creases at that point. Place the zero mark of the ruler on the middle of the bottom crease and measure to the tip of your finger (not your nail) in millimeters. Now repeat exactly the same procedure for your right third finger. To find the 2D:4D ratio, divide the length of your first finger by the length of your third finger. Research shows that the average male ratio is about .98, and a ratio of about .94 would be regarded as especially masculine, while a ratio of 1.00 would be viewed as more feminine. For women, the average ratio is about 1.00, and a score of about .98 would be regarded as more masculine while a ratio of 1.02 would be viewed as more feminine.

CELEBRITY FINGERS

When I first came across research suggesting that the 2D:4D ratio predicted athletic and musical excellence, I wondered whether the same effect might emerge among people who had made a name for themselves in other occupations. However, as measuring the finger lengths of the rich and famous seemed rather problematic, I filed the idea in the somewhat cramped mental box marked "Probably Never Going to Happen." Then, some time ago, I was watching a television program documenting a road trip across America and suddenly had an idea. One of the scenes was filmed in Los Angeles and involved chatting with people walking along Hollywood

Boulevard. In the background I could see the world-famous Grauman's Chinese Theatre, and suddenly the penny dropped.

Since the 1920s many of the world's most famous celebrities have had their signatures, footprints, and handprints set in concrete blocks at the entrance of the theater. Was it possible, I wondered, to accurately measure finger lengths from the casts and thus discover the 2D:4D ratios of some of the best-known figures in show business? My mind started to race. Would leading men have especially high levels of testosterone and therefore especially low 2D:4D ratios? What about comedians? Their success often rests on being verbally skilled and creative rather than having rugged good looks—would that be reflected in a high 2D:4D ratio?

There was just one small problem—I was in London and the casts were in Los Angeles. Never one to let a few thousand miles get in the way of research, I contacted a colleague named Jim Underdown. Jim is a former stand-up comedian from Chicago who now works for the Center for Inquiry, an American organization that promotes the skeptical and scientific investigation of alleged paranormal phenomena. He heads a branch of the organization based in Los Angeles and has been involved in all sorts of strange projects, including examining sightings of alleged UFOs and testing people who claim to have psychic powers.

I e-mailed Jim and asked whether he might be able to help out. More specifically, could he obtain some digital calipers and arrange for a colleague (who was unaware of the 2D:4D theory) to measure as many of the concrete handprints as possible? Jim accepted the challenge. A few weeks later he e-mailed me to say that calipers had been purchased and that he had teamed up with another researcher named Spencer

Marks and spent several days avoiding puddles and security guards, eventually collecting initial data from thirty-seven of the best-known leading men and nine comedians.

The list of leading men read like a who's who of the film industry, including Paul Newman, Bruce Willis, Johnny Depp, John Travolta, Warren Beatty, and Jack Nicholson. Previous work suggested that the average male 2D:4D ratio tends to be about .98. The average ratios for the leading men's left and right hands were both about .96, suggesting that they are an especially testosterone-fueled bunch. The comedians formed an equally impressive group, which included some of the funniest people in the world, such as George Burns, Peter Sellers, Bob Hope, and Robin Williams. Their average left-hand 2D:4D ratio was about .96, but their average right-hand ratio came in at a surprisingly high 1.01.

The work is still in its infancy, but the initial results look as intriguing as they are promising. If the phenomenon is genuine, it might really be possible to discover whether someone has that magic X-factor by simply looking at their hands.

QUICK TIPS FOR GAINING INSIGHT INTO SOMEONE'S PERSONALITY IN 59 SECONDS OR LESS

Ask People About Their Pets. A few years ago I conducted a large-scale online study examining the possible relationship between the personality of owners and their pets. More than two thousand owners rated their personality and the personality of their pets on several factors (e.g., sociability, emotional stability, and sense of humor). In addition, they indicated how long they had owned their pet. Fish owners turned out to be the happiest, dog owners the most fun to be with, cat owners the most dependable and emotionally sensitive, and reptile owners the most independent. Weirdly, the results also revealed telling differences rating pets' sense of humor. According to their owners, 62 percent of dogs had a good sense of humor, compared to just 57 percent of fish, 48 percent of cats, 42 percent of horses, 38 percent of birds, and 0 percent of reptiles.

The findings also revealed significant similarities between the personalities of owners and those of their pets. Interestingly, this similarity increased over time, suggesting that pets may slowly come to adopt their owner's personality, or vice versa. For years, owners have insisted that their pets have a unique personality—not only does my research suggest they might be right, but it also reveals that people's pets are a reflection of themselves. So if you meet someone who has a dog and you want to gain genuine insight into their personality within seconds, ask them to describe the personality of their canine pal.

Bumper Stickers. William Szlemko and colleagues speculated that many people who personalize their car by adding bumper stickers or window stickers may be sending out powerful signals of territoriality, and they were curious to discover if having to share public roads with others could increase the chances of these drivers' experiencing road rage.[16] To investigate, hundreds of participants were asked to report how many bumper and window stickers they had and also to rate their level of aggressive driving. The results revealed that drivers with more stickers admitted to driving more aggressively, including a greater frequency of tailgating and ramming. So if you find yourself driving behind a car covered in stickers, it's probably best to give it that extra inch or two.

All Thumbs. The brain can be seen as working in two general modes. In one mode (often called right-brained), it is more intuitive, visual, and creative. In the other (often called left-brained), it is more logical, sequential, and language-based. In many ways, it is like having an artist and an accountant arguing in your head, and you are flipping between the two. All of us work in both modes, but everyone naturally tends toward one or the other. Right-handers can try this quick test to discover if they tend to be more right- than left-brained or vice versa. Interlock the fingers of your hands and place one thumb on top of the other. People who place their right thumb on top of their left thumb tend to be left-brain dominant, and are thus more verbal and analytical.[17] Those who place their left thumb on top of their right thumb tend to be right-brain dominant, and excel in visual, creative, and intuitive tasks.

Morning or Evening? If you wanted to feel at your best and were free to get up at any time of the day, when would you choose to climb out of bed? At 7 a.m., 8 a.m., 9 a.m., or even 10 a.m? And how about at the opposite end of the day. If you had your way, and were free from all other demands, when would you choose to go to bed? At 10 p.m., midnight, or 1 a.m.? Your answers to those two questions help reveal whether you are a morning type (going to bed early and getting up early) or an evening type (late to bed and late to rise). Recent research also suggests that your answers reveal a great deal about your personality and style of thinking.[18] Questionnaire results from more than 350 people showed that morning types are attracted to concrete information rather than abstract thinking and like to rely on logic rather than intuition. They tend to be introverted, self-controlled, and eager to make a good impression on others. In contrast, evening types have a far more creative outlook on life, are more prepared to take risks, are more independent and nonconforming, and are a little impulsive.

conclusion

Sophie's answer: Ten techniques
in 59 seconds

AT THE START OF THIS BOOK I described going to lunch with my friend Sophie a few years ago. As we chatted, Sophie said that she had bought a book on increasing happiness, and I expressed considerable skepticism about the self-help industry. When I launched into a lengthy account of academic work in happiness, Sophie politely interrupted me and essentially posed the question that acted as a catalyst for this book: are there any scientifically supported techniques that could help improve people's lives in less than a minute? I didn't know the answer, but Sophie's question piqued my curiosity. After surveying thousands of studies in countless journals, I realized that behavioral researchers working in many different areas had indeed developed such techniques. Sophie, here are ten of the most interesting studies that I wish I had known about when you asked. On a good day, I think I could describe all ten in just under a minute.

Develop the Gratitude Attitude.

Having people list three things that they are grateful for in life or three events that have gone especially well over the past week can significantly increase their level of happiness for about a month. This, in turn, can cause them to be more optimistic about the future and can improve their physical health.

Be a Giver.

People become much happier after even the smallest acts of kindness. Those who give a few dollars to the needy, buy a small surprise gift for a loved one, donate blood, or help a friend are inclined to experience a fast-acting and significant boost in happiness.

Hang a Mirror in Your Kitchen.

Placing a mirror in front of people when they are presented with different food options results in a remarkable 32 percent reduction in their consumption of unhealthy food. Seeing their own reflection makes them more aware of their body and more likely to eat food that is good for them.

Buy a Potted Plant for the Office.

Adding plants to an office results in a 15 percent boost in the number of creative ideas reported by male employees and helps their female counterparts to produce more original solutions to problems. The plants help reduce stress and induce good moods, which, in turn, promote creativity.

Touch People Lightly on The Upper Arm.

Lightly touching someone on their upper arm makes them far more likely to agree to a request because the touch is unconsciously perceived as a sign of high status. In one dating study, the touch produced a 20 percent increase in the number of people who accepted an invitation to dance in a nightclub and a 10 percent increase in those who would give their telephone number to a stranger on the street.

Write About Your Relationship.

Partners who spend a few moments each week committing their deepest thoughts and feelings about their relationship to paper boost the chances that they will stick together by more than 20 percent. Such "expressive writing" results in partners' using more positive language when they speak to each other, leading to a healthier and happier relationship.

Deal with Potential Liars by Closing Your Eyes and Asking for an E-mail.

The most reliable cues to lying are in the words that people use, with liars tending to lack detail, use more "ums" and "ahs," and avoid self-references ("me," "mine," "I"). In addition, people are about 20 percent less likely to lie in an e-mail than in a telephone call, because their words are on record and so are more likely to come back and haunt them.

Praise Children's Effort over Their Ability.

Praising a child's effort rather than their ability ("Well done. You must have tried very hard") encourages them to try regardless of the consequences, therefore sidestepping fear of failure. This, in turn, makes them especially likely to attempt challenging problems, find these problems enjoyable, and try to solve them on their own time.

Visualize Yourself Doing, Not Achieving.

People who visualize themselves taking the practical steps needed to achieve their goals are far more likely to succeed than those who simply fantasize about their dreams becoming a reality. One especially effective technique involves adopting a third-person perspective: those who visualize themselves as others see them are about 20 percent more successful than those who adopt a first-person point of view.

Consider Your Legacy.

Asking people to spend just a minute imagining a close friend standing up at their funeral and reflecting on their personal and professional legacy helps them to identify their long-term goals and assess the degree to which they are progressing toward making those goals a reality.

ACKNOWLEDGMENTS

This book would not have been possible without the help and support of many people. First, thanks for the wonderful advice and guidance provided by my agent, Patrick Walsh, and editors Richard Milner, Jon Butler, and Edward Kastenmeier. Thanks also to Clive Jeffries and Emma Greening for providing such insightful feedback at every stage, to Portia Smith for playing a key role in everything, to Jim Underdown and Spencer Marks for measuring the hands of so many famous people, to Roger Highfield for helping to explore the psychology of surnames, to Rachel Armstrong for her insightful comments on romance, to Sam Murphy for her help in discovering the relationship between attraction and sport. Also, special thanks to Pat Hendry and Kirsten Skow, friends to the simple folk. Finally, as ever, special thanks also to the wonderful Caroline Watt for giving far beyond the call of duty. Thank you.

NOTES

INTRODUCTION

1. Tabak, L. (2007, December 18). If your goal is success, don't consult the gurus. *Fast Company.*

2. Rodin, J., & Langer, J. E. (1997). Long-term effects of a control-relevant intervention with the institutionalized aged. *Journal of Personality and Social Psychology, 35*(12), 897–902.

HAPPINESS

1. Lyubomirsky, S., King, L. A., & Diener, E. (2005). The benefits of frequent positive affect: Does happiness lead to success? *Psychological Bulletin, 131,* 803–855.

2. See, for example, Myers, D. G. (2000). The funds, friends, and faith of happy people. *American Psychologist, 55,* 56–67.

3. Brickman, P., Coates, D., & Janoff-Bulman, R. (1978). Lottery winners and accident victims: Is happiness relative? *Journal of Personality and Social Psychology, 36,* 917–927.

4. Cited in Myers, D. G. (2000). The work relating to the relationship between GNP and happiness involved examining data from the World Bank and the "happiness" and "life satisfaction" scales of the 1990–1991 World Values Survey.

5. Diener, E., Horwitz, J., & Emmons, R. A. (1985). Happiness of the very wealthy. *Social Indicators Research, 16,* 263–274.

6. Myers, D. G. (2000). The funds, friends, and faith of happy people. *American Psychologist, 55,* 56–67.

7. Lyubomirsky, S., Sheldon, K. M., & Schkade, D. (2005). Pursuing happiness: The architecture of sustainable change. *Review of General Psychology, 9,* 111–131. Figuring out the genetic component of happiness has involved asking identical and nonidentical twins to rate how happy they are. Identical twins have the same genetic makeup, while fraternal twins do not, and so it is possible to calculate the genetic basis for happiness by carefully comparing the results from the two groups.

8. Borton, J. L. S., & Casey, E. C. (2006). Suppression of negative self-referential thoughts: A field study. *Self and Identity, 5*, 230–246.

9. For an overview of this work, see Wegner, D. M. (1989). *White bears and other unwanted thoughts: Suppression, obsession, and the psychology of mental control.* New York: Viking. The chocolate study is described in Erskine, J. A. K. (2007). Resistance can be futile: Investigating behavioural rebound. *Appetite, 50*, 415–421. I made up the finding about George W. Bush.

10. Zech, E. (1999). Is it really helpful to verbalise one's emotions? *Gedraf en Gezondheid, 27*, 42–47.

11. Zech, E., & Rimé, B. (2005). Is talking about an emotional experience helpful? Effects on emotional recovery and perceived benefits. *Clinical Psychology and Psychotherapy, 12*, 270–287.

12. Lyubomirsky, S., & Tkach, C. (2003). The consequences of dysphoric rumination. In Papageorgiou, C. & Wells, A. (Eds.). *Rumination: Nature, theory, and treatment of negative thinking in depression* (pp. 21–41). Chichester, England: John Wiley & Sons.

13. For a review of this work, see Lepore, S. J., & Smyth, J. M. (Eds.) (2002). *The writing cure: How expressive writing promotes health and emotional well-being.* Washington, DC: American Psychological Association.

14. Spera, S., Buhrfeind, E., & Pennebaker, J. W. (1994). Expressive writing and coping with job loss. *Academy of Management Journal, 3*, 722–733.

15. Emmons, R. A., & McCullough, M. E. (2003). Counting blessings versus burdens: An experimental investigation of gratitude and subjective well-being in daily life. *Journal of Personality and Social Psychology, 84*, 377–389.

16. King, L. A. (2001). The health benefits of writing about life goals. *Personality and Social Psychology Bulletin, 27*, 798–807.

17. Burton, C. M., & King, L. A. (2004). The health benefits of writing about intensely positive experiences. *Journal of Research in Personality, 38*, 150–163.

18. Floyd, K., Mikkelson, A. C., Hesse, C., & Pauley, P. M. (2007). Affectionate writing reduces total cholesterol: Two randomized, controlled trials. *Human Communication Research, 33*, 119–142.

19. Seligman, M. E. P., Steen, T., Park, N., & Peterson, C. (2005). Positive psychology progress: Empirical validation of interventions. *American Psychologist, 60*, 410–421.

20. Van Boven, L., & Gilovich, T. (2003). To do or to have: That is the question. *Journal of Personality and Social Psychology, 85*, 1193–1202.

21. This questionnaire is based on work described in Richins, M. L., & Dawson, S. (1992). A consumer values orientation for materialism and its measurement: Scale development and validation. *Journal of Consumer Research, 19*(3), 303–316.

22. Richins, M. L., & Dawson, S. (1992). A consumer values orientation for materialism and its measurement: Scale development and validation. *Journal of Consumer Research, 19*(3), 303–316.

23. Dunn, E. W., Aknin, L., & Norton, M. I. (2008). Spending money on others promotes happiness. *Science, 319*, 1687–1688.

24. Harbaugh, B. T., Mayr, U., & Burghart, D. (2007). Neural responses to taxation and voluntary giving reveal motives for charitable donations. *Science, 316*(5831), 1622—1625.

25. Lyubomirsky, S., Sheldon, K. M., & Schkade, D. (2005). Pursuing happiness: The architecture of sustainable change. *Review of General Psychology, 9*, 111–131.

26. Chaplin, L. N., & John, D. R. (2007). Growing up in a material world: Age differences in materialism in children and adolescents. *Journal of Consumer Research, 34*(4), 480–493.

27. For a review of this work, see Laird, J. D. (2007). *Feelings: The perception of self.* New York: Oxford University Press.

28. Förster, J. (2004). How body feedback influences consumers' evaluation of products. *Journal of Consumer Psychology, 14*, 415–425.

29. Strack, F., Martin, L. L., & Stepper, S. (1988). Inhibiting and facilitating conditions of the human smile: A nonobtrusive test of the facial feedback hypothesis. *Journal of Personality and Social Psychology, 54*, 768–777.

30. Schnall, S., & Laird, J. D. (2003). Keep smiling: Enduring effects of facial expressions and postures on emotional experience. *Cognition and Emotion, 17*, 787–797.

31. Roberts, T., & Arefi-Afshar, Y. (2007). Not all who stand tall are proud: Gender differences in the proprioceptive effects of upright posture. *Cognition and Emotion, 21*, 714–727.

32. For a fascinating review of this work, see Gosling, S. (2008). *Snoop: What your stuff says about you.* New York: Basic Books.

33. Sheldon, K. M., & Lyubomirsky, S. (2007). Is it possible to become happier? (And if so, how?) *Social and Personality Psychology Compass, 1*, 129–145. Sheldon, K. M., & Lyubomirsky, S. (2006). Achieving sustainable happiness: Change your actions, not your circumstances. *Journal of Happiness Studies, 7*, 55–86.

PERSUASION

1. Lepper, M. R., Greene, D., & Nisbett, R. E. (1973). Undermining children's intrinsic interest with extrinsic reward: A test of the "overjustification" hypothesis. *Journal of Personality and Social Psychology, 28,* 129–137.

2. This experiment was carried out as part of the BBC television series *The People Watchers.* It is based on similar studies in "cognitive dissonance," a term that refers to the uncomfortable feeling that people get when they hold two contradictory ideas simultaneously.

3. For a review of this work, see Kohn, A. (1993). *Punished by rewards: The trouble with gold stars, incentive plans, A's, praise, and other bribes.* Boston: Houghton Mifflin.

4. Higgins, C. A., & Judge, T. A. (2004). The effect of applicant influence tactics on recruiter perceptions of fit and hiring recommendations: A field study. *Journal of Applied Psychology, 89,* 622–632.

5. Jones, E., & Gordon, E. (1972). Timing of self-disclosure and its effects on personal attraction. *Journal of Personality and Social Psychology, 24,* 358–365.

6. Williams, K. D., Bourgeois, M. J., & Croyle, R. T. (1993). The effects of stealing thunder in criminal and civil trials. *Law and Human Behavior, 17,* 597–609.

7. Gilovich, T., Medvec, V. H., & Savitsky, K. (2000). The spotlight effect in social judgment: An egocentric bias in estimates of the salience of one's own actions and appearance. *Journal of Personality and Social Psychology, 78,* 211–222.

8. Raghubir, P., & Valenzuela, A. (2006). Centre-of-inattention: Position biases in decision-making. *Organisational Behaviour and Human Decision Processes, 99,* 66–80.

9. Alter, A., & Oppenheimer, D. M. (2006). Predicting short-term stock fluctuations by using processing fluency. *Proceedings of the National Academy of Sciences, USA, 103,* 9369–9372.

10. Oppenheimer, D. M. (2005). Consequences of erudite vernacular utilized irrespective of necessity: Problems with using long words needlessly. *Journal of Applied Cognitive Psychology, 20,* 139–156.

11. For a review of the research examining the impact of likeability on politics, relationships, health, and the workplace, see Sanders, T. (2005). *The likeability factor.* New York: Crown Publishers.

12. Jecker, J., & Landy, D. (1969). Liking a person as function of doing him a favor. *Human Relations, 22,* 371–378.

13. Aronson, E., Willerman, B., & Floyd, J. (1966). The effect of a pratfall on increasing interpersonal attractiveness. *Psychonomic Science, 4,* 227–228.

14. This study was conducted as part of the BBC series *The People Watchers.*

15. Skowronski, J. J., Carlston, D. E., Mae, L., & Crawford, M. T. (1998). Spontaneous trait transference: Communicators take on the qualities they describe in others. *Journal of Personality and Social Psychology, 74,* 837–848.

16. Small, D. A., Loewenstein, G., & Slovic, P. (2007). Sympathy and callousness: The impact of deliberative thought on donations to identifiable and statistical victims. *Organisational Behaviour and Human Decision Processes, 102,* 143–153.

17. Howard, D. J. (1990). The influence of verbal responses to common greetings on compliance behavior: The foot-in-the-mouth effect. *Journal of Applied Social Psychology, 20,* 1185–1196.

18. See, for example, Razran, G. H. S. (1940). Conditional response changes in rating and appraising sociopolitical slogans. *Psychological Bulletin, 37,* 481.

19. Bodenhausen, G. V. (1993). Emotions, arousal, and stereotypic judgments: A heuristic model of affect and stereotyping. In D. M. Mackie & D. L. Hamilton (Eds.), *Affect, cognition, and stereotyping* (pp. 13–37). San Diego, CA: Academic Press.

20. Martin, P. Y., Laing, J., Martin, R., & Mitchell, M. (2005). Caffeine, cognition, and persuasion: Evidence for caffeine increasing the systematic processing of persuasive messages. *Journal of Applied Social Psychology, 35,* 160–182.

21. McGlone, M. S., & Tofighbakhsh, J. (2000). Birds of a feather flock conjointly: Rhyme as reason in aphorisms. *Psychological Science, 11,* 424–428.

22. Described in Garner, R. (2005). Post-it note persuasion: A sticky influence. *Journal of Consumer Psychology, 15,* 230–237.

23. Caprara, G. V., Vecchione, M., Barbaranelli, C., & Fraley, R. C. (2007). When likeness goes with liking: The case of political preference. *Political Psychology, 28,* 609–632.

24. O'Quinn, K., & Aronoff, J. (1981). Humor as a technique of social influence. *Social Psychology Quarterly, 44,* 349–357.

25. A thorough discussion of the exact circumstance surrounding the attack, and the unreliability of many media and textbook descriptions of the incident, can be found at http://kewgardenshistory.com/kitty_genovese-001.html.

26. For a review of this work, see Latané, B., & Nida, S. (1981). Ten years of research on group size and helping. *Psychological Bulletin, 89(2),* 308–324.

27. Latané, B., & Darley, J. M. (1968). Group inhibition of bystander intervention in emergencies. *Journal of Personality and Social Psychology, 10,* 215–221.

28. Latané, B., & Dabbs, J. M. (1975). Sex, group size, and helping in three cities. *Sociometry, 38,* 180–194.

29. Manning, R., Levine, M., & Collins, A. (2007). The Kitty Genovese murder and the social psychology of helping: The parable of the 38 witnesses. *American Psychologist, 62*(6), 555–562.

30. Goldstein, N. J., Martin, S. J., & Cialdini, R. B. (2007). *Yes! 50 secrets from the science of persuasion.* London: Profile Books.

31. Cialdini, R. B., & Schroeder, D. A. (1976). Increasing compliance by legitimizing paltry contributions: When even a penny helps. *Journal of Personality and Social Psychology, 34,* 599–604.

32. Kunz, P. R. & Woolcott, M. (1976). Season's greetings: From my status to yours. *Social Science Research, 5,* 269–278.

33. Regan, D. T. (1971). Effects of a favor and liking on compliance. *Journal of Experimental Social Psychology, 7,* 627–639.

34. Strohmetz, D. B., Rind, B., Fisher, R., & Lynn, M. (2002). Sweetening the till: The use of candy to increase restaurant tipping. *Journal of Applied Social Psychology, 32,* 300–309.

35. Schneider, M. E., Major, B., Luhtanen, R., & Crocker, J. (1996). When help hurts: Social stigma and the costs of assumptive help. *Personality and Social Psychology Bulletin, 22,* 201–209.

36. Goei, R., Roberto, A. J., Meyer, G., & Carlyle, K. E. (2007). The effects of favor and apology on compliance. *Communication Research, 34,* 575–595.

37. Morris, M. W., Podolny, J., & Ariel, S. (2001). Culture, norms, and obligations: Cross-national differences in patterns of interpersonal norms and felt obligations toward co-workers. In W. Wosinska, R. B. Cialdini, D. W. Barrett, & J. Reykowski (Eds.), *The Practice of Social Influence in Multiple Cultures,* pp. 97–123. Mahwah, NJ: Lawrence Erlbaum Associates.

38. Flynn, F. J. (2003). What have you done for me lately? Temporal changes in subjective favor evaluations. *Organizational Behavior and Human Decision Processes, 91*(1), 38–50.

39. Hornstein, H. A., Fisch, E., & Holmes, M. (1968). Influence of a model's feeling about his behavior and his relevance as a comparison on other observers' helping behavior. *Journal of Personality and Social Psychology, 10*(3), 222–226.

40. Kringelbach, M. L., Lehtonen, A., Squire, S., Harvey, A. G., Craske, M. G., et al. (2008). A specific and rapid neural signature for parental instinct. *PLoS ONE, 3*(2), http://e1664 doi:10.1371/journal.pone.0001664.

MOTIVATION

1. Pham, L. B., & Taylor, S. E. (1999). From thought to action: Effects of process- versus outcome-based mental simulations on performance. *Personality and Social Psychology Bulletin, 25,* 250–260.

2. Oettingen, G., & Wadden, T. A. (1991). Expectation, fantasy, and weight loss: Is the impact of positive thinking always positive? *Cognitive Therapy and Research, 15,* 167–175.

3. Oettingen, G., & Mayer, D. (2002). The motivating function of thinking about the future: Expectations versus fantasies. *Journal of Personality and Social Psychology, 83,* 1198–1212.

4. Deutsch, M., & Gerard, H. B. (1955). A study of normative and information social influences upon individual judgement. *Journal of Abnormal and Social Psychology, 51,* 629–636.

5. Hayes, S. C., Rosenfarb, I., Wolfert, E., Munt, E., Korn, Z., & Zettle, R. D. (1985). Self-reinforcement effects: An artifact of social setting? *Journal of Applied Behavior Analysis, 18*(3), 201–214.

6. Schnall, S., Harber, K. D., Stefanucci, J. K., & Proffitt, D. R. (2008). Social support and the perception of geographical slant. *Journal of Experimental Social Psychology, 44*(5), 1246–1255.

7. Gura, T. (December 2008). Procrastinating again? How to kick the habit. *Scientific American Mind,* 65–74.

8. Zeigarnik, B. V. (1927). Über das Behalten von erledigten und unerledigten Handlungen [The retention of completed and uncompleted activities]. *Psychologische Forschung, 9,* 1–85.

9. Fritzsche, B. A., Young, B. R., & Hickson, K. C. (2003). Individual differences in academic procrastination tendency and writing success. *Personality and Individuality Differences, 35*(7), 1549–1557.

10. Zeigarnik, A. V. (2007). Bluma Zeigarnik: A memoir. *Gestalt Theory, 29*(3), 256–268.

11. See, for example, Singer, R. N., Symons Downs, D., Bouchard, L., & de la Pena, D. (2001). The influence of a process versus an outcome orientation on tennis performance and knowledge. *Journal of Sport Behavior, 24,* 213–222.

Kingston, K. M., & Hardy, L. (1997). Effects of different types of goals on processes that support performance. *Sport Psychology, 11,* 277–293.

12. Libby, L. K., Shaeffer, E. M., Eibach, R. P., & Slemmer, J. A. (2007). Picture yourself at the polls: Visual perspective in mental imagery affects self-perception and behavior. *Psychological Science, 18,* 199–203.

13. Oettingen, G., Pak, H., & Schnetter, K. (2001). Self-regulation of goal setting: Turning free fantasies about the future into binding goals. *Journal of Personality and Social Psychology, 80,* 736–753.

14. Oettingen, G. (2000). Expectancy effects on behavior depend on self-regulatory thought. *Social Cognition, 18,* 101–129.

15. Oettingen, G., & Gollwitzer, P. M. (2002). Self-regulation of goal pursuit: Turning hope thoughts into behavior. *Psychological Inquiry, 13,* 304–307.

16. Wansink, B., Painter, J. E., & North, J. (2005). Bottomless bowls: Why visual cues of portion size may influence intake. *Obesity Research, 13*(1), 93–100.

17. See, for example, Stuart, R. B. (1967). Behavioral control of overeating. *Behaviour Research and Therapy, 5,* 357–365.

18. Martin, C. K., Anton, S. D., Walden, H., Arnett, C., Greenway, F. L., & Williamson, D. A. (2007). Slower eating rate reduces the food intake of men, but not women: Implications for behavioural weight control. *Behaviour Research and Therapy, 45,* 2349–2359.

19. Wansink, B., & van Ittersum, K. (2005). Shape of glass and amount of alcohol poured: Comparative study of the effect of practice and concentration. *British Medical Journal, 331,* 1512–1514.

20. Painter, J. E., Wansink, B., & Hieggelke, J. B. (2002). How visibility and convenience influence candy consumption. *Appetite, 38*(3), 237–238. Wansink, B., Painter, J. E., & Lee, Y. K. (2006). The office candy dish: Proximity's influence on estimated and actual candy consumption. *International Journal of Obesity, 30*(5), 871–875.

21. Chandon, P., & Wansink, B. (2002). When are stockpiled products consumed faster? A convenience-salience framework of post-purchase consumption incidence and quantity. *Journal of Marketing Research, 39*(3), 321–335.

22. Wansink, B., & Park, S. (2001). At the movies: How external cues and perceived taste impact consumption volume. *Food Quality and Preference, 12*(1), 69–74.

23. Bellisle, F., & Dalix A.M. (2001). Cognitive restraint can be offset by distraction, leading to increased meal intake in women. *American Journal of Clinical Nutrition, 74,* 197–200.

24. Wansink, B., van Ittersum, K., & Painter, J. E. (2006). Ice cream illusions: Bowl size, spoon size, and self-served portion sizes. *American Journal of Preventative Medicine, 31*(3), 240–243.

25. Geier, A. B., Rozin, P., & Doros, G. (2006). Unit bias: A new heuristic that helps explain the effect of portion size on food intake. *Psychological Science, 17,* 521–525.

26. Hollis, J. F., Gullion, C. M., Stevens, V. J., et al. (2008). Weight loss during the intensive intervention phase of the weight-loss maintenance trial. *American Journal of Preventable Medicine, 35,* 118–126.

27. Abraham, C., & Sheeran, P. (2004). Deciding to exercise: The role of anticipated regret. *British Journal of Health Psychology, 9,* 269–278.

28. Martin Ginis, K. A., Burke, S. M., & Gauvin, L. (2007). Exercising with others exacerbates the negative effects of mirrored environments on sedentary women's feeling states. *Psychology and Health, 22,* 945–962.

29. Sentyrz, S. M., & Bushman, B. J. (1998). Mirror, mirror on the wall, who's the thinnest one of all? Effects of self-awareness on consumption of fatty, reduced-fat, and fat-free products. *Journal of Applied Psychology, 83,* 944–949.

30. Coelho do Vale, R., Pieters, R., & Zeelenberg, M. (2008). Flying under the radar: Perverse package size effects on consumption self-regulation. *Journal of Consumer Research, 35*(3), 380–390.

31. Jonas, E., Schimel, J., & Greenberg, J. (2002). The Scrooge effect: Evidence that mortality salience increases prosocial attitudes and behavior. *Personality and Social Psychology Bulletin, 28,* 1342–1353.

32. Peterson, C. (2006). *A primer in positive psychology.* Oxford: Oxford University Press.

CREATIVITY

1. Osborn, A. F. (1957). *Applied imagination.* New York: Scribner.

2. Mullen, B., Johnson, C., & Salas, E. (1991). Productivity loss in brainstorming groups: A meta-analytic integration. *Basic and Applied Social Psychology, 12,* 3–23.

3. Ringelmann, M. (1913). Recherches sur les moteurs animés: Travail de l'homme. *Annales de l'Institut National Argonomique, 12,* 1–40.

4. Karau, S. J., & Williams, K. D. (1993) Social loafing: A meta-analytic review and theoretical integration. *Journal of Personality and Social Psychology, 65,* 681–706.

5. For a review of this work, see Latané, B., Williams, K., & Harkins, S. (1979). Many hands make light the work: The causes and consequences of social loafing. *Journal of Personality and Social Psychology, 37*(6), 822–832.

6. Smith, S. M. (2002). Getting into and out of mental ruts: A theory of fixation, incubation, and insight. In R. J. Sternberg and J. E. Davidson (Eds.), *The nature of insight.* (pp. 229–251). Cambridge, MA: MIT Press.

7. Dijksterhuis, A., & Meurs, T. (2006). Where creativity resides: The generative power of unconscious thought. *Consciousness and Cognition, 15,* 135–146.

8. Ulrich, R. S. (1984). View through a window may influence recovery from surgery. *Science 224,* 420–421.

9. Moore, E. O. (1982). A prison environment's effect on health care service demands. *Journal of Environmental Systems, 11*(1), 17–34.

10. Kuo, F. E., & Sullivan, W. C. (2001). Environment and crime in the inner city: Does vegetation reduce crime? *Environment and Behavior, 33,* 343–365.

11. Taylor, A. F., Wiley, A., Kuo, F. E., & Sullivan, W. C. (1998). Growing up in the inner city: Green spaces as places to grow. *Environment and Behavior, 30,* 3–27.

12. Elliot, A. J., Maier, M. A., Moller, A. C., Friedman, R., & Meinhardt, J. (2007). Color and psychological functioning: The effect of red on performance in achievement contexts. *Journal of Experimental Psychology: General, 136,* 154–168.

13. Kahnjr, P., Friedman, B., Gill, B., Hagman, J., Severson, R., Freier, N., et al. (2008). A plasma display window: The shifting baseline problem in a technologically mediated natural world. *Journal of Environmental Psychology, 28,* 192–199.

14. Nemeth, C. J., & Ormiston, M. (2007). Creative idea generation: Harmony versus stimulation. *European Journal of Social Psychology, 37*(3), 524–535.

15. Choi, H-S., & Thompson, L. (2005). Old wine in a new bottle: Impact of membership change on group creativity. *Organisational Behaviour and Human Decision Processes, 98,* 121–132.

16. Dijksterhuis, A., & van Knippenberg, A. (1998). The relation between perception and behavior, or how to win a game of Trivial Pursuit. *Journal of Personality and Social Psychology, 74*(4), 865–877.

17. Vohs, K. D., Mead, N. L., & Goode, M. R. (2006). The psychological consequences of money. *Science, 314,* 1154–1156.

18. Cited in Carey, B. (2007, July 31). Who's minding the mind? *New York Times.*

19. Holland, R. W., Hendriks, M., & Aarts, H. (2006). Smells like clean spirit: Nonconscious effects of scent on cognition and behavior. *Psychological Science, 16*(9), 689–693.

20. Kay, A. C., Wheeler, S. C., Bargh, J. A., & Ross, L. (2004). Material priming: The influence of mundane physical objects on situational construal and competitive behavioral choice. *Organizational Behavior and Human Decision Processes, 95,* 83–96.

21. Förster, J., Friedman, R., Butterbach, E. M., & Sassenberg, K. (2005). Automatic effects of deviancy cues on creative cognition. *European Journal of Social Psychology, 35,* 345–359.

22. Dijksterhuis, A., Spears, R., Postmes, T., Stapel, D. A., Koomen, W., van Knippenberg, A., & Scheepers, D. (1998). Seeing one thing and doing another: Contrast effects in automatic behavior. *Journal of Personality and Social Psychology, 75,* 862–871.

23. Friedman, R., & Förster, J. (2002). The influence of approach and avoidance motor actions on creative cognition. *Journal of Experimental Social Psychology, 38,* 41–55.

24. Friedman, R., & Elliot, A. J. (2008). The effect of arm crossing on persistence and performance. *European Journal of Social Psychology, 38,* 449–461.

25. Lipnicki, D. M., & Byrne, D. G. (2005). Thinking on your back: Solving anagrams faster when supine than when standing. *Cognitive Brain Research, 24,* 719–722.

ATTRACTION

1. Worchel, S., Lee, J., & Adewole, A. (1975). Effects of supply and demand on ratings of object value. *Journal of Personality and Social Psychology, 32,* 906–914.

2. Xenophon. E. C. Marchant (1923, trans.).*The memorabilia, III,* xi. London: Heinemann.

3. Ovid (trans. 1963). *The art of love.* Bloomington: University of Indiana Press.

4. Hatfield, E., Walster, G. W., Piliavin, J., & Schmidt, L. (1973). Playing hard to get: Understanding an elusive phenomenon. *Journal of Personality and Social Psychology, 26,* 113–121.

5. Walster, E., Walster, G. W., & Lambert, P. (1971). Playing hard-to-get: A field study. Madison: University of Wisconsin. Unpublished report.

6. Guéguen, N. (2007). Women's bust size and men's courtship solicitation: A field experiment. *Body Image, 4,* 386–390.

7. Guéguen, N. (2007). Bust size and hitchhiking: A field study. *Perceptual and Motor Skills, 105,* 1294–1298.

8. Guéguen, N. (2007). The effect of a man's touch on woman's compliance to a request in a courtship context. *Social Influence, 2,* 81–97.

9. Major, B., & Heslin, R. (1982). Perceptions of cross-sex and same-sex nonreciprocal touch: It is better to give than receive. *Journal of Nonverbal Behavior, 6,* 148–162. Summerhayes, D. L., & Suchner, R. W. (1978). Power implications of touch in male-female relationships. *Sex Roles, 4,* 103–110.

10. See, for example, Hazan, C., & Shaver, P. (1987). Romantic love conceptualized as an attachment process. *Journal of Personality and Social Psychology, 52,* 511–524.

11. Emanuele, E., Brondino, N., Pesenti, S., Re, S., & Geroldi, D. (2007). Genetic loading on human loving styles. *Neuroendocrinology Letters, 28* (6), 815–821.

12. Based on work described in Hendrick, C., & Hendrick, S. S. (1986). A theory and method of love. *Journal of Personality and Social Psychology, 30,* 392–402.

13. This work was carried out as part of the Edinburgh International Science Festival.

14. Van Baaren, R. B., Holland, R., Steenaert, B., & van Knippenberg, A. (2003). Mimicry for money: Behavioral consequences of imitation. *Journal of Experimental Social Psychology, 39,* 393–398.

15. Reported in Dijksterhuis, A., Smith, P. K., van Baaren, R. B., & Wigboldus, D. H. (2005). The unconscious consumer: Effects of environment on consumer behavior. *Journal of Consumer Psychology, 15,* 193–202.

16. Eastwick, P. W., Finkel, E. J., Mochon, D., & Ariely, D. (2007). Selective versus unselective romantic desire: Not all reciprocity is created equal. *Psychological Science, 18,* 317–319.

17. Chu, S., Hardaker, R., & Lycett, J. E. (2007). Too good to be "true"? The handicap of high socio-economic status in attractive males. *Personality and Individual Differences, 42,* 1291–1300.

18. Kelly, S., & Dunbar, R. (2001). Who dares wins: Heroism versus altruism in female mate choice. *Human Nature 12*, 89–105.

19. Dutton, D. G., and Aron, A. P. (1974). Some evidence for heightened sexual attraction under conditions of high anxiety. *Journal of Personality and Social Psychology, 30*, 510–517.

20. Meston, C. M., & Frohlich, P. F. (2003). Love at first fright: Partner salience moderates roller coaster–induced excitation transfer. *Archives of Sexual Behavior, 32*, 537–544.

21. Cohen, B., Waugh, G., & Place, K. (1989). At the movies: An unobtrusive study of arousal-attraction. *Journal of Social Psychology, 129*, 691–693.

22. Aron, A., Melinat, E., Aron, E. N., Vallone, R., & Bator, R. (1997). The experimental generation of interpersonal closeness: A procedure and some preliminary findings. *Personality and Social Psychology Bulletin, 23*, 363–377.

23. Jones, B. C., DeBruine, L. M., Little, A. C., Burriss, R. P., & Feinburg, D. R. (2007). Social transmission of face preferences among humans. *Proceedings of the Royal Society of London B, 274*(1611): 899–903.

24. Swami, V., & Tovee, M. J. (2005). Does hunger influence judgments of female physical attractiveness? *British Journal of Psychology, 97*(3), 353–363.

25. Aronson, E. (1999). *The social animal* (8th ed.). New York: Worth Publishers. Aronson, E., & Linder, D. (1965). Gain and loss of esteem as determinants of interpersonal attractiveness. *Journal of Experimental Social Psychology, 1*, 156–171.

26. Bosson, J. K., Johnson, A. B., Niederhoffer, K., & Swann, W. B., Jr. (2006). Interpersonal chemistry through negativity: Bonding by sharing negative attitudes about others. *Personal Relationships, 13*, 135–150.

27. Krumhuber, E., Manstead, A. S. R., & Kappas, A. (2007). Temporal aspects of facial displays in person and expression perception: The effects of smile dynamics, head-tilt, and gender. *Journal of Nonverbal Behavior, 31*, 39–56.

28. Gonzaga, G. C., Turner, R. A., Keltner, D., Campos, B. C., & Altemus, M. (2006). Romantic love and sexual desire in close bonds. *Emotion, 6*, 163–179.

29. Kenrick, D. T., Sundie, J. M., Nicastle, L. D., & Stone, G. O. (2001). Can one ever be too wealthy or too chaste? Searching for nonlinearities in mate judgment. *Journal of Personality and Social Psychology, 80*, 462–471.

RELATIONSHIPS

1. Gottman, J. M., Coan, J. A., Carrere, S., & Swanson, C. (1998). Predicting marital happiness and stability from newlywed interactions. *Journal of Marriage and the Family, 60,* 5–22.

2. See, for example, Hahlweg, K., Schindler, L., Revensdorf, D., & Brengelmann, J. C. (1984). The Munich marital therapy study. In K. Hahlweg & N. S. Jacobson (Eds.), Marital interaction: Analysis and modification (pp.3–26). New York: Guilford Press. Jacobson, N. S., Schmaling, K. B., & Holtzworth-Monroe, A. (1987). Component analysis of behavioral marital therapy: 2–year follow-up and prediction of relapse. *Journal of Marital and Family Therapy, 13,* 187–195.

3. Kellerman, J., Lewis, J., & Laird, J. D. (1989). Looking and loving: The effects of mutual gaze on feelings of romantic love. *Journal of Research in Personality, 23,* 145–161.

4. Aron, A., Norman, C. C., Aron, E. N., McKenna, C., & Heyman, R. (2000). Couples shared participation in novel and arousing activities and experienced relationship quality. *Journal of Personality and Social Psychology, 78,* 273–283.

5. Baumeister, R. F., Bratslavsky, E., Finkenauer, C., & Vohs, K. D. (2001). Bad is stronger than good. *Review of General Psychology, 5,* 323–370.

6. Gottman, J. (1984). *Why marriages succeed or fail.* New York: Simon & Schuster.

7. Slatcher, R. B., & Pennebaker, J. W. (2006). How do I love thee? Let me count the words: The social effects of expressive writing. *Psychological Science, 17,* 660–664.

8. Buunk, B. P., Oldersma, F. L., & de Dreu, C. K. W. (2001). Enhancing satisfaction through downward comparison: The role of relational discontent and individual differences in social comparison orientation. *Journal of Experimental Social Psychology, 37,* 452–467.

9. Murray, S. L., & Holmes, J. G. (1999). The (mental) ties that bind: Cognitive structures that predict relationship resilience. *Journal of Personality and Social Psychology, 77,* 1228–1244.

10. Gosling, S. D., Ko, S. J., Mannarelli, T., & Morris, M. E. (2002). A room with a cue: Judgments of personality based on offices and bedrooms. *Journal of Personality and Social Psychology, 82,* 379–398.

11. Lohmann, A., Ximena, B., Arriga, X. B., & Goodfriend, W. (2003). Close relationships and placemaking: Do objects in a couple's home reflect couplehood? *Personal Relationships, 10,* 437–449.

12. Maner, J. K., Rouby, D. A., & Gonzaga, G. (2008). Automatic inattention to attractive alternatives: The evolved psychology of relationship maintenance. *Evolution and Human Behavior, 29,* 343–349.

STRESS

1. Bushman, B. J. (2002). Does venting anger feed or extinguish the flame? Catharsis, rumination, distraction, anger, and aggressive responding. *Personality and Social Psychology Bulletin, 28,* 724–731.

2. Tennen, H., & Affleck, G. (2001). Benefit-finding and benefit-reminding. In C. R Snyder and S. J. Lopez (Eds.), *Handbook of positive psychology* (pp. 584–597). Oxford: Oxford University Press.

3. McCullough, M. E., Root, L. M., & Cohen, A. D. (2006). Writing about the benefits of an interpersonal transgression facilitates forgiveness. *Journal of Consulting and Clinical Psychology, 74,* 887–897.

4. Peterson, C., & Seligman, M. E. P. (2003). Character strengths before and after September 11. *Psychological Science, 14,* 381–384.

5. Peterson, C., Park, N., & Seligman, M. E. P. (2006). Greater strengths of character and recovery from illness. *Journal of Positive Psychology, 1,* 17–26.

6. Krause, N. (2003). Praying for others, financial strain, and physical health status in late life. *Journal for the Scientific Study of Religion, 42,* 377–391.

7. Chafin, S., Roy, M., Gerin, W., & Christenfeld, N. (2004). Music can facilitate blood pressure recovery from stress. *British Journal of Health Psychology, 9,* 393–403.

8. Keller, M. C., Fredrickson, B. L., Ybarra, O., Cote, S., Johnson, K., Mikels, J., et al. (2005). A warm heart and a clear head: The contingent effects of weather on mood and cognition. *Psychological Science, 16,* 724–731.

9. Lefcourt, H. M. (2005). Humor. In C. R. Snyder & S. J. Lopez (Eds.), *Handbook of positive psychology* (pp. 619–631). Oxford: Oxford University Press.

10. Friedmann E., & Thomas, S. A. (1995). Pet ownership, social support, and one-year survival after acute myocardial infarction in the Cardiac Arrhythmia Suppression Trial (CAST). *American Journal of Cardiology, 76,* 1213–1217.

11. Wells, D. L. (2007). Domestic dogs and human health: An overview. *British Journal of Health Psychology 12,* 145–156.

12. Allen, K., Blascovich, J., & Mendes, W. B. (2002). Cardiovascular reactivity and the presence of pets, friends, and spouses: The truth about cats and dogs. *Psychosomatic Medicine, 64*(5), 727–739.

13. See, for example, Turner, D. C., Rieger, G., & Gygax, I. (2003). Spouses and cats and their effects on human mood. *Anthrozoös, 16,* 213–228.

14. Friedmann, E., & Thomas, S. A. (1995). Pet ownership, social support, and one-year survival after acute myocardial infarction in the Cardiac Arrhythmia Suppression Trial (CAST). *American Journal of Cardiology, 76,* 1213–1217.

15. Allen, K., Shykoff, B., & Izzo, J. (2001). Pet ownership, but not ACE inhibitor therapy, blunts home blood pressure responses to mental stress. *Hypertension, 38,* 815–820.

16. See, for example, Lynch, J. J., Thomas, S. A., Mills, M. E., et al. (1974). The effects of human contact on cardiac arrhythmia in coronary care patients. *Journal of Nervous and Mental Disease, 158,* 88–98.

17. Wells, D. L. (2004). The facilitation of social interactions by domestic dogs. *Anthrozoös, 17*(4), 340–352.

18. Hunt, S. J., Hart, L. A., & Gomulkiewicz, R. (1992). Role of small animals in social interactions between strangers. *Journal of Social Psychology, 132,* 245–256.

19. Banks, M. R., Willoughby, L. M., and Banks, W. A. (2008). Animal-assisted therapy and loneliness in nursing homes: Use of robotic versus living dogs. *Journal of the American Medical Directors Association, 9,* 173–177.

20. Wells, D. (2005). The effect of videotapes of animals on cardiovascular responses to stress. *Stress and Health, 21,* 209–213.

21. Cited in Crum, A. J., & Langer, E. J. (2007). Mind-set matters: Exercise and the placebo effect. *Psychological Science, 18,* 165–171.

22. Crum, A. J., & Langer, E. J. (2007). Mind-set matters: Exercise and the placebo effect. *Psychological Science, 18,* 165–171.

DECISION MAKING

1. Stoner, J. A. F. (1961). "A comparison of individual and group decisions involving risk." Unpublished master's thesis, Massachusetts Institute of Technology.

2. Myers, D. G., & Bishop, G. D. (1971). Enhancement of dominant attitudes in group discussion. *Journal of Personality and Social Psychology, 20,* 386–391.

3. Whyte, G. (1993). Escalating commitment in individual and group decision making: A prospect theory approach. *Organizational Behavior and Human Decision Processes, 54,* 430–455.

4. Much of the work discussed in this paragraph is outlined in Janis, I. (1982). *Groupthink* (2nd ed.). Boston: Houghton-Mifflin.

5. Solnick, S. J., & Hemenway, D. (1998). Is more always better? A survey on positional concerns. *Journal of Economic Behavior and Organization, 37,* 373–383.

6. Burger, J. M. (1986). Increasing compliance by improving the deal: The that's-not-all technique. *Journal of Personality and Social Psychology, 51,* 277–283.

7. Santos, M., Leve, C., & Pratkanis, A. (1994). Hey buddy, can you spare seventeen cents? Mindful persuasion and the pique technique. *Journal of Applied Social Psychology, 29,* 755–764.

8. Davis, B. P., and Knowles, E. S. (1999). A disrupt-then-reframe technique of social influence. *Journal of Personality and Social Psychology, 76*(2), 192–199.

9. Freedman, J., & Fraser, S. (1966). Compliance without pressure: The foot-in-the-door technique. *Journal of Personality and Social Psychology, 4,* 195–202.

10. Beaman, A. L., Cole, C. M., Klentz, B., & Steblay, N. M. (1983). Fifteen years of the foot-in-the-door research: A meta-analysis. *Personality and Social Psychology Bulletin, 9,* 181–196.

11. Cialdini, R., Vincent, J., Lewis, S., Catalan, J., Wheeler, D., & Darby, B. (1975). Reciprocal concessions procedure for inducing compliance: The door-in-the-face technique. *Journal of Personality and Social Psychology, 31,* 206–215.

12. Pascual, A., & Guéguen, N. (2006). Door-in-the-face technique and behavioral compliance: An evaluation in a field setting, *Psychological Reports, 103,* 974–978.

13. Dijksterhuis, A., & van Olden, Z. (2006). On the benefits of thinking unconsciously: Unconscious thought increases post-choice satisfaction. *Journal of Experimental Social Psychology, 42,* 627–631.

14. See, for example, Betsch, T., Plessner, H., Schwieren, C., & Gütig, R. (2001). I like it but I don't know why: A value-account approach to implicit attitude formation. *Personality and Social Psychology Bulletin, 27,* 242–253. Dijksterhuis, A., Bos, M. W., Nordgren, L. F., & van Baaren, R. B. (2006). On making the right choice: The deliberation-without-attention effect. *Science, 311,* 1005–1007.

15. See, for example, Gilovich, T., & Medvec, V. H. (1995). The experience of regret: What, when, and why. *Psychological Review, 102,* 379–395. Gilovich, T., & Medvec, V. H. (1994). The temporal pattern to the experience of regret. *Journal of Personality and Social Psychology, 67,* 357–365.

16. Based on work described in Schwartz, B., Ward, A., Monterosso, J., Lyubomirsky, S., White, K., & Lehman, D. R. (2002). Maximizing versus satisficing: Happiness is a matter of choice. *Personality and Social Psychology, 83*(5), 1178–1197.

17. Iyengar, S. S., Wells, R. E., & Schwartz, B. (2006). Doing better but feeling worse: Looking for the "best" job undermines satisfaction. *Psychological Science, 17,* 143–149.

18. Peterson, C. (2006). *A primer in positive psychology* (p. 191). Oxford: Oxford University Press.

19. Highfield, R. (1994, March 25). How age affects the way we lie. *Daily Telegraph,* p. 26. Vrij, A. (2000). *Detecting lies and deceit.* Chichester: John Wiley & Sons. Survey conducted by the Royal and Sun Alliance Insurance Company in 2007.

20. Gramzow, R. H., Willard, G., & Mendes, W. B. (2008). Big tales and cool heads: Academic exaggeration is related to cardiac vagal reactivity. *Emotion, 8,* 138–144.

21. Stromwall, L. A., Granhag, P. A., & Landstrom, S. (2007). Children's prepared and unprepared lies: Can adults see through their strategies? *Applied Cognitive Psychology, 21,* 457–471.

22. Cited in DePaulo, B. M., & Morris, W. L. (2004). Discerning lies from truths: Behavioral cues to deception and the indirect pathway of intuition. In P. A. Granhag & L. A. Stromwall (Eds.), *The detection of deception in forensic contexts* (pp. 15–40). Cambridge: Cambridge University Press.

23. Ekman, P., & O'Sullivan, M. (1991). Who can catch a liar? *American Psychologist, 46*(9), 913–920.

24. Vrij, A. (2004). Why professionals fail to catch liars and how they can improve. *Legal and Criminological Psychology 9,* 159–183.

25. Hancock, J. T., Thom-Santelli, J., & Ritchie, T. (2004). Deception and design: The impact of communication technologies on lying behavior. *Proceedings of the Conference on Computer Human Interaction, 6,* 130–136. New York: ACM.

26. Buehler, R., Griffin, D., and Ross, M. 2002. Inside the planning fallacy: The causes and consequences of optimistic time predictions. In T. Gilovich, D. Griffin, and D. Kahneman (Eds.), *Heuristics and biases: The psychology of intuitive judgment* (pp. 250–270). Cambridge: Cambridge University Press.

27. Buehler, R., Messervey, D., & Griffin, D. (2005). Collaborative planning and prediction: Does group discussion affect optimistic biases in time estimation? *Organizational Behavior and Human Decision Processes, 97,* 47–63.

28. Kruger, J., & Evans, M. (2004). If you don't want to be late, enumerate: Unpacking reduces the planning fallacy. *Journal of Experimental Social Psychology, 40,* 586–598.

PARENTING

1. Rauscher, F. H., Shaw, G. L., & Ky, K. N. (1993). Music and spatial task performance. *Nature, 365,* 611.

2. Rauscher, F. H., Shaw, G. L., & Ky, K. N. (1995). Listening to Mozart enhances spatial-temporal reasoning: Towards a neurophysiological basis. *Neuroscience Letters, 185,* 44–47.

3. Bangerter, A., & Heath, C. (2004). The Mozart effect: Tracking the evolution of a scientific legend. *British Journal of Social Psychology, 43,* 605–623.

4. Chabris, C. F. (1999). Prelude or requiem for the "Mozart effect"? *Nature, 400,* 827.

5. Thompson, W. F., Schellenberg, E. G., & Husain, G. (2001). Arousal, mood, and the Mozart effect. *Psychological Science, 12,* 248–251.

6. Nantais, K. M., & Schellenberg, E. G. (1999). The Mozart effect: An artifact of preference? *Psychological Science, 10,* 370–373.

7. Schellenberg, E. G. (2004). Music lessons enhance IQ. *Psychological Science, 15,* 511–514.

8. Pelham, B. W., Mirenberg, M. C., & Jones, J. K. (2002). Why Susie sells seashells by the seashore: Implicit egotism and major life decisions. *Journal of Personality and Social Psychology, 82,* 469–487.

9. Einav, L., & Yariv, L. (2006). What's in a surname? The effects of surname initials on academic success. *Journal of Economic Perspectives, 20*(1), 175–188.

10. Harari, H., & McDavid, J. W. (1973). Name stereotypes and teachers' expectations. *Journal of Educational Psychology, 65,* 222–225.

11. Murphy, W. F. (1957). A note on the significance of names. *Psychoanalytical Quarterly, 26,* 91–106.

12. Christenfeld, N., Phillips, D. P., & Glynn, L. M. (1999). What's in a name: Mortality and the power of symbols. *Journal of Psychosomatic Research, 47*(3), 241–254.

13. Nelson, L. D., & Simmons, J. P. (2007). Moniker maladies: When names sabotage success. *Psychological Science, 18,* 1106–1111.

14. Mueller, C. M., & Dweck, C. S. (1998). Praise for intelligence can undermine children's motivation and performance. *Journal of Personality and Social Psychology, 75,* 33–52.

15. For a short summary of this work, see Dweck, C. S. (1999). Caution—Praise can be dangerous. *American Educator, 23,* 4–9.

16. Cimpian, A., Arce, H. C., Markman, E. M., & Dweck, C. S. (2007). Subtle linguistic cues affect children's motivation. *Psychological Science, 18,* 314–316.

17. Shoda, Y., Mischel, W., & Peake, P. K. (1990). Predicting adolescent cognitive and self-regulatory competencies from preschool delay of gratification. *Developmental Psychology, 26*(6), 978–986.

18. See, for example, Cameron, C. E., McClelland, M. M., Connor, C. M., Jewkes, A. M., Farris, C. L., & Morrison, F. J. (2008). Touch your toes! Developing a direct measure of behavioral regulation in early childhood. *Early Childhood Research Quarterly, 23,* 141–158. McClelland, M. M., Cameron, C. E., Connor, C. M., Farris, C. L., Jewkes, A. M., & Morrison, F. J. (2007). Links between behavioral regulation and preschoolers' literacy, vocabulary, and math skills. *Developmental Psychology, 43,* 947–959.

19. Duckworth, A. L., & Seligman, M. E. P. (2005). Self-discipline outdoes IQ in predicting academic performance of adolescents. *Psychological Science, 16,* 939–944.

20. Freedman, J. L. (1965). Long-term behavioral effects of cognitive dissonance. *Journal of Experimental Social Psychology, 1,* 145–155.

21. Filley, D. (1999). Forbidden fruit: When prohibition increases the harm it is supposed to reduce. *Independent Review, 3,* 441–451.

22. Tominey, S., & McClelland, M. M. (2008, April). *"And when they woke up, they were monkeys!" Using classroom games to promote preschoolers' self-regulation and school readiness.* Poster presented at the biennial Conference on Human Development, Indianapolis, IN.

PERSONALITY

1. Beyerstein, B. L. (2007). Graphology—a total write-off. In S. Della Sala (Ed.), *Tall tales about the mind and brain: Separating fact from fiction* (233–270). Oxford: Oxford University Press.

2. For a review of this approach to personality, see Matthews, G., Deary, I. J., & Whiteman, M. C. (2003). *Personality traits* (2nd ed.). Cambridge: Cambridge University Press.

3. Goldberg, L. R. (1993). The structure of phenotypic personality traits. *American Psychologist, 48,* 26–34.

4. For further information about this work, see http://ipip.ori.org/.

5. Sulloway, F. J. (1996). *Born to rebel: Birth order, family dynamics, and creative lives.* New York: Pantheon.

6. See, for example, Jefferson, T., Herbst, J. H., & McCrae, R. R. (1998). Associations between birth order and personality traits: Evidence from self-reports and observer ratings. *Journal of Research in Personality, 32,* 498–509.

7. Casanova, G. (1997). *History of my life: Giacomo Casanova, Chevalier de Seingalt.* Vol. 11. (Willard R. Trask, Trans.) Baltimore: John Hopkins University Press.

8. For a fascinating summary of this work, see Manning, J. (2008). *The finger book: Sex, behaviour, and disease revealed in the fingers.* London: Faber and Faber.

9. See, for example, Putz, D. A., Gaulin, S. J. C., Sporter, R. J., & McBurnley, D. H. (2004). Sex hormones and finger length: What does 2D:4D indicate? *Evolution and Human Behavior, 25,* 182–199.

10. Manning, J. T., & Sturt, D. (2004). 2nd to 4th digit ratio and strength in men. Unpublished study, cited in Manning's *The Finger Book.*

11. Manning, J. T., Bundred, P., & Taylor, R. (2003). The ratio of the 2nd to 4th digit length: A prenatal correlate of ability at sport. *Kinanthropometry, 8,* 165–174.

12. Manning, J. T., & Taylor, R. P. (2001). 2nd to 4th digit ratio and male ability in sport: Implications for sexual selection in humans. *Evolution and Human Behavior, 22,* 61–69.

13. Manning, J. T., & Taylor, R. P. (2001). 2nd to 4th digit ratio and male ability in sport: Implications for sexual selection in humans. *Evolution and Human Behavior, 22,* 61–69.

14. Fink, B., Manning, J. T., & Neave, N. (2004). Second to fourth digit ratio and the "big five" personality factors. *Personality and Individual Differences, 37,* 495–503. Austin, E. J., Manning, J. T., McInroy, K., & Mathews, E. (2002). A preliminary investigation of the association between personality, cognitive ability, and digit ratio. *Personality and Individual Differences, 33,* 1115–1124. Wilson, G. D. (1983). Finger-length as an index of assertiveness in women. *Personality and Individual Differences, 4,* 111–112.

15. Sluming, V., & Manning, J. (2000). Second to fourth digit ratio in elite musicians: Evidence for musical ability as an honest signal of male fitness. *Evolution and Human Behaviour, 21,* 1–9.

16. Szlemko, W. J., Benfield, J. A., Bell, P. A., Deffenbacher, J. L., & Troup, L. (2008). Territorial markings as a predictor of driver aggression and road rage. *Journal of Applied Social Psychology, 38*(6), 1664–1688.

17. Ida, Y. (1987). The manner of hand clasping and the individual differences in hemispheric asymmetries. *Japanese Journal of Psychology, 58,* 318–321. Ida,

Y. (1988). The manner of clasping the hands and individual differences in perceptual asymmetries and cognitive modes. *Psychologia, 31,* 128–135. Mohr, C., Thut, G., Landis, T., & Brugger, P. (2003). Hands, arms, and minds: Interactions between posture and thought. *Journal of Clinical and Experimental Neuropsychology, 25,* 1000–1010.

18. Diaz-Morales, J. F. (2007). Morning and evening types: Exploring their personality styles. *Personality and Individual Differences, 43,* 769–778.

Meet with Interesting People
Enjoy Stimulating Conversation
Discover Wonderful Books

VINTAGE BOOKS / ANCHOR BOOKS

Reading Group Center
THE READING GROUP SOURCE FOR BOOK LOVERS

Visit ReadingGroupCenter.com where you'll find great reading choices—award winners, bestsellers, beloved classics, and many more—and extensive resources for reading groups such as:

Author Chats
Exciting contests offer reading groups the chance to win one-on-one phone conversations with Vintage and Anchor Books authors.

Behind the Book Features
Specially designed pages which can include photographs, videos, original essays, notes from the author and editor, and book-related information.

Extensive Discussion Guides
Guides for over 450 titles as well as non–title specific discussion questions by category for fiction, nonfiction, memoir, poetry, and mystery.

Reading Planner
Plan ahead by browsing upcoming titles, finding author event schedules, and more.

Special for Spanish-language reading groups
www.grupodelectura.com
A dedicated Spanish-language content area complete with recommended titles from Vintage Español.

Personal Advice and Ideas
Reading groups nationwide share ideas, suggestions, helpful tips, and anecdotal information. Participate in the discussion and share your group's experiences.

A selection of some favorite reading group titles from our list

Atonement by Ian McEwan
Balzac and the Little Chinese Seamstress by Dai Sijie
The Blind Assassin by Margaret Atwood
The Devil in the White City by Erik Larson
Empire Falls by Richard Russo
The English Patient by Michael Ondaatje
A Heartbreaking Work of Staggering Genius by Dave Eggers
The House of Sand and Fog by Andre Dubus III
A Lesson Before Dying by Ernest J. Gaines

Lolita by Vladimir Nabokov
Memoirs of a Geisha by Arthur Golden
Midnight in the Garden of Good and Evil by John Berendt
Midwives by Chris Bohjalian
Push by Sapphire
The Reader by Bernhard Schlink
Snow by Orhan Pamuk
An Unquiet Mind by Kay Redfield Jamison
Waiting by Ha Jin
A Year in Provence by Peter Mayle